PUZZLE PIECES
TOGETHER

ISBN 978-1-7374176-2-0 (Paperback)
ISBN 978-1-7374176-3-7 (ebook)

Printed in the United States of America

Cover Design by: Nic Youngblood
Interior Design: Heidi Caperton

Scripture quotations from The Authorized (King James) Version. Rights in the Authorized Version in the United Kingdom are vested in the Crown. Reproduced by permission of the Crown's patentee, Cambridge University Press

Text quotations from The Church of Jesus Crist of Latter-Day Saints Book of Mormon.

Published by Puzzle Pieces Together LLC

For information requests visit www.laurajworley.com

PUZZLE PIECES
TOGETHER

Manual  A Pathway to Freedom

Laura Worley   Part 2

This book is dedicated to all those who have suffered at the hands of Satanic Cabal groups. May you all find freedom.

TABLE OF CONTENTS

INTRODUCTION

In this book you will find the pieces to the foundational programming conducted in all MK Ultra programs, which in my experience include the Illuminati, Freemasons, Military, and Fertility Cults, which I refer to as *cults* or *occult groups*.

Many victims of occult groups do not get free from their systematic programming because they lack the necessary puzzle pieces. A person's mind is fragmented while under mind control. Cults consider fragmenting the mind as integral. Cult survivors won't have an expansive memory of their trials, a strategic ruse to conceal the occult system.

Until now, cults have been successful in keeping the Kabbalah Tree of Death hidden from the public. To cultists, the Tree of Death is central to their success. The Kabbalah teaching has been combined with Aleister Crowley's and Manly P. Hall's evil insight to create Lucifer's kingdom through programming.

To understand Lucifer's kingdom, one must understand how God's Kingdom works. Programming can't be understood without looking at its foundation. All programming methods and practices were established through the Tree of Death. Lucifer plagiarized his ideas from God's plan — reversing the Lord's meanings. Satan cannot create. Satan cannot procreate. He lost these rights when he rebelled against God in Heaven. (Refer to *Puzzle Pieces to The Cabal, Mind Control, and Slavery, Part 1*, for a full explanation).

Within the Tree of Death's foundation, all teachings refer to God as Lucifer. Cult members erroneously believe Lucifer created all things, gave life, and even controls human breath. After a cult finishes programming, nothing in a human body remains pure — including chakras, the body's seven energy centers; and bones, muscles, organs, glands, brain, blood, and DNA.

This book contains detailed instructions on how to retrieve what occult groups robbed from members: their intellect, conscience, memories, empathy, and free will. You will learn of a demon's purpose and the layers of demons attached to victims physically, spiritually, and emotionally. Lucifer believes he must prove he's God, having all power over you, he makes people believe he is the one that gives you life and he can take it any time he wants.

It's taken more than 30 years to learn what various cults did to me through programming. The process finally makes sense, the puzzle pieces coming together for a full understanding. It is my great desire to help you understand the occult's inflictions upon cult survivors like myself. Understanding the template of core programming and its specific stages will simplify your deprogramming process. By understanding the core foundation, you will understand the secrets hidden from the world until recently.

I never understood the extent of my programming or why several cult groups committed fiendish acts against me. I thought it was random adversity. This couldn't have been further from the truth. I feel as if I've uncovered a painting that for years had most parts hidden. Now for the first time, I can see the whole painting. I could always guess what programming meant, but unfortunately, I had flaws in grasping the truth. In all my years of working on myself, going to therapy, and spending great sums of money, I've never felt that true change occurred. I was so deeply programmed by the Illuminati; I wasn't able to break free without the deeper understanding I present in this book.

I didn't realize I had a secret weapon hiding inside of me. I knew some of the parts and pieces, but the Tree of Death/Kabbalah teaching and its huge significance was never addressed, not to mention the four worlds attached and the organism's foundational trees. Never once did we find or discuss tree programming, the New World Order (NWO), Army Programming, or Water Kingdom Programming, yet these are essential pieces. You can't become truly free unless the knowledge of the Tree of Death and the foundational programming parts are removed.

Now it's time to get free. If your professional therapist does not understand what's been done to you, show him or her this book. Have the practitioner help you remove the programming. Your freedom will come from knowing the programming in its entirety. I wrote this book as a "how to" manual. If you are unable to work with a professional, ask a trusted friend to help you undo the programming.

Why now? The world is waking up and can see what's been happening for thousands of years — even back to ancient history. The Old Testament is full of stories of sacrifice, idol worship, witchcraft, and civilizations being ruined because of ritual abuse. God is now giving us a chance to stop it. Many people are openly discussing the government-sponsored MK Ultra and the cult's members.

The occult has always worked in the shadows. Now that the cult groups' secrets are becoming known worldwide, their members can no longer kill anyone threatening to reveal secrets. Individuals' programming is breaking down. Cult leaders are becoming familiar faces as they worship Lucifer and perform horrific deeds on babies and children. The good news is, we can stop this. I believe the Lord has urged me to release this book promptly, thereby leading many survivors to freedom.

This book is a sequel to my first book, *Puzzle Pieces to The Cabal, Mind Control, and Slavery. Part 1*. I will not explain the information detailed in that book. Part 1 explores the importance of the Tree of Life and the Tree of Death. You must understand these principles to know why Lucifer has exerted so much energy into making his kingdom like Gods' — only inverted. This book will venture deep into the programming of The Kabbalah Tree of Death's foundation. I will share techniques and methods to remove programming, including integration, and explain the process' order. You will learn the importance of prayer, how to protect yourself, how to cast out demons, and how to renounce curses. The book also contains information on how to manage family programming and addiction.

Various techniques and healing modalities will instruct survivors and professional therapists in releasing painful memories while taking emotional and spiritual health into your own hands. I will provide example prayers for you to cast out entities.

The sad truth is, if you don't remove the Kabbalah Tree of Death foundational programming, you will not get free. Even after many years of therapy, I realized true healing wouldn't come until I acknowledged this important piece. How the cult group programmers must have been laughing! As my memories returned, I began to doubt I was still being controlled, but I was. My core foundation programming was firmly intact. I was shocked by what remained after my extensive counseling and deprogramming.

Although I'm grateful to the therapists with whom I worked for their professionalism and skill, my practitioners didn't have formal mind-control training. However, this book offers enough material to buoy cult survivors to freedom. We can remove the core foundation and integrate the core parts without years of expensive therapy. The survivor can easily go back and clean up the fragments.

Recognition is not my motive for writing this book. I simply want this information available worldwide. I would like to give credit to God for teaching me the principles within this book. He led me to the information necessary to solve the complete puzzle of mind-control programming.

I would also like to thank Amanda Buys, who filled in some of the pieces I didn't understand. This woman has done great work helping survivors. Lastly, I would like to thank my clients, who taught me that God's principles are true, when we found the programming lying deep within. Moreover, almost every bit of information in this book was implicit in my own programming.

It is my calling to help people get free. Some cult survivors are called to tell their stories, while others may feel the need to teach. If you are a survivor, don't worry about what you're supposed to do with the abuse you suffered. If you focus on getting free now, God will grant you discernment later in the journey. God will serve as your chaperon from darkness to light. There once was a time when I felt nothing good would come from my trauma. God had other plans. He gently led me along a route to my current joys of writing books, speaking, and coaching. I'm here because I permitted God to lead me by the hand. I would have never made it this far without Him.

DISCLAIMER

This book can be highly triggering for any person who's been abused and/or underwent any kind of mind control. Please pray and speak to a professional before proceeding to determine whether the book is right for you. If you feel this book's message will benefit you after following your spiritual acumen and professional therapist's advice, you are encouraged to pace yourself and check in with your practitioners as needed. By proceeding forward, you assume responsibility and accountability for your knowledge, and release Laura Worley and Puzzle Pieces Together LLC from any negative outcomes.

I

BEFORE WE BEGIN

SOME FOUNDATIONAL PRINCIPLES

What Does It All Mean?

After all my years of research, I have reached the conclusion all occult groups are rebelling against God. The cult groups worship Lucifer, who is angry and has been rebelling against God since the beginning. All rituals and programming are based on worshiping Lucifer while spitting in the face of God. Biblical principles and commands from God have been twisted by Lucifer as core pillars within his kingdom.

All programming has a spiritual component. When we remove certain layers of programming, we do so in a spiritual dimension of darkness where demons reside. The battles are waged in the spirit realm. To help cult survivors, releasing Lucifer and the spirits following him is necessary. The programming achieved in Lucifer's name is full of illusion. The programming is done in a spiritual realm where the parts of a soul created during programming can execute feats unlike any in a physical body. Parts, also known as alters, are key to programming.

Lucifer is a master of deception and lies. Hence, programming is based on illusions and the world of opposites. Each alter is programmed to believe Lucifer has the qualities of Jesus Christ, and Jesus Christ bears the characteristics of Lucifer. The programs are usually installed through rape committed by a fake Jesus. Lucifer knows if the illusions he cast in cult members' lives were removed, then people could see him as he truly is, and no one would follow him.

Core foundational programming, which is addressed here, is based on spiritual teachings turned upside down and inside out. Lucifer's kingdom is one of total spiritual darkness. Programming and rituals are done so parts of an individual will make oaths and covenants to Lucifer. All ritual sacrifices are an offering to Lucifer, just as an unblemished lamb was an offering to Jehovah in the Old Testament. Similarly, Lucifer requires the sacrifice of a pure, human baby in order to mock God.

It doesn't matter what program a cult survivor is part of, the worship of Lucifer is always the primary aim. Demons will always be attached to people to keep them in line for Lucifer. It's vital to understand the survivor is part of this battle. It is not just about torture and rape; it is about capturing that soul for Lucifer, so God loses one of His beloved children.

Cult survivors are in a spiritual battle whether they want to be or not. That choice was made for them while they inhabited the womb. The only thing that can overcome Lucifer's kingdom is someone with higher authority. Jesus Christ has authority over Lucifer and his kingdom.

We cannot fight a spiritual war without someone of higher authority than Lucifer and his fallen angels. Heavenly Father and His son, Jesus Christ, are the only beings with that authority. Fire must be fought with fire, so to speak, otherwise mankind would be swallowed up by great evil. We have power over all demons and Lucifer when we use the name of Jesus Christ.

In summary, we are in a spiritual battle between God and Lucifer in kingdoms where each of us must choose our side. Cult victims who work through the parts and alters programming removal stage must also choose their leader before integration is possible.

Free Will

Free will is often described as the ability to choose good from evil, right from wrong. This would suggest people make a conscious choice because they have information about each side.

What motivates choice? The answer may seem overly simple, but it boils down to who people follow. If a person chooses to follow God, he makes a choice that allows God to help and guide him. She makes choices based on the teachings of God's Kingdom. If a person follows Lucifer, that individual's choices align with the rules governing membership in Lucifer's kingdom.

In this book, I will not be talking of man's weaknesses or mistakes. This book is directly addressing those who have the desire to follow God and have membership in His kingdom, but have been a member of Lucifer's kingdom by being born into a Satanic cult group. It was not a choice for them in this life. There is no free will when it comes to Lucifer's kingdom.

Free will is a gift from God to all mankind. Lucifer has been trying to take it away ever since God's plan in heaven that everyone got to vote for. God offered a plan of free will, and no matter what happened, God wouldn't take it away from His children. Lucifer had another plan — this one having no free will — wherein no soul would be lost. Free will comes with a cost. People make bad choices with free will; the suffering we may endure because of other people's free will can be a hefty cost to pay. If we followed Lucifer's plan, we would not grow or learn because there wouldn't be free will for thought or action. So, those with a body voted to accept God's plan. All the fallen angels without a body became Lucifer's children. The fallen angels bitterly resent not having a body as humans do.

Let's look at Lucifer's kingdom: There is no free will. Its members must be traumatized, raped, and suffer ghastly indignities to be a part of his kingdom. His subjects are made to believe they are worthless and deserve no happiness or mercy. Lucifer rewards those who endure his tortures. They spend their lives in hell with him, promised they will live in this great hell forever. That is how he "loves." Why would anyone choose this?

Now let's look at God's kingdom: He offers free will. All are inherently loved without doing anything. He believes all are of great worth as His sons and daughters. God is merciful, kind, and He knows we will make mistakes, yet He loves us anyway. There is nothing we could ever do that would stop Him from loving us. Heavenly Father and Jesus Christ offer all people eternal life in love and joy.

No one would ever choose Lucifer's kingdom, right? Lucifer knows that, so his plan is to start in the womb by teaching a baby who he is — and that's God. The baby matures into a child, growing up believing the illusion. This part of an individual's mind has been taught only Lucifer's self-proclaimed greatness. Can that be free will?

For people to have free will, they must know both sides. Likewise, it would not be free will to know only of God's plan. Knowing both sides is key to letting go of the parts that have only absorbed the teachings of evil. It is a powerful healing tool when the alter can see he's been lied to.

Before a cult survivor's recovery, free will is unknown. It is an occult group custom to begin telling cult members at 13 years old they are now making a free will decision. This is a lie. Free will cannot be manipulated. The human soul knows the difference between this so-called choice, and true God-given free will.

When people are under mind control, they are not using free will. If a part has been trained all her life to obey through torture and rape, it's not free will. When a cult leader trains a little girl or boy to have sex with an adult, it's not free will. When a cult youngster becomes a teenager and still uses alters to do horrible things under mind control, it's not free will.

Some therapists say people become accountable at 13 years old. I disagree with this because nothing changed except the person became a teenager. So, if someone under mind control is forced into horrible acts, where is the free will? If someone makes a conscious choice to act differently, he's deciding based on his awareness of the entire perspective.

One of the greatest feelings cult survivors will sense is free will. Survivors are finally cognizant of their world, choosing when, where, and how to participate. They no longer have to act brazenly, violating their moral code.

At some point, survivors must all decide in which kingdom they want to join. For me and my house, we belong to the one true God and His son, Jesus Christ.

What Does It Mean to be Under Mind Control?

To be under mind control means to be under the will of another person. People under mind control are no longer acting by choice. They are being controlled by a spiritual, physical, or mental influence that manipulates individuals from the outside or inside.

Cults have used mind control to assume control of members' cognition to make them conduct acts against their morals and conscious choice. Free will is shattered when someone is under mind control. Cults and demons know they cannot simply abduct free will; they must have permission.

Through torture, the occult can form an opening in someone's mind. The opening serves as a gateway to permit an entity to enter both the mind and the body.

The question remains in many survivors: Am I responsible for what I was made to do? The answer is no.

Logically, people cannot be held responsible if they're in a different state of consciousness. The enigma occurs if the individual's actions go against her morals. For example, the average person would never choose to harm another individual unless the act is in defense. Belligerence, in many cases, bucks a cult member's true identity. Thus, many cult survivors have found that forgiving themselves of evils performed in rituals is onerous, almost impossible. This is natural for any human being with a conscience.

Cult groups know most people do have a conscience. Cults know your act of evil not only violates your free will; it also defiles your soul. The occult grasps that shame and guilt become unbearable. When the apex is crossed, your mind splits as you disassociate.

Let's say you've worked hard to heal yourself and now accept you harmed another. The pain may be too much to handle. This is when you must go to the Courts of Heaven, repent, and ask Jesus Christ to heal your pain. It is truly the only means of having the unbearable pain lifted. (The Courts of Heaven is explained in a later chapter.)

I believe we must acknowledge we've caused damage to others if we survived Satanic Ritual Abuse. We must repent in the Courts of Heaven so Jesus Christ can speak on our behalf, thus revoking the demon's legal rights. Because cult survivors did harm others, demons have a legal right to their souls. The legal claim must be removed for total freedom.

The next step is decisive. We must believe in Jesus's sacrifice. If His blood has spoken for us, we accept His gift of healing, consequently finding peace. We must give all of our pain to Jesus Christ to fully heal us at spiritual, mental, and physical levels.

You did not choose to harm another, so you must forgive yourself. It doesn't mean to shirk all responsibility. However, you must acknowledge your misdeeds and undertake what is necessary in the Lord's eyes to be forgiven.

If something was not the result of our decision, we can be forgiven. However, we still must allow healing to take place following acts of evil that belied our soul.

Just a reminder: Had you behaved as other cult members do, you would not be here reading this book or trying to heal. You are not like them. If you wanted to harm others, you'd still be in the cult.

Your understanding is the main reason I shared this information on mind control. Have this material in mind as you read the following chapters, which may be triggering.

Soul Choice

The soul must make a choice after the conscious and unconscious mind have full knowledge of what happened. The soul must have a full understanding of Lucifer's kingdom and God's Kingdom. There must be a choice with full knowledge of the truth of all things, not the lies of Lucifer. Once the soul has decided, Lucifer or God cannot take that away. The cult survivor has chosen her kingdom. Lucifer often tries to cover up the soul's choice but doesn't have ultimate authority to do so. Lucifer will persuade and create alters that will choose him, but that is not a soul choice. Soul choice cannot be manipulated. Soul choice is using free will at the level of our true self. Our true soul cannot be harmed, hurt, touched, destroyed, broken, abused or changed by anyone.

QUESTIONS OFTEN ASKED

Why Me?

How many times have we asked the question, "Why me?" Why didn't God protect me or help me? Why has this horrible misfortune happened to me?

This will be a process to understand the journey of hell you've endured. But what if you had decided long ago to go on this very journey in order to help others?

It took me a very long time to see that all my suffering would lead me to what I had always wanted, which is helping people, speaking, and teaching. Who knew my suffering would lead me to the giving life I always desired? This indeed matched my soul purpose.

Whatever they did to you, no matter how malicious and disgusting it was, you too can help society. I think we have choices in life. Tragic events happen to everyone. The question is, "What are you going to do about it?"

You are never forgotten by the Lord. If you ask Him for help, He will guide you to the place that frees your soul. Be patient — this will proceed one step at a time. Do not push yourself faster than you are able to go. There is no goal you have to reach within a specific time. It is your journey alone. Do not compare yourself to any other survivors.

To individual survivors, I would say, *You are one of the strongest people on this planet. You survived! Now it is time to heal! Love yourself, forgive yourself, and trust you are a magnificent human being.*

Is it Possible to Overcome the Effects of Abuse?

The answer is, "Yes!" In many ways you already have. You are alive against all odds. You have the tenacity to overcome cult mind control and programming. It will take time, but not years as it once did. Perpetrators of mind control make everything complex — your mind is fractured into many pieces, only carrying some truth. This is accomplished so survivors cannot reveal what the assailants have done. The cult groups know their victims will find healing if they are able to understand what's been inflicted. The cults have concealed the foundational programming well. In the past few years, God has shown us the truth. Since 2020, as their memories return, many survivors' programming is breaking down. I want my readers to own the entire puzzle so they don't spend a lifetime getting free as I have.

Why Has Breaking Free Not Worked?

If you are a survivor and have tried to set yourself free to no avail, it is most likely because you did not know what the cult did to you. Unfortunately, very few professionals know how to break systematic mind control in cult survivors. Still, the circumstances are changing and more information is available. The programming process will be revealed so you can have freedom. You will have the answers to finally undo the programming, pulling the alters back together, so you can become whole, you can become one.

Why Does Understanding
the Programming Matter?

If you don't understand what's been done to you, how can you undo it? That would be like trying to complete a puzzle with only half the pieces. I consulted professionals for decades without reaching the core parts of my programming, which was firmly intact and firmly in control of me. Even though I had recovered much of my memory, the cults were still using me. That is the main reason to understand the puzzle pieces of your own programming. If you don't, they have access. The control will continue.

II

IMPORTANT
SUMMARY FROM
BOOK 1

It's necessary to explain what the Kabbalah is in order to begin sharing the puzzle pieces to the core foundational programming of the Kabbalah Tree of Death. (Before proceeding, read *Puzzle Pieces to The Cabal, Mind Control, and Slavery, Part 1*.)

WHAT IS KABBALAH?

Many people don't understand the Kabbalah teachings; I certainly did not until the Lord showed me when I wrote my first book in 2019. In essence, Kabbalah basically coincides with Jewish Mysticism, but it is so much more. During the years 1500-1800, Kabbalah was considered the true Jewish theology. Many folk customs came from Kabbalah — taken directly out of the Zohar. The power of Kabbalistic customs touched all Jewish life. (For more information, refer to *Puzzle Pieces to The Cabal, Mind Control, and Slavery, Part 1.*)

According to the World History Encyclopedia (2018), "The term Kabbalah refers specifically to the form of Jewish mysticism that became widespread in the Middle Ages.

However, in recent decades it has essentially become a generic term for the entirety of Jewish mystical thought" (para. 1).

Kabbalah represents how people have ascended from the physical to the spiritual world. Kabbalah holds that, through our bodies, anything can be manifested. The cultist groups built upon this idea to include demonic attachments and dark worlds where Lucifer resides.

In many ways, Kabbalah is a rebellion against traditional Jewish beliefs. Kabbalah does touch the magical. Kabbalists study practical and philosophical teachings. Occult groups acquired pure Kabbalistic teachings, inverting them to suit an evil agenda. It is believed the teachings are so intertwined with black magic that many Kabbalists didn't want to be associated with the doctrine in its early days.

Kabbalists saw themselves as the carriers and transmitters of ancient secrets passed down through generations. Kabbalists believe the Bible is primarily for them. The Bible acts like a dictionary and guide for decoding mystical secrets. This ancient teaching was given to specific individuals to decode. Kabbalism believes the god of Kabbalah is superior to the God of the Bible. The name of the highest being is *Ein Sof* (sometimes spelled *Ain Sof*). The teachings of the Sephirot represent being one with Ein Sof. They do not believe in the God of the Bible and consider Him to be inferior.

One of the goals of Kabbalah is to manipulate divine nature, which is where the programming of the Kabbalah tree has relevance. Kabbalah mystics use the Bible as a reference for symbols and story and will invert the meaning God gave them. As you will read in this book, the basis of programming is to create mind-controlled slaves by taking the Tree of Life in God's plans and inverting it to Lucifer's will. Lucifer's tree does not represent love and eternal life in joy and happiness as the Tree of Life does. Satan's tree represents death and hell coalescing into an illusion of glory. The children of Lucifer are taught Lucifer is God and that all the pieces to God's Kingdom were turned into the false story of a wonderful, eternal life in hell with Lucifer.

The most important teachings of the Kabbalah stolen by the occult were represented by the 10-point Sephirot. Each point represented the characters and attributes of God. Each globe represented a world. The inversion of the 10 points of the Sephirot to match occult beliefs was quickly transferred to the teachings of Lucifer's kingdom.

Each of the Sephirot points are deeply sacred and have complex meanings. The components of the Kabbalah Sephirot meanings were to represent God, while the occult uses the Sephirot to represent Lucifer.

The Sephirot are the manifestations of Ein Sof and his magical attributes. These Sephirot are connected by 22 pathways, each based on numbers representing magic. That is why the occult uses numbers for everything. Once again, in God's Kingdom, numbers have a positive representation. Lucifer stole it and now it means the opposite. Each number has a mystical meaning or magical spells attached to it. Some believe Kabbalah is evil because of its ancient quality and historical significance. Kabbalah is a mixture of the Torah and witchcraft.

Here is where I'd like to mention two influential people for their roles in using the teaching of the Kabbalah for the occult. The two men are Alister Crowley and Manly P. Hall. Another well-known figure is Josef Mengele, the Nazi "scientist" who used the Kabbalah's Occult teachings on many children who became the foundation of the Kabbalah Tree of Life upturned to the Tree of Death.

Who was Aleister Crowley?

According to Nachtigal,(2014), "Both of these monstrous individuals were initiated in Luciferian secret societies (para. 2). "Crowley entered every secret organization that would let him join—he was known to be a member of Freemasonry, the Order of the Golden Dawn and the Ordo Tempi Orientis, a German satanic group. He also founded his own magical order: the Astrum Argentum, or Silver Star. After WWI, Hitler was initiated into the Thule Society. The occult Thule Society boasted of distinguished members, including judges, police chiefs, professors, and industrialists. The Master of the Temple was the bald, opiate-addicted occultist Dietrich Eckhart. He trained Hilter in many of the secret teachings of the ancient mystery religions."

"Born Edward Alexander Crowley in 1875," Nachtigal (2014) continued. "Crowley was a pansexual, mystic, occultist, ceremonial magician, deviant, recreational drug experimenter, poet and accomplished mountaineer who was also known as Frater Perdurabo and The Great Beast 666. He founded the religious philosophy of Thelema which enforced an idealist, libertine rule of "Do what thou wilt." The British press named him "The Wickedest Man in the World."

Mclymon (2014) stated, "In 1903, Crowley married Rose Edith Kelly. Interestingly, a huge part of the programming of the Illuminati and Freemasons is based on a core alter personality named Rose. Crowley and Rose Kelly had a baby named Lilith, who represents an entity of sexual iniquity. Kelly went to an institution for alcoholism" (para. 1).

Who was Manly P. Hall?

Manly P. Hall is considered by Freemasonry as an Esoterica Mystic. Hall has been given the highest honors that Freemasonry bestows and yet some of his writings are scoffed at and denied as factual, "lacking proof" by the very people who esteem him. Manly P. Hall was clearly a Luciferian to the core and was proud of it. Hall's writings are the perfect example of the Esoteric/Exoteric knowledge of which he, Albert Pike, and Aleister Crowley reference in their literature.

Manly Hall is the author of more than 150 published books. One of Hall's book titles says it all: *An encyclopedic outline of Masonic, Hermetic, Qabbalistic, and Rosicrucian symbolical philosophy: Being an interpretation of the secret teachings concealed within the rituals, allegories, and mysteries of all ages.*

I really did not want to share too much because I refuse to give undue attention to evil men. However, these men were responsible for part of the template of the Tree of Death's foundational programming taken from Kabbalah teachings.

Crowley and Hall used all manner of teaching that seemed momentous and sophisticated. That is what the devil does. He entices men into hell with his trickery and lies. If two evil men can inspire wickedness in many others, it makes sense that a few good people can inspire greatness. Never underestimate the power one person can employ for good.

III

PUZZLE PIECES TO THE CORE FOUNDATIONAL PROGRAMMING

It has taken many years to find this information, which is so important it's been very well hidden. I've labored for many years to find this information, which is so important it's been very well hidden. In 2019, the Lord began teaching me about the foundation of programming: the Kabbalah Tree of Life/Tree of Death. In my 20 years of counseling, none of this was ever mentioned.

Since my first book, I have learned even more of the hidden pieces of the mind control programming puzzle. When I got stuck in writing the book, the Lord led me to Amanda Buys. Her vast experience in working with survivors filled in the missing pieces for me. I will be sharing many of her teachings from Kanaan Ministries, my experiences with Satanic Ritual Abuse clients, and from my experience as an MK Ultra survivor. These additional insights help survivors become free in the shortest amount of time possible.

The Kabbalah Tree is a sacred symbol to show the beliefs of the Kabbalah teachings and the importance of the Sephirot. This book shows most of the pieces in the programming of cult members by Freemasons, Illuminati, Military, and Witchcraft groups. The Kabbalah Tree of Death is the foundation of all programming explained in *Part 1, Puzzle Pieces to The Cabal, Mind Control, and Slavery*. Earlier, I gave a synopsis of what the Tree of Life represents in the Kabbalah as well as how it was inverted.

The Kabbalah Tree of Life concept was flipped for mind control programming in a spiritual battle between Lucifer and God. When you come to understand the pieces, you will see almost all symbols and allegories come from God despite Lucifer's assumed ownership. It is ironic that Lucifer hates God so badly that he stole every symbol, pattern, and life-giving force God created. To me, this proves Lucifer does not have the ability to create new ideas.

It is my belief there is little time left to help people obtain freedom. We have to do what we can quickly for the cult survivors. Most survivors do not have the money to get professional help for the length of time required to remove every piece of programming. It is not necessary to go after every piece. That is why we must focus on the core parts to be removed in the quickest time.

Indeed, survivors and therapists must address the biggest parts of programming built on the foundation of the Tree of Death/Tree of Life. In doing so, the practitioner must begin at the current age of the client and walk backwards to conception.

Two significant programs are the Water World and the One World Order Army Programming that both connect to the foundation. Every survivor is so different. All I can say is, as a practitioner, I first address the One World Army or New World Order Programming. The programs are crucial to extract from survivors as the plan to reactivate mind control programming begins in 2022 and 2023.

The Water Kingdom or Water World programming is huge and you will have to decide in what part of the removal process it must be addressed. I have just recently found out the Water Kingdom is part of the New World Order Army Programming. It's possible you will have to remove both mind control programs before proceeding to the rest of the removal process.

Each cult survivor will have many programs focusing on different jobs, but these are designed to delay so you never reach the core of programming, which is removal of the Kabbalah trees. There will be 7 trees in the core foundation programming, and I have found additional trees can be built for a specific purpose in the survivor's teenage mind. In my example of removal of the Tree of Death, I will show you the main pieces that absolutely must be removed. Also, I will explain how a few additional trees can be built later in the teen years, which was part of my programming.

Again, the survivor and therapist will have to work together to find all the pieces to the core foundational programming. Sometimes in the beginning of sessions, you may have to start where the survivor is comfortable and work on memories. Survivors often say, "I do not have a lot of memories." Just start with what the survivor does know. This will lead to the client remembering more. Please use the tools and methods in the back of this book.

After you've finished removing the core foundation, don't worry if a few straggler programs remain. You can take care of the small pieces later. Let me give you an example of what I mean. I had gathered all the foundational pieces I have listed, the Water Kingdom, and Army programming, but most of the small pieces had collapsed. I never once had to address Alice in Wonderland or the Wizard of Oz because they are distractions. If you focus on these kinds of programs; you will never get free. Occult groups know that! The Illuminati/Freemasons are masters of illusion and distraction. (The groups use Alice in Wonderland and Wizard of Oz programs significantly, but they are not the core foundation. I can tell you from my own experience because I focused on these programs though it did not set me free.)

This removal process is for the individual. You will be shown the construct of the program with all its pieces so you understand all of it. The biggest point I can make here is every survivor is different and will have different program pieces. Up to now, every survivor I have worked with has the foundational programming of the Kabbalah Tree because it is an allegory to the Illuminati/Freemasons' doctrine. This crosses over into additional occult groups. Please make sure you don't leave out the Druids. They will have ancient teachings for programming. Many survivors will have this programming.

If you are a survivor and have a family, you will have to go to your partner and/or children next. As I will explain later, you, your partner, and children may have a great deal of programming to remove. Don't become discouraged at what I just said. The most important thing is to remove your own programming. You will find it begins to loosen up the entire family's programming. As a mother or father, you will be able to accomplish a great deal for your children. Spouses or partners must realize they will have programming if they've lived with a survivor for any period, even if that time was not in the partner's childhood.

Let us begin...

First, this process — and any removal process — must begin with a client's prayer for protection. The cult survivor must pray for himself, his family, and anything else he loves. You and the survivor will then bind all fallen angels under the authority of Jesus Christ. You will send them away so they don't interrupt the work. Throughout this process, you will state the prayer more than once to cast out the demons, which are layered into the programming. When you eliminate fallen angels attached to one set of programming, another set of fallen angels linked to other programming fills in. You will know what I mean in the next example. (See chapter "Prayer and Casting Out Demons" for further understanding.)

You then have the client say, "I command all of my parts wherever they are to come back into my body now. Wherever you are (listing specific places such as the underworld, Water Kingdom, hiding places, etc.), you must come back now! You will have them go to a safe place where they cannot be harmed. They will not have any power to interrupt or sabotage the session. In this safe place there will be no communicating with demons. We put the safe place under the authority of Jesus Christ so we can ensure safety and compliance. The alters must learn the truth about Lucifer and who he is and the truth of Jesus Christ. The alters can decide whom to follow when they are ready. We do not push the alters to choose. All illusions will be removed and no lies can be told while alters are in a safe place or during session time. It is very important to set up how the session must go. Setting boundaries help the session to go more smoothly. (Say whatever else you feel inclined to.) The point here is that the parts must no longer be blinded by Lucifer and his demons. The parts believe what they're told about the specific world in which they live. That is why a survivor's parts must face the truth of their fragmented lives. They also need to know they won't be hurt while the practitioner and client work. I often allow survivors to enter a healing bubble filled with the frequency of love. I command all entities to have no power over the survivor, as the bubble is under the authority of Jesus Christ — no demon will have the ability to breach this healing bubble. The alters and demons will have no ability to communicate during the session. I even do this for the angry parts and the witch parts. In this bubble, the parts do not wield any power to sabotage the session. They will see all that takes place without illusions. Just make sure the parts/alters understand they will not be harmed, but they also have no power to sabotage or lie in this place of safety.

All parts have to be shown the truth. This is so important. For the first time in his life, a survivor gets to exercise free will, he gets to choose a side. The alters may have to be taught the essence of free will because they have never had the ability to choose. This must be thoroughly explained to the parts before the team's work is done. I learned this fact a few years ago and it's been confirmed many times working with clients.

In this example, I removed the New World Order programming first. Each case may last many hours or a few. If cult survivors were taken back in the years 2011-2020, they will have an updated and installed New World Order Army programming with current instructions in addition to the programs lying dormant for many years.

Next, I went to the vast Water Kingdom connected to the foundation. When I say vast, I mean it may require 15 hours or more to remove. Again, every survivor will be different so the procedure could take less time. A survivor may not even have this program at all.

In another example, the practitioner and survivor will have to work closely with the Holy Spirit for guidance. I have been using Muscle Testing and Body Code for the last six years to help my clients remove programming. At times, a practitioner may be stumped, though Muscle Testing on the client will direct her easily. The survivor's unconscious was programmed to not share information, but the cult never implanted programming to thwart Muscle Testing and Body Code. I have been able to use Body Code as a guide to ask questions. The client and I uncover the truth very quickly.

IV

THE ORDER
PROGRAMMING
IS INSTALLED

THIS IS NOT THE ORDER YOU REMOVE TREE OF DEATH PROGRAMMING. YOU MUST START WITH THE SURVIVOR'S AGE TO WORK BACK TO THE WOMB IN THE REMOVAL PROCESS. IT WILL BE EASIER TO UNDERSTAND IF YOU KNOW THE ORDER THE PROGRAMMING IS DONE.

IT ALL BEGINS IN THE WOMB...

First Important Core Part of the Programming

It's important to explain that the first split of the survivor's mind is at conception. At that moment, a cult survivor's mind is split in half. From that point on, half of the mind is all Lucifer gets. All programming and teachings of spiritual darkness will transpire in that half. The unconscious mind believes there are two people. Lucifer does not get the whole mind in God's Kingdom. I believe God doesn't allow Lucifer to control the whole person because everything Satan does is against all of God's Laws. So, from the first split at conception all that will be done to the baby is in only half of the baby's mind.

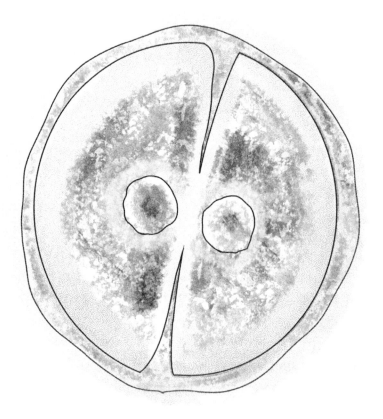

PICTURE BY NIC YOUNGBLOOD

The core self exists before anything is done to the baby. To program a human being, there must be a way to create an illusion for the infant and child to believe. The trauma is so severe, the core self will split to survive. That split part of the mind will believe Lucifer's teachings in the womb. The core self's job is to keep us safe. It's a brilliant way to survive, taking the trauma and putting it in a compartment. Eventually that compartment will not remain closed when cult survivors hit their 30s and 40s. Membrane walls start to break down and memories begin to surface. In programming, the splitting is done purposefully. The cult knows the child will split when there is too much trauma. When the baby or child splits, this is when the cult will create an alter to fully integrate with the Occult teachings.

At conception there will be the first split in the baby's mind. I call the first split the "Twin." Other's might call the first split at conception another name. To me and other survivors, it feels like a Twin. The part in the back is the dark side belonging to Lucifer's kingdom that knows nothing else. The Twin is split many times throughout a survivor's life. The survivor is in the front; the twin in the back withstands all the trauma, abuse, and programming.

It is an incredibly weird feeling. My conscious self that has a high moral code was absolutely horrified at what parts of me had not only experienced but acted out. I felt as if I were two people. "There is no way this thing can exist in me," I thought. I hated the Twin and all the other parts for what they had done. For many years I could not accept this dark part of me that could do awful things. It was absolutely not possible. In some ways I can't believe it now. It all seems like a movie. In many ways it played out like a movie.

An alter or part of myself was made to watch a movie over and over until I believed the lies and illusions. The occultists started the horror movie in the womb and never ceased until a mindless robot formed.

As for information about Satanic Ritual Abuse, we are learning more and more. Thank goodness. I am sure 5 years from now we will discover a speedier way to remove programming. I am banking on it! For now, I have found this is the most timely, accurate information — not to mention the most hidden.

TEMPLATE OF THE SEPHIROT TREE

The template of the Sephirot Tree is formed in the womb to create the Tree of Death. The Kabbalists call it the Tree of Life. Next is a diagram of a metaphorical lightning bolt to the baby in the womb. Definitions of each globe will appear later.

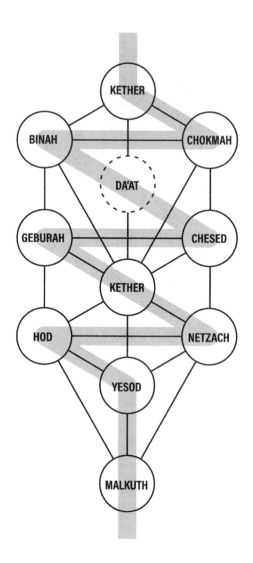

Lucifer fabricates a template of the Tree of Death in the womb. The baby will sense a lightening bolt has invaded the womb. As far as I know, there are 7 rituals performed on the pregnant mother to ensure a template has been formed to accommodate large downloads of programming. This is when the Stronghold Demon, who has the most authority of the fallen angels and is appointed by Lucifer, is downloaded. In my first book I called the Stronghold Demon "The One."

Before babies are even born in cults, they've been severely traumatized and abused. Tragically, the abuse is unleashed upon every child in occult groups. It is unbelievable infants live through it.

The cult groups all rush to capture the child at conception. If a cult group has claim to the first split, the group contends it has the most control. Let's say the Fertility Cult is the first one to reach the infant after the first split occurs. The Fertility Cult will promptly attach the Stronghold Demon that stays with the child for life, literally growing up alongside him or her. Now let's say the Druid Cult discovers the child, pouncing in next to capture him or her. The Druids also cause a split and download an ancient demon in the family line. Now, in swoops the Illuminati/Freemasons to capture the baby and trigger a third split.

Stronghold Demons

A Stronghold Demon is assigned to you for the rest of your life starting at the split in conception.

A Stronghold Demon's task is focused on bringing victims down into misery and hell. Lucifer and the spirits that followed him have fallen from heaven and are very angry with not having a body. Lucifer will assign each fallen angel to a person for that individual's life until death unless the demon is kicked out. Many do not make it to the point of expelling the demon. Most people never even realize or remember the acts done to them by cults.

When a child is in the womb at conception, Lucifer grants a demon the right to have full-time access to a body. This demon will be with the child over a lifetime. To achieve all that Lucifer requires to do in his kingdom, the Stronghold Demon will have complete control over the child. The Stronghold is an illusion over the child. He or she believes the demon is a best friend and that he or she cannot live without it. The Stronghold has disguised itself to look like something comforting to the child. As the child grows, he or she learns the only way to live is to have the Stronghold present at all times.

This Stronghold will give permission for all other demons to attach to all the creations of the different worlds in the Tree of Death programming. The Stronghold has the most power; like in humans, the part that is the first split has the authority over all parts.

The Stronghold Demon must keep its victims in pain and punishment so it remains attached to them. The demon tells children this is for their own good, this will make them strong and happy.

If the Stronghold Demon wins over the soul and the person ultimately goes into Lucifer's kingdom, the Stronghold is rewarded by Lucifer by being given another person in the family line. The Stronghold then has a higher ranking. The more souls he wins for Lucifer, the higher his ranking in Lucifer's Fallen Angel Army. The cult's hierarchy is modeled after Lucifer's hierarchy.

You cannot expel the Stronghold Demon unless you have integrated all programmed parts/alters. In the final step you must be working with the part called Twin that was the first split. Twin has to tell the Stronghold to go. No other part can make the Stronghold leave. You must work backwards, integrating all parts so that you end up at the very first split. The first split's name is often Rose or Adam but not always.

The ultimate goal is to bring back the parts to Conception Identity or twin for complete integration. The Core Split at conception will have to be worked with a great deal because the survivors' parts/alters are 100 percent loyal to Lucifer's Kingdom. This Core Part has their partner, the Stronghold Demon, who must be released in order for the Core Part at conception to be integrated, which enables the survivor to become whole in the mind, body, and spirit.

Don't worry if you do not yet understand what I am saying. In another chapter we will talk about core parts and integration. You will understand as you keep reading.

The Twin cannot integrate fully until you work with your own family's programming. When family programming is removed, then the Twin can be made whole through complete integration.

Remember I am showing you the order cults do the programming. THIS IS NOT THE ORDER YOU RE-

MOVE THE PROGRAMMING. START FROM SURVIVORS AGE NOW AND WORK BACKWARDS TO THE WOMB AND THE FIRST SPLIT AT CONCEPTION.

Here are some pieces that you must remove in the womb. This is not a complete list. This can help you understand what you will have to find in the programming to remove.

Remove:

- All Seven rituals done to mother and baby in the womb
- The template of the tree
- Lighting or energy used by Lucifer to claim baby as his
- All trauma
- All downloads
- All curses
- Family History this is where the child's bloodline comes in. This is a huge download of iniquity from the beginning of time.
- Remove all they were trying to create for the character of the person and put them back to what God created or in other words who they truly are.
- All core parts must be integrated back to the first split.
- Take away all illusions so the parts can see the truth.
- Always remove the alarm systems. Do not forget this, very important!

One of my clients was literally downloading instructions to be transgender in the womb. Cults think they have authority to create a baby in the manner of the True God; however, the true God is Lucifer to them. Occult groups believe they have all the power to do this; the real God of Heaven and Earth is wrong. They damn well know their acts mock God and lie to the children, transforming them into awful creatures. In God's eyes, they are not! The demons know who you *really* are — so they feebly try to conceal you. The fallen angels have one job and one job only: To destroy you. They start destroying people in the womb if the family belongs to the occult. My husband had a demon attached to him in the womb from his ancestors' iniquity. It wasn't the same kind of attachment as his family members were not cultists, but whatever was in the family line allowed this demon to be passed down generations. We released demons right to legally torment him. By the blood of Jesus Christ; the demon's right to the family bloodline was revoked.

One person's programming in the womb was to be a queen in the family bloodline, an entirely different ritual performed on babies in the womb. As a practitioner or survivor, you must discover what was done to the baby and who they were assigned to become by Lucifer. The pieces of the programming listed here are just a fraction of what has to be removed in the womb. It is your job as a professional or survivor to find out exactly what happened.

You will have to at some point separate the Stronghold Demon, the one with the most authority over the survivor.

Survivors have grown up with the Stronghold, who won't let go easily. You will have to call all parts of the soul back from the Stronghold. When all parts are called back, the Stronghold has to be bound and put under Jesus Christ's authority. "The One" will now have to look at the truth. Survivors will not be made to choose anything, but they must now look at the truth of who the Stronghold and Lucifer are. You must take away all illusions.

The witchcraft parts are 100 percent loyal to all things that are witchcraft, which ultimately means Lucifer's Kingdom. I can tell you from my own experience it is not easy for the twin to renounce everything they have ever known. The Twin will worry about what is going to happen to them. You will have to find a way to create a safe way for the alter that was from the first split to be made whole and willing to join the true self and be willing to work as one.

Examples of Womb Programming from my clients. This will give ideas of additional things to look for to remove in the deprogramming process.

FIVE EXAMPLES OF PROGRAMMING IN THE WOMB

What I am about to tell you may blow you away and probably stir up anger. I will share what was done to five different people while they were in the womb. The mother was able to identify what was done in her womb to her child so she could remove her child's trauma. Once you remove your own foundational programming, you will now have to attend to the children who developed in your womb.

You might be wondering, "How can I remove something from my child?" The child was in your womb; thus, you can remove what happened while he or she was in your body.

The evil people doing the programming are traumatizing you while getting to the baby from conception on. I know it is crazy, but this is what they do.

It is a miracle any child can live through this while developing in the womb. The first example shocks me the most. It causes outrage to know these evil people would go this far.

EXAMPLE A

For four months before conception, a mother endured great torture to prepare the womb. The occultists were literally creating a separate womb so the baby would not be connected to the mother. It gets even worse. The baby was designed to be given to a politician as a slave before the baby's conception. I still can't believe anyone would go this far to make someone a slave.

Here are the pieces we removed for both the mother and baby. It is remarkable the mother endured this for her child.

Puzzle Pieces to Programming

- For 17 weeks the mother was being tested to set up an artificial womb before the conception of a female infant.
- The cult members were fabricating a second womb where they began implanting images.
- The cult tested mother to see what she could tolerate.

- The cult inflicted trauma to produce emotions of shame, worthlessness, and shock.
- The cult implanted the instructions, "You do not have parents, you only hear and know us."
- The cult manufactured a hell hole in which the baby was conceived.
- Drugs were given to cause supernatural abilities in the baby.
- Captured baby's experiences in images to show the baby how to survive.
- The conception happened in a lab where the father ejaculated; the parents felt shock so the baby would feel shock.
- First split occurred at the baby's conception.
- The womb had been designed to condition the child's nurturing. The cult controlled it all.
- The baby had to complete a template already set up.
- Mother and baby were to never connect in any way.
- The parents were not allowed to be parents.
- Baby grew up in a womb created by Lucifer, not the way God created.
- In this fake womb the child was allowed to only feel fear, terror, worthlessness, loneliness.
- Parts of the mother and baby were hidden from one another, the parts had to return and reunite.
- The cult created a trauma so the spirit left the mother's and baby's bodies and the Stronghold Demon could be downloaded.

- Began creating the template of the Kabbalah Tree of Death with all points.
- Removed lightning from baby and mother.
- Established connection between the baby and Stronghold.
- The mother lives outside of her body most of the time the baby can be controlled; the baby cannot find its mother.
- Stronghold gives permission to other entities to attach to the points of the template.
- Right before the baby's birth, the demons and cult made the baby believe its mother was dead and the only way to survive was to swear allegiance to Lucifer.
- The programmers began alien programming and connected the baby to the planet Mars. They also made her believe she had a past life.
- Programmers put toxins in the mother's body to build her immune system. Most people would fall ill, but these special children did not; the baby adjusted to the toxins to survive.
- Invested more effort to ensure the child would not feel love.
- The programmers fashioned a so-called super soldier.
- This political figure possessed the five parts of this baby's soul as her owner.
- In the counterfeit womb in the mother's body, the politician's face was presented to the developing baby as if the politician was her real mother.

A lot more was done to the infant and mother to create a slave baby the way the cult wanted. Once again, Hillary Clinton strikes again! Yes, she was the one who had this done. How many people has she done this great evil to?

What we found is it did not matter what they did. The infant baby in the womb did know the identity of her true mother. She actually turned out exactly the opposite of what they were trying to create. The mother said the daughter was very loving and compassionate all her life. She was very intelligent. She accomplished a great deal in her life. The mother did not know for certain all her actions as an adult slave.

We have to assume this child did not escape the programming and yet the cult did not make her into a non-feeling robot. This makes me believe there is a higher part of ourselves the cult cannot reach no matter how hard they try. They can't destroy us completely.

I will never cease to be amazed at the lengths the followers of Lucifer will go to make a human being a robotic slave. It makes me so happy to hear success stories. In the end they do not win!

EXAMPLE B

This example is someone who had three trees created in the womb for her baby. Three groups created a tree they would oversee and work in unison. This client had seven pages of information we found, so I will not reveal all of it here. I will help you to see the main picture. This example will show how the cult began teaching the infant she was transgender; the cult also tried to change the baby's gender. This was another heinous example.

Puzzle Pieces to Map Out

- The cult laid a curse on the baby, as they always do, but the baby was to become ill if she ever grew close to her parents.
- The alter split was from the Fertility Cult that created a hidden tree.
- The cult anchored the baby to a Greek Goddess demon.
- A high-up leader in this witchcraft group wanted this baby and was to have all power over the child. Once again, the baby was stolen from mother and father.
- As the baby grew in the womb for about 7 months, the high-up witch inflicted another curse that the baby would be only theirs.
- This baby was to be the carrier of the ancestors of the Fertility Cult. The cult downloaded all of the family line into the baby.
- Instructions were given: "You must honor your family heritage. We picked you to represent our family line. You must always be loyal to us. We are your only family."

- The cult anchored her to a covering so she would never get free of them.
- The cult began building a different tree with each point meaning something completely different. It was as if they were building her character in the download of evil commandments.
- The cult anchored the goddess entity to the child with a specific ritual.

We then had to remove a great deal from the witch part of the mother that allowed this. The mother witch part felt very honored the cult had picked her baby for all the honors. We had to remove all permission given by the queen witch in the mother for all of this to occur.

- In this case, the Fertility Cult had the first split at conception.
- This Stronghold represented all witchcraft but was not the Illuminati/Freemasons' Kabbalah Tree of Death.
- We believe many children have this special download and connection to the goddess entity. Significant work was invested into creating the baby's understanding of what had to be obeyed in the world.

There was more, but this will give you an understanding. We will go to the Illuminati Tree of Death Installation that happened to the same baby.

Pieces

- The cult completed the following in the order the cult usually reserves for the template of the Kabbalah Tree of Death
- The cult downloaded a stronghold demon that invited the other entities to be attached to the points on the Sephirot tree.
- The baby was given a curse of instructions. One was, "You are mine and I can do anything I want with your body."
- They selected this baby to be the queen.

Here I am unsure of the overall meaning, but at the end we put it together the best we could.

- They downloaded three god entities.
- Programming was connected to the third eye, which they went into great detail to accomplish.
- The cult was tying everything into her body, connected to her chakra energy centers.
- A couple of months before the baby's birth, the cult traumatized her so she'd leave her body to be escorted to meet Satan. He gave her the gift of inversion with these instructions: "I am everything you need. Don't listen to anyone else."
- A darker satanic energy downloaded into her from this meeting.

- The cult captured her female to be transgender by creating a male part tied to an entity to create the illusion.
- Did a lot with balance and hormones in the infant's body in the womb.

We had to remove a lot around the transgender identity. This may explain why, in the last several years, we're having such an increase in gender issues. The transgender is a symbol of Baphomet, whom all Luciferians worship. That is why the cults want everyone to have the female and male parts. I had no idea this was being done in the womb. I knew the vaccines that are given to children had fetal cells that may confuse the baby if the infant has another gender in its body. This is nothing but giving a big middle finger to the real God. They're messing around with things they have no right to.

Third Tree from Druids

- Many ancient beliefs were downloaded here from the Druids.
- The cult downloads the colors that represented the world in ancient times.
- Here it becomes complicated. The cult needed a male body to perform the rest. They picked the father to be possessed by the god entities for specific rituals.

- The instructions were: "You will have only an incestuous relationship." (The cult believes incest is the only way to have a holy union. This is another way Satan rebels against God in the most rebellious way.)
- The cult connected the child's immune systems together somehow.
- Thus, the baby would carry the three goddess entities when the three male entities wanted to take over for these sexual acts; they possessed the father's body.

Removing the programming was difficult because the mother had an alter that would step aside and let this all take place, but the father had no idea any of this was going on. Needless to say, we had to bring in the father and remove all this for him, the mother, and the baby. This is so heartbreaking and a sure way to destroy families. That is what Lucifer does. He destroys families in the worst way; when you get these cult groups involved they often take over the whole family.

(On a side note: It is not uncommon to find more than one cult group has tried to capture the baby so the cult has the right to own the baby for Lucifer.)

Example C

This female baby came from the Fertility Cult or witchcraft. There are many curses and many spiritual downloads of evil.

The cult will teach babies to hate males, especially the father.

- Fear and terror are the first emotions created in womb.
- Stronghold is immediately given permission to take over the baby.
- A disconnection from the mother and attachment to the witches must be made.
- This baby was instructed to never get her needs met by the mother.
- Download of ancestors.
- This particular baby was selected by a family to be the head queen. She was to direct the rest of the siblings and even the parents.
- If the Fertility Cult is present, the mother will always have a witch part that cooperates with all the cult's agenda, so permission must be renounced by the survivor.
- The cult disconnected the baby's body from her spirit because the cult wanted the baby's spirit captured.
- The female baby was instructed to never be close to the father or she'd be punished.
- Many spells were cast on each stage of fetal development.
- Many witch parts were instructed to protect the baby because she had queen status.
- The baby would only know the witch parts and not know the real mother.

- The cult placed coven energy around the bay to always be theirs to protect.
- Images of leaders were placed in the womb so the baby would know who to obey.
- The cult will always attach programming and alarm systems to the body's organs.
- Placement of Core Foundational Tree template installed.
- The download takes place around the witchcraft rules.
- Instructions given that when the baby is old enough, she will rule over the coven.

This is a short version, but we found something unusual. The grandfather, who was the son of the high witch, was able to sneak in some programming in the womb. The grandfather somehow connected himself to her and stole a part to be in him. There were many pieces to this, but some pieces are the same as the above examples. This story is not as happy. While the cult did not achieve all they wanted, the mother reported the child had done exactly as programmed. The child was a constant source of conflict in the family whenever they'd get close. The adult female never felt anyone had done anything for her as the programming demanded. The mother reported this child could never accomplish enough, and nothing seemed to match reality. The child would continue to say she always had to be responsible for her siblings, except the siblings and parents did not see it that way. This was really just the witch part talking. The baby's witch part believed she was responsible for the family. In the world of witchcraft, that was true. The one thing they did not get was this baby's soul. She remains a kind and thoughtful human being, successful in life and loved by everyone.

Example D

This example, a female baby, was mostly accomplished in the womb and included the grandfather's Satanic control.

- The first split was executed by the grandfather.
- The cult downloaded messages, such as "Your mother does not want you" and "You are mine."
- Many negative emotions were downloaded to create terror, fear, hopelessness, and shame.
- The cult slipped a cover over the baby's mind so she couldn't see her true self.
- The cult downloaded many emotions and torture experiences into the mother; if she were to interfere with her father's control, he'd kill her.
- Many negative statements were inserted into the mother and baby.
- The cult took different parts of the baby's humanity and hid these parts around the world. (The professional must call parts back and send them to Jesus Christ for healing. When the tortured parts are whole, return them to the baby.)

- The cult downloaded the Kabbalah tree template.
- The cult downloaded the Stronghold Demon.
- The grandfather connected himself to the child for eternal control. Parts of the child were in him and parts of him were in the child.
- The cult built a wall around the baby to prevent a mother-child connection.
- Many alarm systems were downloaded into the baby.
- The cult erected a castle in the womb for programming.
- The cult used the entity *Hypo Campus* to erase all the baby's memories.
- The cult abused the mother, by, for example, hitting her in the stomach.
- Shock and torture were incessantly used to create imbalance in the nervous system.
- The mother was being starved as the catalyst to the baby starving.
- The cult decreased the mother's heartbeat so the baby thought her mother was dead and would promise to be loyal to the grandfather.
- Baby was allowed to feel all the mother's trauma.
- Ancestral control was given over to the child.
- The cult started many programs in the womb and attached to the body's organs.

This example has pages of downloaded information, apparently focused on making the child feel worthless. This child seemed to crossover throughout her life. The grandfather had a hold on the family and told them he was god and they better obey him. Any child his daughter had would be his only. A lot of ownership instructions and entities accompanied the ritual to make it seem real. The mother reported her child seemed to always struggle in life but had a heart of gold and made everyone laugh. In many ways, the grandfather's intentions succeeded. The sad thing is the child was incredibly talented and intelligent but could not see her gifts. The grandfather's deep download of worthlessness seemed to prevail in the poor baby, who didn't deserve this. No one does. The acts are so wrong on so many levels that no words are adequate. The mother reported her adult child is starting to turn things around. Always have hope. Never give up on anyone.

Example E

This female infant had a mixture of Fertility Cult, Illuminati, and Military programming in the womb. The grandparents even tried to sneak in some evil downloads—all to own her poor innocent soul.

- The cult performed the following curse: "If she ever removed any of this, she'd get terribly sick. She would spend her life depressed, lost, and hopeless."

- This is where it becomes confusing: The grandparents were in control of the mother's witch parts. Because cult members did not live by the mother, they used witch parts to do the programming while the baby was in the womb.

You may be saying, "What?" This is hard to understand, but it's possible for an ancestor to take over a person's body with an entity's help. Entities can receive permission by a family member to dominate the witchcraft part in the mother. The cult took over the mother's witchcraft part and completed the programming through the mother to her womb. Yes, insane, but this is what cults do.

- The mother's witch parts were taken over by entities with ties to the Fertility Cult and the grandparents began to install the cult's doctrine.
- The grandparents implanted many orders, such as "Hate everyone and be angry all the time, your parents are not your real parents, hate your father," and "Your father will never have your love or connection."
- Somewhere amid the mess, the Illuminati programming began with the tree and the Stronghold Demon. Those who implanted this were completely different people. (I believe this piece was tied to the military.)
- The grandparents tell the children they've been chosen to be the programmers from the family line, an-

choring the line to two different commonly used military programs.
- The baby is confused because different groups and ancestors are fighting over who will own the baby, and who will have instructions for the baby's life, which sometimes may conflict.
- The baby is told to be loyal to the cult, which creates several splits.
- The mother receives many instructions from the three cult groups. Many times, the groups act as one because they include the same people with membership in different cults.
- Before the baby's birth, the foundational programming template is installed; there are many commands, emotions, and orders downloaded through the template.
- The cult has captured the whole body for Lucifer's control.

This example required about three hours to list everything to be removed. I am completely astonished by the abuse inflicted on a poor little baby in the womb. The mother reported the child has a strong spiritual connection to God and is a loving mother. The mother does not recall much of what happened after the pregnancy, but we feel the cult did not let this baby go and performed the usual programming. The child was extremely intelligent and the mother believed the military used her and her child as a team. While she probably hasn't escaped the CIA programming, it seems like God has stepped in to provide her with all the things forbidden by the cult. She has a happy family to this day. She does struggle with depression from time to time, but her depression could be from bloodline demons.

What is my take on all of this? If I were to focus on only the evil thrust upon these babies in the womb, I would probably despair. But that is not what I feel: I see in myself and clients that the cult did not win. Yes, they inflicted a lot of damage, but they did not win. Just in these five examples, each of these children developed into strong individuals. The cult did not achieve its objective. I would say the cult did not even come close. Why? Why did they not get the zombie, hardened soldiers they wanted? I believe it is because the true soul of the person could not be overpowered. It still blossomed in each of these examples.

One more insight about the examples: Each child's family had a common denominator. The child learned about the true God the Father and his son, Jesus Christ. Did this teaching stop what happened? In some ways I believe the children were protected. God won't interfere with free agency, even with people who use free will for evil. God does help us to endure trials better than we could withstand alone.

I'd like to make one more point. These children were raised in highly dysfunctional homes where the whole family suffered cult abuse, but the parents showed their children love and gifted them with education, family activities, work, and prayer.

All of this made a difference in the cults' failure. These groups will work so hard to prevent family love or God's love in the survivor's life. Love and our loving God heal. He always does; that is why cults torture you over and over. Just remember, the cult members go to such extremes in their attempt to block love. Love will set you free from their control.

God will not halt our afflictions, but He can help us through it. He can infuse us with the strength to take one more step when we believe we cannot. You have made it this far. Never give up and do not quit. This is what the cult groups want and we must never again do anything they want. You are a warrior. You can make it the rest of the way. You are a powerful soul who has looked evil in the face and survived. Now is the time to heal to prevent this evil from happening to anyone else. God needs all of His warriors to dismantle Lucifer kingdom. God needs everyone. You did not withstand this for no reason. Ascertain God's plan for you, His promise to create beauty from awfulness. If you reach out to the true God, He will help you understand how you can now use all of your trials for good.

WHAT ENCOMPASSES
THE FOUNDATION?

It is important to understand The Tree of Life according to Kabbalah and how the tree was inverted, fashioning The Tree of Death. Here are the original teachings from Kabbalah that represent the characteristics of who they believe is God.

THE KABBALAH SEPHIROTH (SEPHIROT)REPRESENTING THE TREE OF LIFE

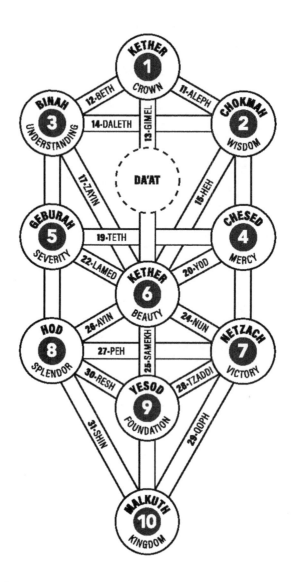

(The ten points can be spelled differently just like Sephirot and Sephiroth are the same but spelled differently.) In my first book I explained the Sephiroth Points. Different articles offer slightly different descriptions of each point. This is a quick reference.

This is the original intention of the Kabbalists; the positive side of the Tree of Life:

1. **Kether – Crown:** Known as Adam, male and female, remaining nine worlds come from Kether, neutral, balance.

2. **Chokmah – Wisdom:** First power of consciousness, wisdom, foundation of mercy pillar, male force, right brain.

3. **Binah – Understanding:** Reflects pure light of Chokmah, Pillar of Judgement, refers to left brain, female.

4. **Chesed – Mercy:** Pillar of Mercy, right shoulder or arm.

5. **Geburah – Judgment:** Left shoulder or arm, courage severity.

6. **Tiphareth – Beauty:** Center of the whole system, from Chokmah and Binah, balanced vertically and horizontally, represents the sun in the planetary system, four elements, the heart. The Tree of Life's center, energy from this sphere feeds all the others.

7. **Netzach – Victory:** Right hip, support.

8. **Hod – Glory:** Left hip or leg, emotion, passion, finds balance in Yesod, world of Unconscious.

9. **Yesod – Foundation:** Serves Sephirot above channel to Malkuth, associated with sexual organs.

10. **Malkuth – Kingdom:** Connected to Kether, "as above, so below," base of being.

11. **Da'at – Knowledge:** Secrets come from here, an awareness connection, key that includes sex chambers. Full life force, all spheres connect as one. Silver cord will be connected here.

This is how the globes of the Sephirot appear on the body.

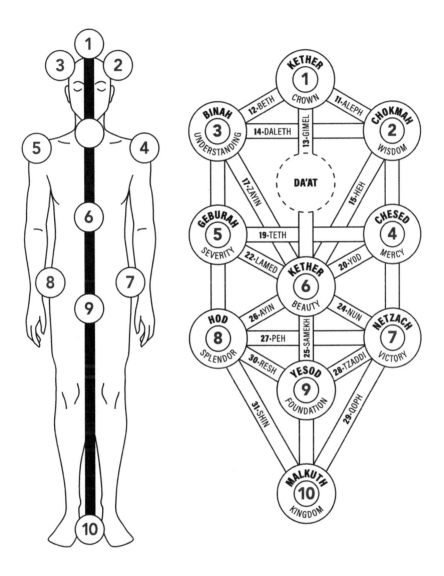

Evil aspects are downloaded into the person to create the Tree of Death. The Tree of Death represents the new person Lucifer wants created. The point is to cover up the true person so there is nothing left of God's creation. Each globe will be downloaded into the child with a great evil and a specific demon to each globe. Each globe acts as a separate world with parts created for specific jobs for that world. The parts are not aware of what occurs in the other points of the Sephiroth/Tree of Death. Each globe will have its own color, symbols, codes, and alarm systems. As each globe works separately, the programming works as a whole. In the removal process, decide which globe will be removed first and how the globes must be removed as a whole. As you will see, this is only the beginning of the foundation.

Each Column of the Sephirot

THE PILLARS

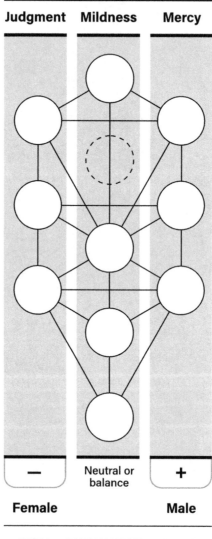

Judgment	Mildness	Mercy
—	Neutral or balance	+
Female		**Male**

FORM   CONSCIOUSNESS   FORCE

The three pillars will be found in the Sephirot. The middle pillar, a pillar of balance, connects to the second heaven of Lucifer. Kether and Malkuth are on the top and bottom of all trees. Kether and Malkuth are infused with sexuality. Metatron is connected to the middle pillar.

CHAKRAS

Chakras are energy centers heavily utilized by Lucifer's kingdom to feed off its members. The chakras or energy centers are a constant source of energy for the building of Lucifer's Kingdom, for feeding the cosmic trees, and for almost superhuman jobs of cult members. This is a map of a chakra system God created in each of us as humans. Let's begin with what we know about chakra systems.

CHAKRAS

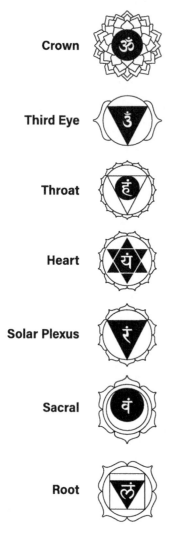

Crown

The Crown is the 7th Chakra located at the top of the head. It represents higher consciousness. The cult will do many download of the demons here.

Third Eye

Third Eve is the 6th Chakra and is located in the center of the forehead and above the eyebrows, which represents intuition, creativity, and connection to God. The cult will do a lot in this area to close it off the pineal gland in the person.

Throat

The Throat is the 5th Chakra and is located in the center of the neck. It represents the ability to speak and communicate. The cult will do a lot of, "Don't talk or tell" here.

Heart

The Heart is the 4th Chakra and is located in the center of the chest. It represents love, self-love, and relationships. The cult will build wall upon walls to cover up the heart. They do not want any survivor to feel love because it heals.

Solar Plexus

The Solar Plexus is the 3rd Chakra and is located below the chest.It represents self-esteem and will power. The cult will beat those down before the survivor is even born.

Sacral

The Sacral is the 2nd Chakra and is located below the navel. It represents creative and sexual energies. The cult takes over right away to exploit all things sexual.

Root

The Root is the 1st Chakra and is located at the base of the spine. It represents the foundation of which we build our life, safety, security and stability. In the cult there is none of these attributes, only fear and terror 24/7.

There are seven energy centers running along the spine of 33 discs.

This is the Energy System of a Survivor with Tree of Death Foundational Programming

CHAKRAS

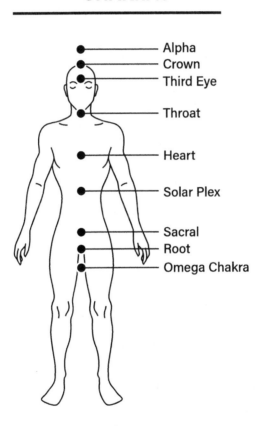

This is an artificial energy system with nine energy points created when the survivor is a baby. The two points form a closed current running through the body, magnifying the person's electromagnetic field. The two extra energy centers guarantee the person can achieve superhuman feats for the cult. The two extra energy centers are called Alpha and Omega.

Alpha is 8 inches above the crown chakra and Omega is 8 inches below the root chakra. Both of these centers are created early, possibly starting at 3 to 6 months of age. Both centers are connected to the Cosmic Tree of Death in Lucifer's second heaven (Buys, 2020, Restoring).

Joseph Mengele used this programming. A mind-controlled survivor will usually be constantly tired due to their energy being consumed — like a vampire lustily consuming blood — to feed the Cosmic Tree or Lucifer's kingdom.

Alpha is 8 inches above the crown chakra and Omega is 8 inches below the root chakra. Both of these centers are created early in the survivor's life, possibly starting at 3 months to 6 months. Both centers are connected to the Cosmic Tree of Death in Lucifer's second heaven.

Alpha energy center is corded to Metatron.
Affiliated to the snake and other entities.
Magnifies electromagnetic field.
Helps to feed the Cosmic Tree.
Omega Energy system.
Corded to Shiva, the god of destruction.
Affiliated with the snake and phallus.

Both of these centers work together and with the seven other energy centers.

Dismantling can be dangerous due to some survivors being programmed since inception. You must decide when to remove it.

Map out all pieces to the programming and its connections. Muscle test to see when and where you should remove the two extra energy systems and return them to God and his authority.

There may be more than one chakra system. You will have to find the chakra system inserted last and remove it first.

Each chakra point has programming, is assigned a god, and contains:

A Hebrew symbol
Codes and numbers
Trigger words
Alarm systems
Suicide systems
Color
Personality with a specific job or jobs
Drugs
Alarm systems of all kinds
Specific Jobs

Often, the meaning of the chakra system correlates with color and description — except the opposite. For example, the Sacral point relates to sex and creative energies. Monarch programming will be connected to this chakra point as well as the Tree of Death. It's up to the professional and survivor to find all particular pieces of the Chakra programming. This information will help you have a good start.

BIRTH OF THE CHILD

Recently I have discovered that during the process of the child going through the birth canal, cults have figured out a means for the child to die and then be resuscitated. When the child returns to life, the cults say that your God, Lucifer, has brought you back to life and given you breath. The cult says you must be loyal to Lucifer, who created and saved you. The newborn has already been programmed through the womb to accept Lucifer. Now, as the child proceeds through the birth canal, there is a sealing of the teachings learned in the womb.

This is a client's quote: "I had a dream that when I was held in the birth canal I actually died and was born dead then resuscitated. I believe it was done so I would not be born in the image of God as when they revived me, they said, "Here with the life of our Lord's breath is this child," followed by, "The life of Lucifer has returned to this body. You will have a true life with the lord." (Lord means Lucifer)

Soon after the baby is born, the cult will begin the ritual where a three-way rape will take place, causing the baby's mind to split three times. The three-way rape will be done many times through the survivor's life. Apparently, cults are doing this digitally to the "new generations' for the same effect of torture to the point of mind splitting. This is a core event that must have all its pieces removed.

Once the child is born, the cult will immediately begin the installation of the Tree of Death. The best way for you to understand the installation process is for me to share a story I heard at a 2004 seminar. The story is graphic. I offer a warning if you are a survivor; the following details could be highly triggering.

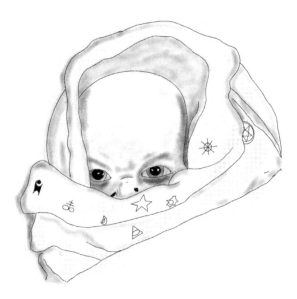

PICTURE BY NIC YOUNGBLOOD

Installation of the Foundation Explained

This is a Satanic Ritual Abuse's story of how the downloaded Tree of Death was installed.

Sarah's Story — The Tree of Death

According to the manual *Mind Control: An Introduction*, "On the day of her birth, Sarah's father gripped the wooden mallet he used to drive wooden pegs into wooden beams. He tapped her forehead with it. Her body instantly went into convulsions; for a short time, she stopped breathing. Sarah's torment was not due to the tap of the mallet but to the download of spiritual evil assigned to her body by her father's will.

"The little girl's sensory experience told her the mallet had been smashed into her head, that her head swelled to several times its normal size, and that her life had been spared only by the goodness of the gods of her ancestors. Sarah was later told the group had gathered to pray, asking their gods to "test" the girl to see if she "was strong enough to live." Because Sarah survived, the cult assumed their gods had chosen and healed her and now "owned" her head. She was later taught that her three gods were joined together in a jeweled crown, which floated between her skull and her brain, guiding and directing her life and will. She was convinced the seed of the Tree of Death had been planted in her body on her day of birth.

"Three months later, Sarah was laid on the wooden altar, and her father punched the infant in the chest with his fist, temporarily stopping her heart. The baby briefly turned blue, then returned to pink as the heart resumed its rhythm. Sarah's experience told her that her entire body burned as if an internal fire had exploded in her chest — a sensation produced by the download of spiritual evil accompanying the punch. She was led to believe the god of the heart had restarted her heart and spared her life. Since she lived, the god was now the source of "beauty" within her heart. He would guide and control her emotions. She was later taught that her burning sensation meant the Tree of Death's seed had sprouted.

"When Sarah was six months old, she was tied to the wooden altar, legs spread wide, and her hymen ruptured with an intricately carved wooden rod. Because Sarah was female, her mother had inflicted her agony. The little girl's experience was that a red-hot steel rod had been thrust completely through her body, a sensation produced by the download of great spiritual evil accompanying the penetration. With the removal of the rod, Sarah perceived that all of her blood had been drained from her body and that the gods of her ancestors had graciously spared her life. She later learned the rod's sensation was Tree of Death's rapid growth along her spine as the tree had been watered with her blood and could mature. But, as it was explained each time she was raped, the tree would have to be watered regularly with her vaginal blood until she began producing menstrual blood.

"The infant was 9 months old when the toes of her left foot were punctured with a sewing needle and the right foot was squeezed. Sarah's experience told her a venomous snake had struck her big toe, a female black widow spider bit her second toe, a bee stung her third toe, a wasp pierced her fourth toe, and a scorpion stung her little toe. The download of spiritual evil had formed those pictures in her mind in addition to the illusion her foot and leg had swollen to gigantic proportions. The cult also created the sensation of excruciating pain and the picture of the father carrying her body into his shop and squeezing her right foot in a big vice, completely crushing it. Sarah heard the noise of her foot bones being crushed. The cult persuaded Sarah that she carried great spiritual power; otherwise, she would not have survived the venom or foot crushing. She was convinced the Tree of Death within her had its roots in agony and venom.

"The bee sting was added to the left ear on her first birthday. The bee had been inserted, stinger first, into her ear canal, the insect tormenting her until it stung. A leather-making steel awl was pressed into the right ear, causing great pain. The little girl's experience was that a queen bee had crawled into her left ear and laid its eggs, they had hatched, and the larvae were eating her brain. The tremendous download of spiritual evil that accompanied the bee sting had created this picture in her mind. The picture created in her brain was the awl puncturing the eardrum, all the fluid of her brain's right side running out her ear. The cult later informed Sarah they had invited one of their gods to heal the left side of her brain and give her wisdom; they had invited another god to heal the right side of her brain and give her understanding. The constant ringing in both ears, she believed, was a constant reminder that only cult members had wisdom and understanding, so it was useless to attempt to find it anywhere else. She was convinced the Tree of Death had begun to branch out, its two columns controlling both sides of her body.

"At 15 months, Sarah's right shoulder was dislocated and her left-upper arm bone broken in a fracture by the stomp of her father's heavy boot. A major download of spiritual evil was passed into these two parts of her body to take control. "Judgment" was to rule the left arm and "mercy" the right.

"Molten gold was poured into Sarah's shoulders, creating intricate occult shapes within her bones, even replacing a bone in one arm. The burning sensation was long-lasting, over several weeks, as the gold cooled and her shoulder and arm healed. She was convinced the Tree of Death had fully branched out within her body and that she was trapped eternally between "judgment" and "mercy."

"The horse's iron-shod hoof whizzed past Sarah's face as Blackie, the plow horse, kicked back in annoyance. Sarah's father was tickling the horse with a cornstalk while her mother held the 18-month-old behind the horse, trying to gauge where the hoof would fly so she could move Sarah into harm's way. The next kick brushed the girl's left leg, causing her mother to adjust her hold a bit, nodding her head again. Tickle, kick, wham! This time a direct hit, just below the little girl's waist. Sarah's mother checked. Yes, the leg was definitely hit hard enough, but was it broken? As she flexed the girl's leg, Sarah's mother saw it bending in an unfamiliar place.

"Yes, it was broken, and Sarah was unconscious from the pain. The mother laid her daughter on the straw. The father moved beside her, grabbed Sarah's right leg, and with a strong jerk and a twist, quickly dislocated her right hip.

"Sarah's experience was that her lower body had been consumed in liquid fire, that acid had been poured into the hip socket and cobra venom injected into the other leg.

"The picture created by the spiritual evil assigned by both parents was that the Tree of Death had thrust its roots down Sarah's legs to reach the venom and acid within her marrow. Sarah was later instructed that these were gifts from the gods named "Glory" and "Victory" as she gave them her legs. Sarah was convinced the Tree of Death was fully grown in her body. It would rule her life forever and she would never turn from the path of her ancestors. On Sarah's second birthday, her body's 10 sacred locations were joined together with the sacred 22 paths. Sarah received a special sucker as a birthday gift from a man she had never seen before.

"By 24 months of age, as Sarah licked the sucker, she ingested the mild hallucinogenic drug. That night she was placed on the stone altar, a knife tip scratching paths connecting the 10 special places of her body dedicated to various gods.

"In Sarah's sensory experience, the knife cut deeply into her flesh as wires were laid alongside her bones to connect the 10 places with 22 paths. Each wire glowed red hot in response to the man pronouncing the correct path name. The flesh healed without leaving a scar. A picture was created by the spiritual evil downloaded with the drug and a verbal description of the installer's actions. The man then stood between the father and the mother, placing his left hand just below Sarah's throat and leading a strange chant. The picture in Sarah's mind was a bright white ball of light materializing in the man's right band, floating in the air, moving into her throat, not painful but very warm. Suddenly she felt peaceful and was floating in warm water. Sarah later learned the Tree of Death had blossomed, providing her with an 11th special place where she could access the secret knowledge of the universe. Sarah was now connected to the most secret source of illumination, to the 'light bringer' himself, and had become part of the Illuminati."

Sarah's story was shared at a 2004 seminar for therapists. Steve Oglevie, a trainer who had worked with 300 Satanic Ritual Abuse survivors then, gave out a huge manual called *Mind Control: An Introduction*. The book contained her story as a survivor who endured a brutal Tree of Death installation.

In my first book I did not detail survivor installations, but I felt I should share a fuller story of cults. I would like to note Sarah's story is different from what Amanda Buys teaches on the order of installation of the Sephiroth Tree of Death. My own programming was not in the order of Amanda's teaching. So, I am left to believe the order for each survivor may be different. I am sure you will be sick of me saying this, but you have to determine the order of installation for every survivor yourself. All of this is a guide.

Steve Oglevie in 2004 said the cults did not really use the Tree of Death Programming anymore, and I never addressed it in my work. At the time I did not think anything of this story. I did not like reading it, but that was as far as it ever went. It is amazing how our minds can shield the truth from us when we are not ready for the information. It is interesting that Steve Oglevie too was led astray by believing the Tree of Death is not the foundation to all programming. Buys said the same thing. She said when they came upon the trees, they were led astray by someone on her team telling her this was not important. I also find it interesting I was shown the information about the Tree of Death and how important it was in 2019. Then it seemed Dan Duval of Bride Ministries came out publicly sharing about the Tree of Death. To me this is amazing! The Lord is equipping professionals to help survivors become free. It really has been the last three years when so many people are starting to remember their abuse and programming. The Lord is on our side and helping us.

For the younger generations, the cults are using new technologies to install the Tree of Death. This way the child will not show any bruising and they can even make the pain of the programming ten times worse. The unconscious mind believes the movies downloaded with drugs, trauma, and torture. With this new technology, the cults are making it much harder for survivors to break loose from this signif- icant foundational programming, but God will always be more powerful than what man creates. We will win. More and more people are enlightened about what the government and cult groups are doing.

Hopefully, you can see the horror each survivor encounters during the Tree of Death's installation. The tree is installed in a manner that ties the person to Lucifer. By the time cults finish, survivors believe a tree has fully grown in their bodies. The body and tree are one. The cult groups connect this tree to the organs, chakras, nervous system, DNA, glands, etc., to represent Lucifer. The cults say the Tree of Death is the Tree of Life. They must capture the whole body, spirit, and mind. From this teaching of the Sephirot, everything is inverted in the child's mind. I wish I could say the terror stops here, but in many ways, it is just of the beginning. All training will be built on the Tree of Death Programming.

The worlds of the Kabbalah Tree of Death are created with a purpose. The worlds signify the different levels and how they connect. Each teaching corresponds to a specific age of training, including the precept Lucifer's kingdom will be completely built by the time the survivor reaches 16- or 17-years of age. A special training exists that starts at 17-years and must be completed by 19 years.

VI

BUILDING OF THE
FOUR WORLDS

Now each child will begin to build Jacob's Ladder which will consist of five more trees that lead to the four worlds and the Cosmic Tree. A tree will be created in the underworld making a total of seven trees comprising the core foundation.

9

THE FOUR WORLDS

The next information came from Amanda Buys, an amazing woman. As far as I am concerned, Amanda has saved my life and many others. I was taught fully about the importance of the Tree of Life and shared that knowledge in my first book. I understood the Tree of Death is the foundation of all cult programming. As I wrote this book, God showed me so many things. I came to a period when I knew there was more information, but I was stuck. I prayed for help and guidance of where I could find more information because the Tree of Death was so well hidden. I certainly got a strange answer. I was told to go back to the post I saw a few months earlier about a woman teaching about MK Ultra. I thought, "Yeah, right, I am going to find something two months ago on Telegram social media." I did it anyway;

to my surprise, I found it. I had looked at Amanda's website previously but nothing registered. Well, this time what did I see? Videos on the Kabbalah tree. I thought, there is no way someone else is talking about this. Not only was Amanda talking about the Kabbalah tree and how Lucifer reversed it, but she provided so much information. I felt I had hit the motherload of information. I was overwhelmed by the amount of information. I watched Amanda's videos on the Kabbalah tree three times and many other videos. I read many of Amanda's manuals in a couple of months.

I personally want to say how grateful I am to Amanda for all her years of research and experience. I know others have contributed to her work, but this is key to total freedom. The Lord has pushed me to finish this book quickly because so many people are awakening as their programming breaks down. It is so important to all survivors wanting to get free from all mind control. It has been so well hidden that as soon as I mentioned the Kabbalah tree in an interview, a group of "Cultists" attempted to kill me, which I will explain at the end of this book.

The practitioner will have to discern the individual's programming but also must understand the four worlds and how they function in deprogramming and the names of many entities that must be called and cast out.

Here is a picture of the four worlds. Each world has a Sephirot tree.

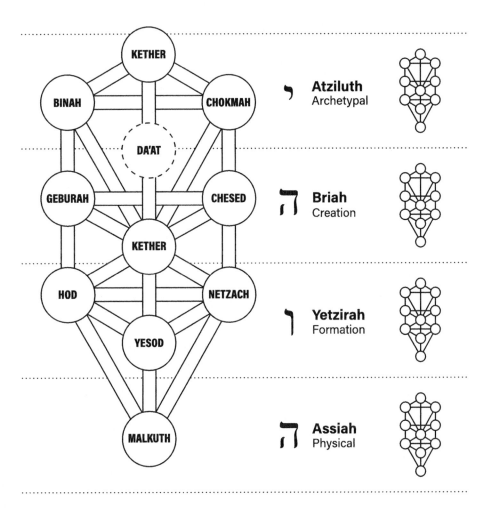

Atziluth
Archetypal

Briah
Creation

Yetzirah
Formation

Assiah
Physical

Four Worlds

Each Sephirot tree has 10 points called the 10 emanations that are the foundation of all creations. Each of the 10 points is located in each of the four worlds: Assiah, Yetzirah, Briah, and Atziluth. The Kabbalists call them the 10 roots of the Tree of Life. All these worlds are inverted for the purpose of programming survivors for mind control. Each survivor has the four worlds as a part of their programming. Each world will be worked on by the survivor to reach the highest world where Lucifer is. These trees are connected to the original Tree of Death in the body.

Atziluth

First and highest world is called Atziluth.

The element of fire is connected to Atziluth, the world where Lucifer stole the names of God to use for himself. The names connect to the Sephirot, which connects to one of God's names with a specific meaning.

Atziluth is a world of archetypes from which manifestations happen. This world vibrates at a high speed of pure vibrating energy. As you move down the world, the energy and power decrease.

Atziluth is where Lucifer is.

The next four charts, from Amanda Buys and Kanaan

Ministries, contain such important information to become free. I learned about the four worlds from Amanda. I believe God told me to find her because she had the missing pieces I could not find. So grateful.

(Restoring the Shattered Soul; Book 116-DID-SRA_Book_3_June-20.pdf /page 21-24)

SEPHIROT POINTS	NAMES OF GOD AND MEANING
1. First Crown	Eheieh: I am (that I Am)
2. First Wisdom	Jehovah: essence of Being
3. First Understanding	Jehovah Elohim: Gods of Gods
4. First Mercy	El: God the Creator
5. First Severity	Elohim Gibor: God the Potent
6. First Beauty	Eloah Vadaath: God the Strong
7. First Victory	Jehovah Tzaboath: God of Hosts
8. First Glory	Elohim Tzaboath: Lord God of Hosts
9. First Foundation	Shaddai, El Chai: omnipotent
10. First Kingdom/Second Crown	Adonai Melekh: God

Briah

The second highest world is Briah, meaning creation.

Briah has the water element. The highest ranking fallen angels reside in this world. Metatron is the ruler of this world. Briah mirrors down, reflecting to the next lower kingdom, Yetzirah.

Briah manifests worlds of creation. Seven days of creation are involved. You will find many rituals of programming are seven days.

Amanda Buys said, "In the World of Briah, the 10 spheres of light are called the Archangels of Briah. Their order and powers are as follows":

SEPHIROT	NAMES & MEANING
B1...Second Crown	Angel of Presence-Metatron
B2...Second Wisdom	Raziel...revealed to Adam the mysteries of the Kabbalah
B3...Second Understanding	Tsaphkiel: the contemplation of God
B4...Second Mercy	Tsdakiel: the justice of God
B5...Second Judgement	Samael: the Severity of God
B6...Second Beauty	Michael: Like unto God

B7...Second Victory	Haniel: the Grace of God
B8...Second of Glory	Raphael: the divine Physician
B9...Second Foundation	Gabriel: the Man-God
B10...Second Kingdom/ C1...SecondCrown	Sandalphon: the Messias

Yetzirah

Yetzirah is on a level created beings will take shape and form, a reflection of Briah's power.

The world of Yetzirah connects to the element of air. This world is where ideas and patterns are formed; Amanda said it corresponds to the Garden of Eden.

The power controlling the world of Yetzirah controls the world of Assiah. The world of Nephilims contains evil celestial creations.

Amanda Buys' Kanaan Ministries chart.... **Yetzirah... Hierarchy**

C1...Third Crown	The Cherubim, Chaioth, Ha Kadosh, the Holy Animals
C2...Third Wisdom	The Cherubim, Orphanim, the Wheels

C3…Third Understanding	The Thrones, Aralim, the Mighty Ones
C4…Third Mercy	The Dominations, Chashmalim, the Brilliant
C5…Third Severity	The Powers, Seraphim, the Flaming Serpents
C6…Third Beauty	The Virtues, Melachim, the Kings
C7…Third Victory	The Principalities, Elohim, the gods
C8…Third Glory	The Archangels, Ben Elohim, the sons of god
C9…Third Foundation	The Angels, Cherubim, the Scat of the Sons
C10/D1…Third Kingdom/ Third Crown	Humanity, the Ishim, the Souls of Just Men

Assiah

THE FOURTH AND LAST STAGE

Assiah connects to the earth elements. It is the material world of action. This world connects to the solar systems. Most programming has the planetary system where this world will connect to the next system of programming. Remember, one thing connects to the next. All worlds and spheres present before are actualized here, the material world of matter, which corresponds with unbalanced energies. This world represents action.

The information in this chart is from Amanda Buys' Kanaan Ministries. She said Crowley and Hall had differing opinions on how the globes should be arranged, so she included both. Crowley represents Thelema; Hall represents Freemasonry.

	Crowley	Manly P. Hall
D1…Fourth Crown	Pluto	Rashith H. Galagalum, the Primum Mobile, the fiery mist which is the beginning of the material Universe
D2…Fourth Wisdom	Neptune	Masloth, the Zodiac, the firmament of the fixed stars
D3…Fourth Understanding	Saturn	Shabbathai, the sphere of Saturn
D4…Fourth Mercy	Jupiter	Tzedeg, the sphere of Jupiter
D5…Fourth Severity	Mars	Madim, the sphere of Mars
D6…Fourth Beauty	Sun	Shemesh, the sphere of the sun

D7...Fourth Victory	Venus	Nogah, the sphere of Venus
D8...Fourth Glory	Mercury	Kokab, the sphere of Mercury
D9...Fourth Foundation	Luna	Levanah, the sphere of the moon
D10...Fourth Kingdom and Crown	Earth	Cholom Yosodoth, the sphere of the four elements

"There are 10 arch-demons that are connected to the world of Assiah," Buys said. "They are counterparts of the archangels we saw in Briah. The ten orders of demons and the ten Arch-demons of the world of Assiah are as follows:"

ARCH DEMONS OF ASSIAH...HIERARCHY	
D1...Evil Crown	Thaumiel, the doubles of God, the two-headed; Satan and Moloch
D2...Evil Wisdom	Chaigidiel, this who obstructs; Adam Belial
D3...Evil Understanding	Satharial, the concealment of God, Lucifuge
D4...Evil Mercy	Gamchicothe, the disturber of things, Astaroth
D5...Evil Severity	Golab, incendiarism and burning; Asmodeus
D6...Evil Beauty	Togarine, the wranglers; Belphegor

D7...Evil Victory	Harab Serap, the dispensing Raven, Baal Chanan
D8...Evil Glory	Samael, the embroiler; Adramalek
D9...Evil Foundation	Gamaliel, the obscene; Lilith
D10...Evil Kingdom/Evil Crown	Nahemoth, the impure, Nahema

The charts below show each point on the Sephirot Tree and how it connects to the four worlds and the Planetary system. Every survivor has this programming that connects to foundational trees and to the planetary systems.

1 KETHER

Atziluth (Lucifer)	Eheieh - I Am [that I AM]
Briah (Fallen Angels)	Metatron, Angel of the Presence
Yetzirah (Nephilim)	The Cherubim, Chaioth Ha Kadosh, the Holy Animals
Assiah (Solar System)	Pluto
Tree of Evil (Solar System)	Thaumiel, the doubles of God, the Two-headed; Satan and Moloch

② CHOKMAH

Atziluth (Lucifer)	Jehovah–Essence of Being
Briah (Fallen Angels)	Raziel—the herald of Deity who revealed the mysteries of Kabbalah to Adam.
Yetzirah (Nephilim)	The Cherubim, Orphanim, the Wheels
Assiah (Solar System)	Pluto
Tree of Evil (Solar System)	Neptune

③ BINAH

Atziluth (Lucifer)	Jehovah Elohim—God of Gods
Briah (Fallen Angels)	Tsaphkiel—the Contemplation of God
Yetzirah (Nephilim)	The Thrones, Aralim, the Mighty Ones
Assiah (Solar System)	Saturn
Tree of Evil (Solar System)	Satharial, the Concealment of God, Lucifuge

4 CHESED

Atziluth (Lucifer)	El—God the Creator
Briah (Fallen Angels)	Tsaphkiel—the Justice of God
Yetzirah (Nephilim)	The Dominations, Chashmalim, the Brilliant Ones
Assiah (Solar System)	Jupiter
Tree of Evil (Solar System)	Gamchicoth, the Disturber of things, Astaroth

5 GEBURAH

Atziluth (Lucifer)	Elohim Gibor—God the Potent
Briah (Fallen Angels)	Samael—the Severity of God
Yetzirah (Nephilim)	The Powers, Seraphim, the Flaming Serpents
Assiah (Solar System)	Mars
Tree of Evil (Solar System)	Golab, incendiarism and burning; Asmodeus

6 TIPHARETH

Atziluth (Lucifer)	Eloah Vadaath—God the Strong
Briah (Fallen Angels)	Michael—Like unto God
Yetzirah (Nephilim)	The Virtues, Melachim, the Kings
Assiah (Solar System)	Sun
Tree of Evil (Solar System)	Togarine, the wranglers; Belphegor

7 NETZACH

Atziluth (Lucifer)	Jehovah Tzaboath—God of Hosts
Briah (Fallen Angels)	Haniel—the Grace of God
Yetzirah (Nephilim)	The Principalities, Elohim, the gods
Assiah (Solar System)	Venus
Tree of Evil (Solar System)	Harab Serap, the dispensing Raven; Baal Chanan

8 HOD

Atziluth (Lucifer)	Elohim Tzaboath—Lord God of Hots
Briah (Fallen Angels)	Raphael—the divine Physician
Yetzirah (Nephilim)	The Archangels, Ben Elohim, the sons of god
Assiah (Solar System)	Mercury
Tree of Evil (Solar System)	Samael, the embroiler; Adramalek

9 YESOD

Atziluth (Lucifer)	Shaddai, El Chai—Omnipotent
Briah (Fallen Angels)	Gabriel—the Man-God
Yetzirah (Nephilim)	The Angles, Cherubim
Assiah (Solar System)	Luna
Tree of Evil (Solar System)	Gamaliel, the obscene; Lilith

⑩ MALKUTH	
Atziluth (Lucifer)	Adonai Melekh—God
Briah (Fallen Angels)	Sandalphon—the Messias
Yetzirah (Nephilim)	Humanity, the Ishim, the Souls of Just Men
Assiah (Solar System)	Earth
Tree of Evil (Solar System)	Nahemoth, the impure; Nahema

(Amanda Buys, Kanaan Ministries, Kabbalah teachings videos 1-4)

THE TRIADS

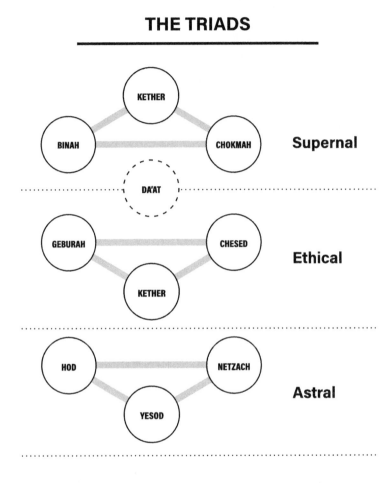

Triads are shown in these three images.
This image is the Sephirot being separated into three triangles that correlate to the three spiritual
worlds separated by veils.
Each Triad is connected to the three non-physical worlds listed. Each Triad has its own meaning in
programming that must be removed.

You have learned the 10 Points of the Sephirot Tree or the
Tree of Death and the meaning of Kabbalah, both the positive and negative, including how the cult uses the Kabbalah

for demonic programming. You have learned how the trees connect to the four worlds and what the four worlds represent. So far, there are six trees in the Core Foundation. Now we proceed to how a cult survivor climbs Jacob's Ladder and progresses to the four worlds just described.

VII

STARTING TO CLIMB
JACOB'S LADDER

After the cult installs the Sephirot tree, the survivor develops skills to ascend Jacob's Ladder through each step of the four worlds. The four worlds are spiritual realms in the Kabbalah. Assiah has the spiritual and physical combined. The four worlds are connected at the bottom and top of the Kabbalah Sephirot Tree.

Climbing the ladder is part of the foundation and will represent the cult's members ranking. Everything in this world is about moving up the ladder to beat the other person's ranking at the top. Lucifer's Kingdom established the process this way. You are always having to fight your way to the top. Each year requires a different training. Each person must complete their training. Each step requires more torture and trauma and instructions from the demons. The higher you ascend in the four worlds, the more torture you've survived; your reward is getting closer to Lucifer. This is how Lucifer brainwashes the survivor to believe it is good to be tortured — then later you can live with him in Lucifer's Heaven.

At the bottom of the Sephirot Tree, survivors begin their climb from Assiah. When they reach the world of Briah, the climb will become much harder and the fallen angels' authority has increased. Not many people make it to the highest part of the Sephirot in Atziluth due to the horrific abyss that must be traveled across. This will include a ritual with Leviathan the snake. If you get through, you will be in the world with Lucifer. You will not be able to cross, however, without the help of an entity called Metatron.

WHO IS METATRON?

In Kabbalah mysticism, Metatron is the fallen angel who must be called upon to travel through the worlds to reach Lucifer. As I looked on the internet, I found that the Metatron archangel is revered as the one authorized to guard the secrets of God's Heaven. Because the occult has inverted the true spiritual meanings, we must now view Metatron in the negative. In Kabbalah, the stories all sound pleasant, but as we know there is nothing nice about the cult's evil goals.

Metatron is said to represent the patterns of creation. The Sacred Geometry conveys the shapes of the world. So, if Metatron's cube is a symbol for good, how does Lucifer turn it into evil? If the original Metatron was intended to create balance and harmony, what does the angel mean for evil? Could the evil Metatron's purpose be to create disharmony in the mind and body of cult members so they can receive Lucifer's evil? Is that what they have done? The occult captures all things for Lucifer; however, are individuals' body, mind, and spirit equipped to handle this dark energy? Because Lucifer wants to be God, Metatron must be the keeper of Lucifer's secrets. He is the next authority under Lucifer. In their effort to be close to Lucifer, individuals must learn the secrets of Lucifer. Metatron is a very powerful demon. Metatron represents Lucifer in all his business.

Metatron is found on the Tree of Life/Tree of Death in between Yeshod and Da'at. There are 13 circles to represent Metatron in the Sacred Geometry figure.

This picture represents the Metatron Cube in Sacred Geometry.

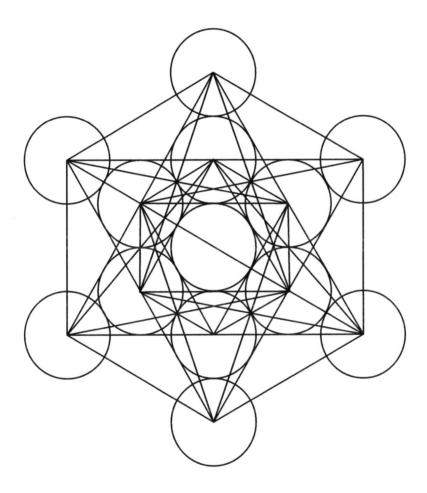

This is a picture of the Merkabah, the six-pointed star that transports cult members to all four worlds.

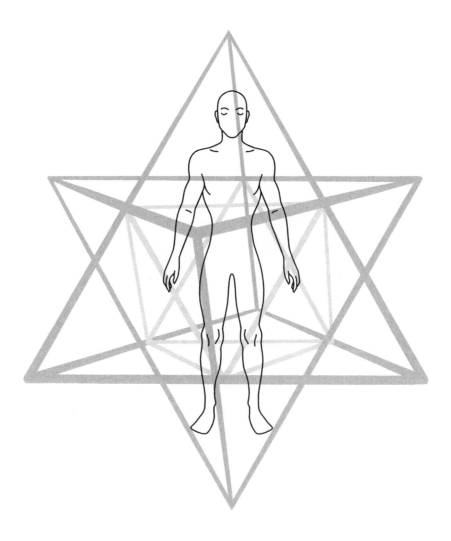

11

THE COSMIC TREE

Cosmic Tree

PICTURE BY NIC YOUNGBLOOD

* The Cosmic Tree is in the 2nd Heaven with Lucifer.

* The survivors energize this tree with their iniquity.

* Evil acts provide Lucifer with energy to act upon humanity in darkness. Every member of Lucifer's Kingdom must feed the Cosmic Tree.

The Cosmic tree is both receiver and giver of all energy. The tree contains the light Lucifer stole from the children of the cult groups so he could imitate a light similar to God's. There is no glory in Lucifer's kingdom. Even though all survivors are taught this glory will come. The energy centers or the two extra Chakra centers of every survivor feed the tree and receive dark energy from Lucifer. Disconnecting the energy centers requires care because the action is dangerous. Also, remember to bring the survivor's life force back from the 2nd Heaven.

The Cosmic Tree is always being fed by mind-controlled slaves by taking all their energy. Many survivors will complain of severe fatigue. If you are a servant to Lucifer, your energy is being sucked out constantly. You are expected to feed the tree until you die. The Cosmic Tree represents a great deal in Lucifer's kingdom. It is the life force connecting all cult survivors.

LEVIATHAN

Somewhere in the beginning of creating the foundation, Leviathan will be downloaded
and is a part of the Tree of Death/Tree of Evil.

Leviathan is a snake and is highly revered in the world of Lucifer. This very evil snake is part of the Kabbalah tree and Water World. The snake begins at Malkuth on the Sephirot tree and when it reaches the genital area it splits into two snakes representing both male and female. The snake runs up the spine and is part of the energy centers. Leviathan represents ancestral sin. This depiction of the snake is deeply sexual and is a part of many rituals. The snake is recognized by medical staff. Most professional offices have the symbol of the two snakes.

On the Sephirot Da'at in the Kabbalah teaching, mankind has lost a great deal of knowledge. In the last days Leviathan will restore this secret knowledge, which comes down to technology and the acquisition of transhumanism.

Leviathan and the child's experiences with Leviathan are introduced early because of the programming they intend to do to the survivor.

As the mind control slave ascends the rankings, the slave must eventually experience a ritual that will allow a crossover into Lucifer's kingdom of hell. The ritual is abominable to any who experience it. The following is paraphrased from survivors who experienced the Leviathan ritual: They entered a pit of poisonous snakes knowing they would be bitten. They had to navigate a gulf to reach Lucifer. By now, the cult survivors had developed the ability to call on different entities to help them. They find their way to Leviathan, a ghastly snake that ultimately consumes them. You may have seen a picture of Leviathan eating his tail. This symbolizes the serpent devouring the earth. It will devour cult survivors; if they find their way out, they are worthy to enter the place where Lucifer dwells.

Early in the programming, it is taught Leviathan is inside survivors The cult groups carefully build on this programming until their members have to cross the abyss to reach Lucifer.

Once cult members have found their way to Leviathan, they must fornicate with the entity and find their way out of the snake. Leviathan does not let them out until they give up part of themselves inside Leviathan. The sacrifice has to be recovered in the removal process. The recovery entails a great deal; a practitioner will need a lot of information from the survivor. Below are the parts required to be addressed. You will have to remove all of this.

Then the removal process from the Sephirot tree will be another removal process. I am not sure if Leviathan can be completely removed until the four worlds and Tree of Death are removed.

Map out the Puzzle Pieces of Leviathan. Here are some pieces you will have to complete:

- Remove all rituals with Leviathan.
- Remove all promises and oaths
- Remove all snake bites and poison
- Physical, sexual, and emotional trauma
- Call back the humanity out of Leviathan
- Release Leviathan out of survivor

- Remove dragon sex
- Remove all Nephilims connected
- Remove all entities involved
- Rewards given for surviving the ritual
- Survivor will have to renounce ranking for achieving this and all rewards promised
- Promises of eternal sexual bliss
- Remove infinity loop that the survivor can never leave
- Participation in the Feast of Leviathan
- Feast of Leviathan meaning
- Tail in mouth symbol
- Renounce connection to Metatron
- Remove all rewards Lucifer gave you for surviving the rituals to get to his kingdom
- Part or parts of the survivor will be in the infinity loop. You must call them back.
- Kosher serpent, dragon, Metatron are connected as one. Disconnect them inside the survivor
- Remove the Kosher serpent, dragon, and Metatron from the Tree or Trees of Death and all trees they could be connected with.
- Check and remove additional serpents.

TREE IN THE UNDER-
WORLD 7TH TREE

This is where the saying, "As above, so below" originates.

"As above, so below" is a good analogy. The survivor begins climbing Jacob's Ladder; at the same time, the survivor is ascending the underworld while the seventh tree is being built in the underworld.

With each step into another dimension, the survivor will confront different levels of demons or fallen angels. (Refer to the *Demons* chapter for further understanding of demons and their levels of authority.)

The Tree of Death and the Tree in the underworld are connected together; one above so below. In the removal process you will find these two are the last to remove in the removal process. Practitioners will find this is by far the most complex of the programming. Here is where the Stronghold demon will be watching over and protecting the Trees. There will be extensive kill programs if removed. If I did not use Body Code, Muscle testing, and Jesus helped to remove this part the client would be in deep trouble. There is no way a survivor can tell you all the program pieces here and will not know all the alarms that could go off. I am not saying this to scare you. Just remove the Tree of Death and Tree of the Underworld with extreme caution.

I want you to understand when we get to this part of the deprogramming process all of the core foundation has been removed. The first tree and the tree in the underworld is the last step. The other trees have to be removed first and you work down to the first Tree which is the foundation. You may find that the Grid is holding everything in place as well. Usually, remove the Grid before you begin the process.

Remember the demons have no intentions of letting the person go. You will need all the spiritual help you can have. This cannot be done safely without the help of Lord Jesus Christ. After I Map out all the pieces to the programming; I will have the survivor go to the Courts of Heaven. We will go to the courts and share all the programming we have found. Jesus will help us address all demons that will be fighting to keep possession of the person.

Please do not remove the two trees separately. You must map out all pieces of the trees and Grid and anything else muscle testing finds. When all information has been found and you know what has been done in the programming; it is ok to move ahead and remove the programming altogether. I need you to hear this very important fact. Never, Never, remove anything until you know you have all the pieces. The unconscious mind can tell you how to remove the program. In this case, you have to understand all of each piece for you to remove anything. If you go ahead and start removing these two trees without fully understanding what has been done, the client could be severely hurt.

The unconscious mind believes there is a tree throughout every part of the body. Every part of the person's mind, body, and spirit has been captured by the trees. The programmers set up the tree to kill the person using the roots. One client said the roots of the tree will strangle him from the inside out if he gets free. Many parts/alters will be in the underworld with a part of the person's humanity that will be trapped for eternity in hell.

Be well prepared when removing the foundation and the tree in the underworld. When I say this is the Core Foundation and everything is built on it, I mean it! Be Careful!

These entities are connected to each globe installed on the Sephirot Tree in the underworld.

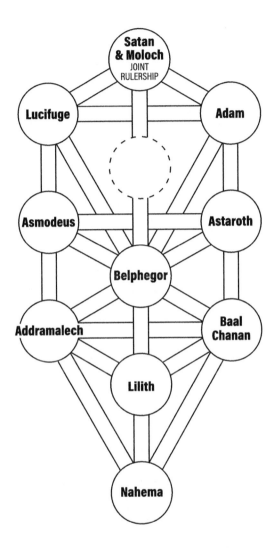

Seven trees have been listed — the foundation of all survivors' programming. Other trees, not part of the core foundation, may be constructed.

VIII

PIECES TO REMOVE AS YOU ADDRESS ALL FOUNDATIONAL PROGRAMMING

More Important Puzzle Pieces that must be removed from the survivor.

LUCIFER TRAPS THE 5 PARTS OF THE SOUL

Five Parts of the Soul (Buys, 2019, Restoring):

1. Nefesh- Soul of vitality, in blood, lowest level of soul, breathing and beating heart, element earth and connects the world of Assiah.

2. Ruach- Spirit, in heart, translated as wind, energizes a person's consciousness, element air, connects the world of Yetzirah, corresponds to water and fire.

3. Neshamah- Breath of life, water Briah in brain, level of higher soul and consciousness, source of individual identity, functions at unconscious level and source of ego, corresponds to water and the world of Briah.

4. Chaya- Connection to everything living, connected to fire and the Atziluth world.

5. Yechidah- Singular one, the body's highest plane of the soul and the one that connects to God, connects to Adam Kadmon and is in contact with all life and all of creation.

Lucifer traps all parts of the soul. You will have to release all of this. Let go of the breath of Lucifer. True Neshamah must be restored and reconnected to God.

Renounce death experiences where Nephilim breathed in Lucifer as the cult downloaded into the survivor.

Muscle test or ask the survivor where the above can be removed.

Capturing the parts of a survivor's soul is a big deal. Breath is what gives us life. If Lucifer captures your breath, you believe Lucifer can give or take away breath. This is a lie; only God can do that.

15

5 ILLUMINATI GOALS AND 5 "I WILL'S"

[Contribution from Amanda Buys on page 177 of her 2020 manual, *Recap, Refresh, and Recalibrate for the Journey Forward*. I agree with her statement, but I had not seen the information written this way. I would like this chapter of goals and "I will's" to be her concise explanation. I have spoken extensively about the goals; below is exactly what Amanda said regarding the goals and "I will's."]

Goals of Illuminati

1. Abolition of monarchies and ordered governments

2. Abolition of private property and inheritances

3. Abolition of patriotism and nationalism

4. Abolition of family life, the institution of marriage, and the establishment of communal education of children

5. Abolition of all religion

How do I know this is true? Because this has been in my New World Army Programming all my life and the lives of my clients. (Refer to the New World Army programming chapter.)

This must be renounced as there is a survivor's part that's made oaths to carry out the cult's plans and be loyal to the Illuminati.

Five "I Will's" that must be accepted by survivors.

1. I will ascend into heaven;

2. I will exalt my throne above the stars of God;

3. I will sit also upon the mount of the congregation, in the sides of the north;

4. I will ascend above the heights of the clouds;

5. I will be like the most high.

This is done because Lucifer is angry with God and is replying to this scripture: Isaiah 14-12-24

"How are thou fallen from heaven, O Lucifer, son of the morning! How art thou cut down to the ground, which didn't weaken the nations! For thou has said in thine heart... then goes through the five I wills but opposite."

This will be said many times in a survivor's lifetime.

16

SILVER CORD AND GOLD CORD

The Silver Cord acts as an umbilical cord to the soul as it leaves the body. When souls are traveling out of their body into other places, they are still bound to the body by the Silver Cord. It is unbelievable to me how much the search engines hide concerning the sections of the Kabbalah covering the functions the Silver Cord inverted. The Silver Cord is not considered evil, but the Illuminati/Freemasons' mind-control programming utilizes it for evil.

I say the cord is being used for evil because the cults teach members how to leave their bodies and fly to wherever they desire. If the cults are having a big ritual and you don't physically live nearby you are expected to leave your body to attend the ritual. Disobeying the cult by not being at a ritual in spirit form can result in death or at least punishment. I remember many years ago I would say I have not seen the cult members in years. All the while I was spiritually leaving my body while sleeping, attending every ritual.

All survivors will have a Silver Cord that must be addressed. I would like to share a story about a Gold Cord. In one survivor's experience, we found a Gold Cord. I kept asking, "Do you mean a Silver Cord?" She kept saying, "No. It is gold." The discrepancy was because the survivor was ordained to be a queen while in the womb due to her family line of ancient Druids. Some of the Druid family line programming is extremely intense, downloaded with high-ranking demons.

If mind control programming related to the Silver or Gold Cord is present, curses are attached. There will be many negative emotions connected to the cord, and survivors' ancestors may be attached to their Silver Cord.

I believe when the soul leaves the body, the individual feels a sense of freedom; the cult somehow connects the cord to evil to trap the survivor. The Illuminati and other groups do not want members to ever feel free.

The Silver or Gold Cord is connected to Da'at on the Sephirot Tree in the heart area where the cord is the keeper of secret knowledge. The cord protects the person from not being lost when the soul leaves the body. The body learns to adapt when the spirit leaves as the body is still connected through the Silver or Gold Cord.

"As long as the silver cord isn't broken" said Buys (2019, *DID/SRA training video*), "it allows your spirit to travel through the second heaven or to other earthly places (astral places). You are not allowed to cut the silver cord because if you do that person dies. What must we do? We must ask the angels to bring the person back to their bodies.

"The cord allows cult members to have a seat in the 2nd Heaven-survivor's bloodline; disembodied spirits can be attached to the silver cord through knots. The survivor's bloodline can be attached to this silver cord. The connection offers ancestral spirits a form of eternal life. Because of the cult's iniquity, these dead human spirits do not immediately go to Sheol but are kept in a holding place belonging to Satan" (15 of 19).

When a royal bloodline survivor is conceived, a myriad of dead human spirits will be assigned to the silver cord and can function as one. The spirits can push back their host and control the body for a limited time, usually during rituals or for special assignments.

According to Buys, we commit murder if we cut the silver cord. I believe the best we can do is remove all evil from the cord, including curses, the family bloodline, dead human spirits — cutting off permission for the cult to use the silver cord as an entryway to the survivor's body. I know Amanda's statements are true; when the "queen" client had the gold cord, the cult used it to download all the Druid ancestors. Later we realized an ancestor and powerful entity would possess her body during rituals. The ancestor came from some type of royalty.

OTHER PROGRAMMING
YOU NEED TO KNOW

Core Events and Core Parts are the focus in the removal process. During this process, it is possible that certain programming will be found. Many programs are distractions that won't lead to freedom and require much time. Just make sure the path is necessary before you go down it. Some of the programming will just collapse as you focus on the core events. It is quite possible you may have to remove a specific program before you go any further, which is ok.

It is common to have the following in programming:

- ALICE IN WONDERLAND
- WIZARD OF OZ

- SLEEPING BEAUTY
- CAROUSELS
- CLOCKS
- COMPUTERS
- CUBE
- DOORS
- SAFES
- BOXES
- JEWELS
- DIAMONDS
- KEYS (Keys are very, very, very important.)
- ALL KINDS OF TECHNOLOGY (MAKING FANTASIES)
- BOOKS
- IDOLS OF EVERY KIND (God said you will not worship idols of false gods, so good Luciferians do exactly what God said not to.)
- NUMBERS IMPORTANT TO ILLUMINATI- 3, 5, 7, 13, 33, 666 (Numbers have a meaning. They were important to God too. Lucifer stole numbers to make them negative. Seven is important to God's Kingdom. Seven days of creation. Lucifer's kingdom uses seven days for rituals.
- SYMBOLS ARE VERY IMPORTANT METAPHORICALLY AND HAVE A HIDDEN MEANING
- SECRET HAND SHAKE TO INFORM A BROTHER

- SPECIFIC WORDS
- INVERSION- EVERYTHING IS INVERTED TO A SURVIVOR. (You say, "I love you" and they hear, "I hate you.")

(PLEASE CHECK PUZZLE PIECES TO THE CABAL, MIND CONTROL, AND SLAVERY, PART 1 FOR ADDITIONAL PROGRAMS.)

IX

CORE EVENTS TO
BE REMOVED

We covered the pieces survivors must remove to find freedom. They are the basic puzzle pieces that go into programming. Now we address the events that will be removed and different ages integrated. The womb programming begins at conception. We have talked about birth. Now we will learn about the rest of the events. The next event is one of the most important events, which occurs at 13 months.

13TH-MONTH RITUAL

Important Core Event- 13 Months

13 Months Old

PICTURE BY NIC YOUNGBLOOD

The 13-month-old ritual contains one of the most horrific experiences imaginable. The cults use the 13-month-old ritual to trick babies into believing they will be saved. The cults say, "Do you want to meet Jesus? He will save you. All you have to do is open your heart to Jesus and all this pain will go away." Up to this point, the 13-month-old has been severely traumatized starting in the womb. The baby, of course, wants to be saved and the pain to stop. The cults continue with their lies so the baby opens up its heart to Jesus. Jesus immediately comes in and loves the baby, promising He will always be there and never leave. At that moment the baby is whole. The trauma is healed and the mind becomes one. For the first time, the baby feels whole and loved. All the separate parts the 13-month-old had are now one as God intended. This is the first time the baby's mind is whole. Then, all of a sudden, after this wonderful feeling of wholeness and love from Jesus, the cult invades with the three-way rape. Cult members say to the baby, "See — Jesus lied to you, he doesn't love you, you have been tricked. We will be the only ones here for you." The baby is absolutely horrified and splits again three times. This is where the three-way rape happens, causing three core splits from the whole. They will now cover and wrap the 13-month-old, in death. Masking the true self as much as possible is a continual process throughout most of the survivor's life.

The 13-month-old will be the most hated by all of the survivors alters. The cult members teach the alters that the baby is the cause of the reason they have been so tortured. At the 13-year-old ritual, the cult will have tricked the teenager to hate this baby at 13 months, so she will have to kill the baby. This killing represents the core self -connected to God. The cult wants to obliterate the true self. This ritual is another way of destroying the survivor's connection to God and destroying the soul God created. By 13-years-old, most of the child's programming is finished.

I cannot imagine anything worse than fooling a child into believing the only being who can save the child let him down in the most heart wrenching way. The cult's mind-control continues to reinforce hate of Jesus Christ because Jesus is the only one with authority over Lucifer and his fallen angels. I believe that in this moment what occurs between the baby and Jesus is not lost but serves as an anchor to the child's soul. The child may sense there is something beyond what the cult taught. In some ways, I think the Satanists sabotage themselves because they show the baby there is a Jesus. At some level, the true self knows the cult is not God as it professes. I believe Jesus does experience everything the child goes through and does not leave the child. We must remember, when we think Jesus does not love us or understand us, we need to know He felt everything we've experienced in the Garden of Gethsemane. He knows what it feels like to be raped and tortured — he felt it for you too. All we have to do is come to Jesus and accept his gift and the power of his spilled blood as atonement for us. Jesus will help us through the healing process. It is painful and many ask, "Why did he not protect me? He cannot interfere with free will. What he can do is help us endure.

As for the 13-month-old ritual, the three core parts created by the three-way rape will be connected to three domains. The domains connect the baby to very powerful, evil demons, and each domain has a purpose. The demons below will stay with the survivor for life.

The First Domain – Apollyon

The Second Domain- Nimrod

The Third Domain- Michael

In each domain, the demons are connected to different parts of the baby. Apollyon represents a beast and is connected through sodomy using the anus as its pathway. Nimrod uses the pathway to the vagina and represents strong sexual pleasure. Michael is connected to the penis in the mouth for oral suffocation. Michael represents religious false light and teachings. Cult groups will build upon these downloads of demons for the rest of the child's life. Survivors must contact this core part/alter repeatedly for integration.

Below is more information on the three domains. Survivors and Professionals will have to remove all the pieces of the domains, casting out these entities as they work their way back for integration and to when the demons were downloaded in the first installation.

3 DOMAINS

Each domain will have 13 parts, 0- to 13-years-old. Core shields in the domain are daughter, mother, and wife, which can be queens in the system. Each core part has an alter system. So there are many wives, mothers, and daughters. (Opposite for male.) You will have to find the one with the most authority and work with that part. Core (Parts) are connected to domains.

First Domain: Apollyon

Character represented by Satan, pure beast, evil, rage against Christians, the Beast, underworld (Buys, 2019). Fake internal system, 13 /alters/parts, child driven to supernatural rage, enabling entity Apollyon to possess a body to do horrific things. Captures soul through sodomy. Sexual acts the domain's focus including bestiality and domination. The cult will cage children and treat them like an animal and force them to have sex with animals. There will be a daughter, mother and wife of the beast with many alters behind them. Some parts could be called names such as Hitler or King George. There will always be a beast alter that will act like an animal. All teachings are reinforced through anal sex (Buys, 2019).

Second Domain: Nimrod

Character represented by Apollyon (Buys, 2020). May represent the Antichrist. He was first transformed into a hybrid and is known as Alexander. Encapsulates Body-first orgasm. Super human strength with high energy. Behind transhumanism. Supernatural sexual experiences. Rules over sexual pleasure. Demonically charged orgasm. First Nephilim son was called Nimrod. In this domain you will find parts called vagina, orgasm, and other sexual names (Buys, 2020).

The 13-month-old is the daughter of Nimrod and knows him as the Savior (Buys, 2020). The 13-year-old knows him as her Nephilim son, and the 26-year wife knows him as a husband and is addicted to their supernatural sex; she also will be known as the queen. Opposite for male (Buys, 2020).

Thirteen parts in this domain are connected (Buys, 2020). There will be a daughter, mother, and wife in this domain with many parts behind each one. Opposite for male (Buys, 2020).

Third Domain: Michael

Fake prophet, entities, Metatron, most spiritual, fake light, quantum level might not need body to function (Buys, 2020). Tantric sex used to steal energy, seduction and pleasure. Religious programming. 13 parts, energy centers maximized here, fake miracles and healings. Claims the spirit when a person is brought to death by oral suffocation. The energy centers are maximized in this domain to create supernatural powers from Michael (Buys, 2020).

The three downloads are done at the same time when the cult does the 3-way rape. I hate writing about the horror of what they do, but if we don't know what their deeds are, a survivor cannot get free.

When I first watched the seminar with Amanda Buys. I was unsure what to think about domains. So, I decided to see if my clients had the domains. Guess what I found? Amanda had shared a new piece of the puzzle. To make a long story short, there it was: the Domain system. Then I started to see how the cults were using the domains to tie in the family and download the ancestors' iniquity from the family's bloodline. The more I worked with the three Domains, the nastier the work got. There is evidence: clients reported being taken over by one of the three entities to perform terrible things. All while the survivors were not in their bodies.

This part I did not expect because I did not hear it in the seminars. The 13-month-old ritual is not only a big event for the baby, but also for the parents. To participate in the ritual, the parents are possessed by a blood ancestor or one of the three entities. The parents are being tied to the 13-month-old for different purposes. The parents are under complete mind control and will be transported to a younger self. I have found that parents' teenage alters are used because by this time they had become very angry.

I'm going to share a client story including a hard part for him to accept. The survivor's daughter had been selected in the womb to be a queen from the Druid ancestors. From the beginning, he was connected to his daughter in a King role, and her as queen. The programming process for this young girl was to be connected to only the King — her dad for bloodline purposes. We found that each time he was taken over by the entity Michael to be with the Queen, the daughter was possessed by a goddess entity and the ritual would continue for the Druids. To the Druids, Illuminati, Freemasons, and other occult groups, incest symbolizes a pure blood relationship — the only allowed. It is sick but true. Why is it true? Because Lucifer is in a war with God. God said incest is forbidden, so the cult groups made it their No. 1 rule. They think it's the only way to keep their cult bloodline pure.

Map out the following for the survivor. The map may be different in every case. These are the most important alters/parts to remove. Rely on the survivor to help in the removal.

- Release three-way rape
- Everything the cult did to make the child distrust Jesus must be restored
- Layers of death wrapped around the child
- Renounce the huge demon download
- Disconnect the three core shields from the three domains
- Remove all teachings and connections from domains
- Cast out Apollyon, Michael, Nimrod
- Bring 13-month-old's humanity back
- Disconnect from Lucifer
- Mother goddess disconnection
- Work with all the Daughter, Mother, and Wife systems parts

The parts must be integrated back to the 13-month-old many times and then to conception for full integration. (Explained in the Chapter of Core Parts.)

Remove charts of gods, the teachings of the specific demons called Apollyon, Michael, and Nimrod. I have found there are demons with much more power that are well hidden; people are not aware of the demons and they're not openly discussed. They are to never be mentioned, just like the hidden 13 members of Illuminati.

Each Core Part must walk back to find the baby hidden from the other parts because the 13-month-old knows Jesus and has been covered up. When a core part is taken back to find the baby, you will need to know the condition of the baby.

- Can you find the baby?
- What condition is the baby in?
- Are you able to retrieve the baby from its secret place?

If the survivor's part is able to retrieve the baby; I have Jesus put his hands on the baby to give it a blessing to heal the baby from all abuse and from everything in the ritual. The 13-month-old baby must be whole before each Core Part can integrate. (Explanation at end of book)

I would like to share this as one way to complete integration. I believe that integration can happen in many ways according to how the survivor's mind works. The point here is that we want to find the 13 core parts to integrate with the 13-month-old and back to the first split at conception. (See the Integration Chapter for more information.)

THE 3-YEAR-OLD RITUAL

This ritual is performed in every survivor I have worked with including myself. Parts of the ritual were covered in my first book. Please refer to Part 1 for more information. Practitioners or Survivors will have to remove all things about the ritual.

"Three Years Old"

PICTURE BY NIC YOUNGBLOOD

The 3-year-old ritual is a very important event in a survivor's life. The child has proven she can live through all the torture necessary to have the Tree of Death fully implanted in the body mind, and spirit. The child has sufficiently proven itself to the cult, and this is the first acceptance for Lucifer. Because the child has lived through the installations of the tree up to this point, she is brought for acceptance and the first and sacred seed is implanted from Lucifer.

This important ritual includes the trauma over Jesus Christ, so the child fully accepts Lucifer. The child will receive hallucinogens and experience a warm, inviting atmosphere; for example, a light where angels may appear and a figure that resembles Jesus. When the child wants to go to who they think is Jesus; immediately another horrific experience will happen. I've heard survivors say they were saved by Jesus at 3-years-old. Maybe this is true, but this is a part of a ritual. I know for sure that the survivor is going to a person that is acting like Jesus and is part of the ritual. I believe it is possible that the survivor is left with the memory of being saved and feeling this good feeling to hide the rest of what happens in the ritual.

This child has been prepared carefully thus far to receive Lucifer's seed. The child is not to suffer any sodomy because the child must be pure when the seed of Lucifer is given. The child has had objects inserted in their bottom to prepare for the coming seed. One client described objects being placed in the bottom, each getting a little bigger to handle an adult penis. The child receives the seed of Lucifer by sodomy; from that moment on, the captured child must protect Lucifer's seed with every ounce of energy they have. After the child receives the seed, she is considered worthy before Lucifer.

I will spare you the remaining gory details of the ritual, but the child is once again accepted by the cult. A wall must be built around the tree where the seed and child are kept. This is when the cult begins to use complex programming. During this ritual, powerful demons are downloaded to ensure Lucifer's Seed is protected and the child can never get away.

After the ritual is complete, the core foundation of Lucifer's Kingdom is considered firmly planted; because of the child's worthiness, they will be blessed with the seed of Lucifer. Lucifer has accepted the child of 3 years. At 3 years, the child also may receive a title denoting authority in Lucifer's kingdom. As the child grows, each age will be captured in the tree. The cult will go to great efforts to build a wall of protection so the child never escapes. Cult members will continue to build upon the Tree of Death throughout her training, which will continue through 17- or 19-years-old.

Three parts are created: a seed part, a tree part, and a son or daughter of Lucifer part. Each part/alter will once again be connected to Nimrod, Apollyon, and Michael of the three domains. The three parts here are connected to the core parts developed at 13 months.

This daughter of Lucifer — or in some cases a son — is 100% loyal to Lucifer. The child will have complex programming. A son's name may be Adam, for instance, or a daughter's name Rosette.

Remember, with each numerical age, the programming must be connected. The cult once again connects the seed, tree, and son or daughter of Lucifer parts to Apollyon, Michael, and Nimrod.

For the ancient Druids, I believe the seed of Lucifer has been carried since the beginning of time. The seed must be transferred by someone who carries the ancient seed in their family line. The Druids have different programming that includes ancient teachings and powerful demons that are attached to the seed.

PICTURE BY NIC YOUNGBLOOD

Remove every part of the ritual.

Identify the acts committed against survivors and map out the pieces for removal. The practitioner may need to plan on a few hours to gather all the programming pieces. Do not start a removal process without making sure you have enough time to finish it. Many strong demons would have been downloaded to protect the tree, seed, and Lucifer's captured child. Once you begin messing around with programming, the demons will try to attack. You must remove it all at once so the demons don't have a chance to harm the survivor. (Mapping Out the process is sufficient if you can't do it all at once.)

This program removal will be complex and may include layers of alarm systems, suicide programs, bombs, and booby traps. The cults connect all this programming to organs, glands, the nervous system, and chakras. The procedure must be completed many times. Below are pieces of the ritual that absolutely will be a part of all 3-year-old rituals. Use Body Code and Muscle Testing for the rest of the programming that must be removed. (Go to the Chapter on Body Code and Muscle Testing near the book's end.)

- The ritual itself
- Rape
- Implantation of the seed
- Acceptance of group
- The Tree of Death Download training

- Renounce Lucifer's acceptance of the child and seed being placed into the tree
- Remove all oaths and promises
- Release download of demons
- Stronghold Demon and the original split must be disconnected from the seed and renounced.
- Monarch training starts at about 3 years for those who were assigned the jobs; all titles and jobs must be renounced.
- Have Jesus destroy any ability for Lucifer's Seed to recreate itself.
- Remove illusions about Jesus Christ, such as He raped them.
- The wall or walls have to be removed, but be very careful. Complex programming and alarm systems are attached.
- Remove the many guards to protect the wall, tree, seed, and parts.
- The cult will have the child connected again with the chakra system.
- Disconnect the survivor from Apollyon, Nimrod, and Michael.
- This programming will have death programs, which means if you remove the program the survivor will die. That is why practitioners must have all the pieces to the program before removal. The cult will have connected a trigger tied to the heart or somewhere else, so the heart stops if removal of the program takes place.

- The cult will have connected the survivor to the Cosmic Tree, so disconnect here.
- The cult will have conducted the Bible trauma here.
- The ritual will have the child reject Jesus. For the ritual to be effective it is crucial for the child to reject Jesus and fully accept Lucifer. Find all pieces connected to Jesus in an evil way and make sure the identity of Lucifer and Jesus is corrected in the truth of the way it is.

The above is a fraction of what you need to locate and address. It is impossible to find every piece unless you use the techniques; I will show you. Each piece of a ritual and a program is important to find because there is meaning in the actions and words. There is always a reason something is done. Nothing is done randomly.

Identify other programs connected to the 3-year-old ritual, making sure they are disconnected. We are unraveling a carefully constructed puzzle where one layer leads to the next. This is why we must start at the age of the survivor and work our way back to the womb. Hopefully, you can see what a mess we'd have if we didn't follow the correct order to remove programming.

Once all programming and ritual pieces are removed, you will need to address the parts/alters. This is when integration will need to take place, but it may possibly take some time to occur. The best way to accomplish integration is for the survivor to see the whole truth about what happened and to see who Jesus Christ really is and who Lucifer is. Just let the survivor know he or she will be safe and not pushed into anything. Survivors can freely choose who they want to follow. Sometimes you have to explain what choosing means because they have never had the right to choose anything. (Go to the Integration Chapter for more information.)

SACRED GEOMETRY

Sacred Geometry and Forms of Life are very important in the teachings of Freemasonry and Kabbalah. Sacred geometry ultimately represents every shape in the universe and was created by the true God. Lucifer understood its importance and used it in mind-control programming.

The Seed of Life comprises seven circles.

SEED OF LIFE

In programming this seed is the most sacred above all things. It is to be protected by the survivor even unto death. Lucifer wants to ensure his seed continues at all costs.

The following information is from *Puzzle Pieces to The Cabal, Mind Control, and Slavery, Part 1.*

The Seed holds all of Satan's kingdom, laws, and authority to act in the child's name and have complete power over the child's free will. The Seed is highly revered in Satanic cults.

The Seed represents three things: Placeholder, Beginning, and Permission for Satan to have control of another's mind and body.

The Seed entraps the human soul. If everything leads back to the seed, we must acknowledge the importance of keeping the survivor trapped in the illusion of the Twin and the One Demon.

- The Seed represents the capturing of the spirit to make the person a part of Satan's kingdom.
- The Seed now represents Lucifer's children.
- The Stronghold or The One is attached to the seed and protects it.
- The Seed is where the One Demon is protected and is the root of all his evil.
- The Seed cannot be destroyed.
- The Seed will forever reproduce itself.
- A part of humanity is trapped in the seed and is in a great deal of pain.
- The Seed holds the lineage of the family's past, present, and future, so no family members get free.
- The Seed represents the Creation and the secrets of Satan's kingdom.
- The Seed allows Satan to control the survivor's mind and grants permission to possess the body.
- Satan told God he would possess the bodies created for Adam and Eve. God then responded by saying he would put enmity between man and Satan. That does

not mean Satan did not find temporary ways to steal the mind and the body of individuals.

- The Seed is protected by many demons and alters created with the Tree of Death.
- The Seed is planted in the root chakra and considered to be the root of all life and controlled by Satan.
- The Seed is considered sacred, and all things must be sacrificed to protect it.
- The Twin is the main protector of the Seed.
- The Seed is the placeholder for Satan and the trinity to reside.
- The Seed is the portal in which Satan comes into the body.

The seed is a representation of Lucifer capturing another child of God and saying this person is mine and now is no longer a child to God. The child is now fully Lucifer's even though the child's capture will be reinstated many times throughout the child's life in many rituals.

FLOWER OF LIFE

The Seed of Life will expand into the Flower of Life. This Flower of Life represents our Life Force energy. Everything in the universe is woven within a repeating pattern that shows itself through this sacred flower and represents the thread of our being across all dimensions. The Tree of Life comes from the Seed of Life and on the Tiferoth of the Sephirot. (Amanda Buys)

The Flower is a very important part of the foundational programming and is attached to the tree. If you look at the second picture, the Sephirot Tree is in the middle of the Flower. In the middle of the tree is the Seed. If you remove the tree, the flower can continue to bring back the tree. The Flower in the programming must be completely removed. It seems the Flower will forever reproduce itself, but Jesus Christ can destroy it and all it means.

It is interesting to me that the programming is based on the sacred geometry where all shapes and patterns are based. This is what I believe is called the universal creation based on a set of certain shapes and patterns from which all things are created.

The Seed of Life, the Flower of Life, and the Fruit of Life are the foundation of all fruit shapes and patterns. It is interesting that in programming you can have the same fruit on the tree that must be earned by training, rewards, and surviving rituals. Also, if you look closely, Metatron Cube has the Fruit of Life for its basic shape. I am really blown away at all the programming one might think is random but actually conveys a significant meaning. It seems the more you learn, the more there is to learn.

Because the Tree of Life, Seed of Life, Flower of Life, and Fruit of Life are connected you will have to remove them all.

FRUIT OF LIFE

Rose and Adam

Rose is a name that represents a small and older part that can be the first split at conception. (This does not mean this will be the name.) The name Rose is a representation for many things. Roses are sexual symbols. Rose symbolizes a vagina. Sexual goddesses could be part of the system. The Small Rose (a child alter) is connected to the foundation of the Kabbalah Tree of Death and the Seed. In some survivors, Rose can be a main programming system. Rosette can mean a bloodline back to Cain. Rose or Adam will function in the worlds of Atziluth with Lucifer. I was taught by a therapist that the first split was called a witch twin. A witch twin is the first split at conception. After publishing my first book, I realized there is a better word for the first split, which acts as a twin — a twin being taught the opposite of what she's learned in her core self. The twin is being taught to worship Lucifer. Most survivors agree this feels like a twin. I prefer to call the first split at conception; a twin.

Rose is connected to a seed of life. She is considered the fruit. She is the totality of everything created as a mind-control slave. A goddess entity will come up in Rose called Venus but I have found other names. Well-hidden systems surround her to protect her. Rose will be the last core alter/part a therapist finds in the survivor. She is 100% committed to Lucifer's kingdom and is the one the Stronghold demon is connected to for a lifetime starting at conception.

Big Rose will be a warrior and has earned her ranking. She will have a lot of training and skills. She has been made to believe she has chosen Lucifer's Kingdom with free will. She believes Lucifer thinks she is very important and will often be told "very special."

Rosette, (Rosie) and Big Rose

XI

MONARCH PROGRAM

MONARCH PROGRAM

To all Grandmothers, Mothers, and Daughters

Once the Monarch programming begins in the family, it is passed down through each generation. This does not stop unless someone in the family line wakes up and does something to stop it. If you are in the presidential level of programming, secrecy is guaranteed. You have skills they need and want, and you learn quickly. You can split your mind easily to create different personalities.

Each Monarch level is earned by great torture going through the 13 levels of training. The person in training must pass many tests. My first book included a scene with a hardened school classroom where you were never good enough despite your actions. The child may have accomplished amazing feats but is told he did a horrible job and

201

is completely worthless. The cult blames the child for not doing the task well enough and blames the child that the other kids were punished or killed. The teachings from the cult will be blame, blame, blame. The cult needs the child to feel worthless.

At age 7, I began to see important people high in the government and in foreign countries. The government used military men that are traitors to their county to cover up what was happening to the children. Many military people were ensnared in the MK Ultra programming. Many of them would have to escort me to meet someone. The main person escorting me was Kissinger, who seemed to escort me to the most important people.

Monarch programming includes all things sexual. Monarch slaves know how to please every type of pervert. The sexual techniques are taught by the worst perverts of all — the CIA and M16. Monarch programming techniques are continually updated with technology and new ideas of perversion.

Common names include Kitten programming and Gumby programming to make children believe they are very flexible. The whole monarch system is based on a cocoon turning into a butterfly — another perverted program. Many alters will complete each mission. The trauma is so great there are many splits. Ultimately, the training goals are designed for the child to feel nothing. His work is merely a job. The child will be the perfect robot. Most children will not be present in their bodies to shield themselves from atrocious sexual acts. They learn to have no reaction to the sexual act.

The Presidential Alter in Me

This is what I wrote a while ago as I tried to understand what being a presidential model meant. I had five core alters with many parts behind them in a system: Number 1 was a messenger, Number 2 handled all sex, Number 3 was the recorder, Number 4 took orders, and Number 5 was a hidden alter stealing all memory from me. I had names in the programming for each alter. The Sex Kitten is in the Monarch Programming and instructs in all sexual acts. Each job was required to be done exactly or I would be punished severely.

Information codes had to be provided for access. The messenger and receiver attached to photographic memory. Trauma holder, sex holder, and file box were there when the trauma was too extreme for me to handle. Reporter is always present in case anything fails. There must be a full account by a part not connected to trauma or sex.

I had file boxes in my memory just for Nixon, and a few others. To get into the file boxes, the person will have correct codes made for only them. Kissinger wanted file boxes on everyone I met so he could use the information to hurt them. I suppose it was for blackmail purposes. Although I was communicating with government officials who interacted with other countries, Kissinger made me tell him everything. He had an override code for all information and a part just for him, a common practice in programming. The programmer has a secret part. Cult members all do it because they are psychopaths with huge egos and a yearning for power.

Certain scenarios were established for me to practice. When I made errors, I was punished by torture. A lot of practice with instruction was necessary to be a messenger and sex toy. This is where the CIA teaching came in. Just imagine that a young child 3 to 7 being taught sexual acts an adult would not do in the bedroom with their partner. I learned quickly because of the consequences if I did not. No Child could perform these acts without splitting the mind many times.

In my writing about my past; a part carrying memories about Nixon came out. A part/alter was created to be Nixon's private girl toy. This part responded only to his voice and password. Each password served a different purpose. I was created to do his will.

Kissinger would take me to a big room with a red bedspread. I always shared a secret message and received one from Nixon. Each time, the message was activated by a programmed sexual act. At times I was escorted through a tunnel where Kissinger met me. He often escorted me to black limousines where men with dark skin spoke a language I did not understand.

In other experiences, I had to speak German often, and French, Russian, and Latin to priests.

Many times, I was turned over to Gerald Ford, who hurt me physically every time by performing anal sex; afterward, I would withstand clots of blood coming out.

I met Bill Clinton when I was 13 while he was governor. I don't recall much about him. I had a file box for Clintons. The rest of my story starts as a 17-year-old with Hilary Clinton mainly, though Bill was involved a little.

The Monarch program is only one part of the MK Ultra programming I received. I'd like to share an earlier piece of writing that will strike a chord for many enduring similar monstrosities.

All my life I have been a guinea pig to these evil humans that acted as animals. Each new cult member or scientist was eager to play and practice. Each discovery remade me into something new. I was viewed as a robot. They had permission to do what they wanted every day with no oversight, no one to punish them for their crimes, and no one to protect me.

The cults manufactured the perfect weapon. When you control another person's mind, you can do anything. There are no boundaries; the possibilities are limitless. Just imagine this much power in another human being. The cult members are drunk with power, using it to injure children. Usually, the children's parents are under mind control, unable to protect their offspring. Truly — the child is in the grips of hideous, obscene monsters. My abductors didn't care how much humiliation, shame, and degradation I suffered. The freaks actually felt immense pleasure in my pain. The greater the pain, the more potent their high felt. Evil must own pain to live with all its demons. As I fell victim to their power, my tormentors relished millions of dollars. When do all the survivors get compensation from the governments for such anguish?

I was only 2-years-old when the government started its experiments on me. In 1961, government officials were already experts in using mind control. They used patterns or templates to solidify the programming foundation in every survivor.

Each decade, the government would learn more and gain more technology to experiment on me and many others in the MK Ultra program. After all the decades of drugs, prodding, operations, and experiments of every kind, the government could not destroy my humanity. The cults captured parts of me, but my soul they could not destroy. It was not theirs to take. They could only have it if I granted it. As the torment increased, so did the light in my soul. By my teen years, I had encountered many near-death experiences. While the cults were downloading their demons and evil, I was talking to Jesus and he was strengthening me. That is why I am so convicted in Jesus Christ. I know He exists. I felt His love on the other side. I know He is real and I know they can never take Him away. I know without a doubt my soul exists — I existed before and I will exist after I die. My soul is not for sale.

They know they can't destroy my soul, so they just cover up that part of me that is untouchable. The rest is filled with their lies and illusions. They tried to obstruct me from finding the truth, but I did find the truth, and I did remember.

It's crucial for the occult to steal our free will; most people would not obey the cult's sick orders if they had free will. That is why cults must use mind control. If survivors remembered half of their torment, they would not live. And yet we do. What a powerful statement of who we truly are. We are so powerful and strong, we can live through the overwhelming torture, rape, and abuse of every kind. We are not weak. We are more than cults told us we were.

The programmers' goal is to fracture the mind thoroughly to hamper recollection of a cult's secrets. A survivor usually has pieces that come over time. It takes time to make the mind back whole again.

Joseph Mengele was one of my programmers. I had several. They created an illusion in my mind which they had no right to and made me believe I had a tree growing in my body. Programmers play many other games such as implanting codes, colors, symbols, and commands, leaving their signature last. After all, programming cannot be without their name and special psycho brand. Cult members tortured me until my mind split — at that moment, they designed a part to control. They could do it over and over and keep achieving more splits for more games and illusions. All the while they think they are God with their awesome ingenuity. Always outsmarting the next programmer.

There were many times the programmers' experiments would test how far I could go. It was thrilling for them to see a person forced past a breaking point. The programmers are the developer of a game. My job was to prove if their game would work on a human being. The programmers were past feelings and I feel full of demonic control.

The occult descends into depths of depravity few can imagine. What's more, governments all over the world are experimenting on the most vulnerable citizens, the children. I pray we'll annihilate the cults for the pain and misery they've caused.

If you're a survivor of MK Ultra programming, trust your strength. You would not have made it this far if you were not strong. You can outsmart the cults and get free. They are weak. Anyone who inflicts such malevolent programs against another individual is weak, powerless, pathetic. Cult members are nothing to be respected or revered. Hold on. Just take one step at a time. You can make it.

The Lord showed me that anything done under mind control lays blame at the feet of the controller. Oftentimes we cannot forgive ourselves for what we were made to do. If you are under mind control and someone tells you to do something awful, it is not free will. The cultists who taught you, designing parts of you to commit evil, will lay down and answer to the Lord for this. It is important in the healing process to acknowledge what we have done — and if necessary, repent. We have the Savior's love.

XII

BREEDER FOR
THE CULT

Early as 9-years-old

Breeders are for producing babies in the cult for sacrifice in Satanic rituals. The girls in the cult begin having babies after they have their periods. Often, the girls receive drugs to start their periods; drugs also are given to conceive multiple babies at once. The age of a breeder can begin as young as 9 years, and breeders usually don't reach their late teens or early 20's. A Breeder can have as many as 20 to 30 pregnancies for the cult for different purposes in the cult rituals. No pregnancies go to full term. Sometimes they may let a breeder reach 7 months for a specific ritual if the pregnancy can be hidden.

More than not, cult babies are offered to the high priest or the individual with authority for the group's specific ritual.

The cult will make the child believe he acted in ways he didn't. The mother will be forced to watch the sacrifice of their child. The cult requires the Breeder to commit ill acts against the baby to further split his mind. The goal is to have the alters/Breeders not care about the child or to believe this is a job with no meaning. A breeder has often broken a survivor to never return. Imagine a child of 11 years forced to have a baby and possibly twins. The young girl will have babies — often without drugs — and the family doctor will deliver the babies in secret. The infant won't be allowed to bond with the mother. The babies are immediately taken away.

The breeder has no memory of having the baby or being pregnant. If the mother and father are under mind control, they were programmed to not notice or remember the child's pregnancy. The babies are delivered between 4 to 5 months so no one outside the family knows. The cult often hides the mother in her last few months.

These babies are basically ordered. The Cult wants one at a certain age for a certain date; the planning of pregnancies will coincide with well-planned times and purposes of the rituals. A nettlesome problem may arise when different groups want a baby from the same mother.

Here is a map of puzzle pieces you must address. Again, not in order.

Ask the mother: at which age did you begin? What is the last age the survivor was pregnant? Now work your way to the first time a survivor had a baby. Sometimes you can just do them all together. This will be challenging to address. You will have to manage the survivor's traumatic emotions here through Body Code or Tapping. If this is the first time a survivor is aware of pregnancies the survivor will need time to reflect. There will be a need to grieve.

Pieces to Breeder Programming and Job

Remove programming to create the parts to accomplish the job: Breeder, Colors, codes, alarm systems, suicide programs, etc.

These babies are in God's hands, not Lucifer's. We call humanity to return to the babies and send them where they belong in Jesus' arms.

We renounce all that was stolen from the babies from all the people who sacrificed them.

Renounce any baby still being used to feed the Cosmic Tree or any person or place.

Make sure they are removed from every dimension, including the underworld and Lucifer's heaven.

Cut all generational cords of all this evil.

Remove all downloaded entities at each birth still attached to the survivor.

Remove all permission given from the survivor.

Release all meanings to the ritual.

Remove loss frequency of the survivor.

Remove menstrual blood curse and return it to how God intended.

Remove curse of the womb for Lucifer.

Remove implantation of sperm with each perpetrator.

Remove all drugs while pregnant, to get pregnant, or to have multiple pregnancies.

Remove the belief the survivor is a creator with Lucifer and these children are his.

Call survivors back from all the places they went to have the babies.

Remove connections to the Tree of Death and all Sefirot globes and pathways.

Make sure the survivor's parts are aware of what occurred.

Remove the symbol of Lucifer's seed.

Repent for any part the survivor had in the death of a baby.

Muscle test for anything else that must be removed.

You are now ready to say a prayer over the individual pieces and to use the magnet to remove energy out of mind and body across the general meridian, which can be down the spine or over the head; starting at eyebrows, go over the head, and down to the neck's base 10 times. To remove entities, go the opposite direction; start at the base of the neck over to the eyebrow in the middle of the head. (Explanation in Chapter of Techniques)

Test to see if anything else has to be done? Continue to repeat until finished.

XIII

NEXT IMPORTANT
EVENT IN CORE
FOUNDATION

13-YEAR-OLD COMING
OF AGE RITUAL

PICTURE BY NIC YOUNGBLOOD

Each age has programming and trauma. To remove the programming quickly, we will go to the next age of 13 years. This is a very important ritual as now the child is perceived as an adult. He or she is taught they have free will here and can choose the kingdom of Lucifer. The cult believes 13 is the coming of age. The teenager can freely choose to accept all that's been taught in Lucifer's Kingdom. The cults teach the teens they all of a sudden have free will. This is not the truth. There is no free will in Lucifer's kingdom. I say this is not the truth due to one question… If you are under mind control and drugged, parts of you are programmed; then how are you choosing Lucifer's kingdom under free will? No one who experiences this ritual is wide awake. All of a sudden, the cult lets you choose what you want to do? You are not allowed to say no. Not ever. Nonetheless, this is how it works in Lucifer's kingdom. As a 13-year-old, you are choosing to be part of Lucifer's kingdom under a mind-controlled part — and don't forget, the young person is always drugged for the illusion to become real.

The 13-year-old will be tortured and raped by 13 people. The teenager will be extremely angry; she will summon the anger from every part so she becomes filled with rage. The cult will provoke so much anger in the teen, she will be able to kill anything.

Until this moment, all the parts hate the 13 -month-old baby and blame him or her for all the problems. Now the cult tells the young teen it will summon all the parts they hate about themselves so they now have the chance to kill the baby. Blinded by rage, the teen can do this easily as the acrimony is uncontrollable. He or she agrees to let Apollyon enter their body. The teen stabs the baby many times, convinced the 13-month-old is part of themselves, the one who joined Jesus' side long ago. The cult always keeps this part hidden from the survivor. The teen is heavily drugged, so the ritual's illusions seem real. Please don't forget — it's all free will in cult members' eyes. The cult manipulates all of it.

The 13-year-old swears covenants and oaths to join Lucifer's Kingdom willingly. She or He will be made to beg for Lucifer's acceptance. The teen renounces everything about God. The hate is huge by this time because of the consistent, organized grooming to hate God for 13 years amid torture. She will state the "5 I Will's". After this long ritual, Lucifer will accept her. The teen believes Lucifer is really there for them — and they are so special. When I worked with a client at this age, the client was in shock upon realizing Lucifer was not really there. This is where professionals must force survivors to face facts, to know all of this was a big lie. Lucifer does not love them and will never do anything for them. The promise to spend eternal life with Lucifer is also a lie. Lucifer has no power to offer anything eternal. He will be under Heavenly Fathers and Jesus Christ's authority for eternity, suffering the consequence of his evil against the children of men. Lucifer has no power to choose where anyone will spend eternity. Lucifer cannot offer paradise either. This is common in programming. The parts believe if they do their job for the New World Order, paradise is the reward.

Survivors will be stunned to realize it's all a lie. But the truth must be known by all the parts/alters who have been lied to.

Now the teen will be impregnated by a demon, a grand illusion. She will bear a Nephilim son. This is when she becomes a mother. So, she was a daughter between 13 months and 13 years. The ritual is the first seal earned by the survivor, designating every cult member's position to Lucifer on the slave chart. As a mother, the teen will be seriously addicted to her Nephilim son and she will have a few more. (This is from Amanda Buys.) After the ritual, the 13-year-old receives her first star and seal to Lucifer, one of five earned through the survivor's lifetime. Coming of age is a big deal in cult groups.

We have now entered a spiritual darkness that becomes difficult to understand. I just see it as programming we have to destroy. There is no greater evil that exists compared to our current discussion.

Map out **the puzzle pieces of incidents at the 13-year-old ritual, then remove.**

This is not in order. Just be sure all the pieces are included.

Start with the removal of all alarms, suicide programming, bombs, booby traps, and anything else that may inflict harm.

In the process of Mapping Out all pieces of the ritual and programming, you will find more than one set of alarm systems to be triggered. The complex programming means if you remove one thing, the removal can trigger

something else. Even in the Mapping Out process, a survivor can be triggered by an alarm system going off. Use
the techniques to remove alarms and trigger programming
each time and continue to move forward to map out all of
the 13-year-old ritual. DO NOT REMOVE ANYTHING
UNTIL THIS IS FULLY DONE.

Release ancestors' iniquity.
Release emotions: anger, rage, sadness, etc.
Release trauma.
Release near death experience
Remove all words when the survivor leaves her body.
Cast out demons or anything downloaded.
Remove barriers (such as a wall) built.
Remove any ranking or status.
Keys.
Renounce permission.
Renounce all demons and god entities.
Remove layers of death around.
Remove 1st seal which is the "Coming of Age" ritual at
13-years-old.
Call back the survivor from another dimension or any-
where else.
Renounce the "5 I Wills" of Satan.
Release rage and hatred toward Jesus, Christians, and
anything representing God or against Lucifer.
Address the killing of a baby. Repentance here is neces-
sary.

Remove acceptance of Lucifer and whatever that entails.

Remove the baby from a fallen angel, bring back the baby's captured parts to send back to the baby; have Jesus heal the child.

Remove all Nephilim connections (there may be significant programming here).

Remove lies.

Bring survivor's humanity back from different places and underworld.

Speak now to Rose or Adam to ensure they see Lucifer's truth.

Repent for her or his parts/alters and return parts to core personality.

Remove all alarm systems from where they are attached.

Remove connection and permission to the Silver Cord so dead human spirits, entities, and ancestors cannot re-enter.

(This is only a brief list of the "Coming of Age" Ritual that must be removed.)

LASTLY, THE SEAL AS A SLAVE OF 13 AND THE FIRST EARNED STAR AS A SLAVE OF LUCIFER may have significant programming to remove. Be sure to remove the star and its meaning.

KEYS WILL ALSO BE GIVEN AT DIFFERENT STAGES OF TRAINING THAT MUST BE RENOUNCED.

There is a lot that goes into this ritual because the teen is accountable for all things in Lucifer's Kingdom. The 13-year-old declares "yes" to all things Lucifer by the 100% loyal parts.

The survivor's parts/alters believe Lucifer loves and accepts them. They have earned their first sealing to Lucifer. This ensures the parts are always Lucifer's and no one can break the seal. The survivor knows he or she must continue training while proceeding to the highest rewards, rankings, and keys. They will have relentless battles to prove their worthiness. It is the only way residents may live in Lucifer's world. The next goal is to progress to Lucifer's heaven/hell. Few reach the goal due to the extreme torture.

By 13-years, the survivor's 13 core parts are formed with many programs and countless parts behind the core parts/ alters. When a survivor has finished training, he or she will have hundreds, maybe thousands of parts. You would never be able to retrieve each one. Hence, we must focus on the 13 core parts. The focused process eventually reunites all parts of the mind. On occasion, survivors and professionals have to start with the integration of parts before they reach the core parts; this is ok. The core part or the part with the most authority in a system can decide for all parts. When the core part is ready for integration, the other parts come together without the survivor having to work with each part. Again, there is more than one way to integrate parts and return the mind to wholeness. Please trust your intuition, your client's intuition, and God's Help. All of this material is only a guide. (Check Chapter for Integration.)

17-YEAR-OLD RITUAL

PICTURE BY NIC YOUNGBLOOD

Most of the basic training for recipients of Illuminati programming will be conducted from about 16- to 17-years-old. Seventeen years through 19 years is the next stage of training — similar to attending college. Many survivors I have worked with have a 17-year-old ritual. For me, this ritual is absolutely huge.

In this example, the seven-day ritual creates another tree separate from the foundation of the seven trees. This programming is performed for specific reasons that pertain to the survivor.

In my case, this tree was part of the process to become Hilary Clinton's slave. If I survived the seven-day ritual, I'd be given to her as a slave. The tree had a different meaning than all my prior programming. In the process of getting free, I have been led back to my 17-year-old more than any other age as so much going forward was tied to this tree.

One thing the programmers will not do is mess with the carefully crafted foundation. If they do, the whole operation could fall. So, they created another tree connected to the foundation but not in a way that destroyed all previous programming of my first 16 to 17 years.

In my first book, I explained this ritual, but for seven days I was being tortured, raped, starved, and given nothing to drink. The continual programming was to create a slave part to fulfill Hilary's wants. This part would be totally loyal to her and cater to her every whim. On the last day of the programming, I received beer — it was programmed for me to believe that only beer would save me and relieve my pain.

The seven days of vicious abuse by many men almost killed me because of its intensity. They all took turns in the programming and there were different rooms in which this took place.

In order to remove this tree and the programming, you must map out the pieces. The Mapping Out helps to see programming on a conscious level and then to renounce and release it through different methods. I do not address specific codes and symbols in the programming because the survivor doesn't need them removed. Addressing codes can be removed in a general way. It cuts out the possibility of the mind being triggered because the person said out loud a code and to an unauthorized person. If the unconscious mind is told to gather them all up this allows safety for the survivor and also goes much quicker. You must command the unconscious mind to gather the codes and turn them over to Jesus Christ to be destroyed with the other puzzle pieces. (Check Chapter Techniques and Removal)

It's important to know keys are earned at each stage of programming. The keys may signify training and rank completed and must be destroyed, but first the survivor's part must renounce all ranking or rewards.

The ritual has many meanings, supplemented by some of the highest-ranking Illuminati. I do not know if every survivor has the 17-year-old ritual, and only a few have what I experienced. All of my clients do have a 16- or 17-year-old ritual for different purposes. It is so important to understand this ritual's purpose.

You know the Sephirot tree has 11 points. I was given 13 points on the Sephirot tree. You will have to confirm whether any extra globes were earned if the survivor experienced the 17-year-old ritual.

The cult programmed the ritual to connect to my chakras. The male abusers called in Egyptian gods/entities. The download of demons and sacrifices will always serve a purpose. Seven demon gods were downloaded into me at each daily ritual. Because Hilary was high up in The Illuminati, she had earned slaves. In this case, the slaves and slave line are granted as her eternal possessions. If I was accepted by these gods/demons in the ritual, I would be given to Hilary the queen.

What I am sharing is from my experience. The foundation of energy systems are put in early, but when the cult built a tree separate from the seven foundational trees at 17 years, it created a new system connected to the chakra system with a whole set of meanings, alters, and jobs with additional god entities. You will have to check which survivors have this. Sometimes, the seven points represent seven kingdoms having individual entities and bloodline connections; in my case, the cult assigned the seven points to the hidden seven leaders, one room for each leader. The second chakra system did not have nine more points, only seven. If the survivor has this, you will remove it at the age of installation. THIS IS NOT THE FIRST CHAKRA SYSTEM. I wanted to state what happened to me because of the high level of programming I had. This information may help, though only some survivors may have experienced it.

The installation of the tree at 17 years ran independently of the foundation of the seven trees. One reason this was done was for me to manipulate the elements of fire. Cult members had already taught me how to manipulate the fire energy from the chakra system in my body — an additional source of energy. This feat was also accomplished for the Druids, an ancient, noble group. The part fabricated in this ritual comes out and creates fire only if one of the seven men summons it for the One World Army.

When I had the seven-day ritual at 17, the cult tested me at the end. Cult members had tortured me in every way possible to make me fierce. Because I was already being used to manipulate the fire element, cult members connected to my anger that they had created. The cult connected to my spine. They used the Demon Apollyon to control my mind, body, and spirit to create a second energy source used in the One World Government. The rage of Hitler was downloaded, which caused me to seizure. Something materialized in my liver concerning blood and urine, my heart beat rapidly, and my adrenaline shot up. I do not believe any of this is possible without demons. It is similar to the cult's actions in the water world. I was feeling great pain in my liver, my body covered in sweat.

At the 17-year-old ritual, I grew terrified of unexpected experiences. Apollyon, Metatron, Michael, and Nimrod were familiar in my life as a survivor. Just as the 13 men are only a front for the real 13, so it is with the familiar demon's people talk about. Each demon has a different ranking granted by Lucifer. A prominent demon was summoned by the seven Druid members — a demon I had never seen. The demon had power that overshadowed the power of Apollyon. He is a demon with great authority only the highest mortals can request. He appears only to help establish the One World Government. I recognized that demon at the ritual in 2015 to announce the New World Order. Members of the cult called upon the highest demons for turning the keys to receive the three men responsible for the One World Government's inception. The demon will guarantee Earth is burned through fire. Does that sound familiar? Is that not what is going to happen when Christ arrives? He will burn the wicked. They once again have stolen God's plans. They've confirmed all the good people who won't follow Lucifer will be burned when the Earth becomes his. If you ever want to understand God's Kingdom as a survivor, just turn Lucifer's kingdom exactly opposite of God's; you will know how Lucifer stole everything.

To remove all that's been done over these seven days, I had to map out the pieces. Pages of information demanded hours to complete. For privacy reasons, I'm not including all of it.

Here are the map pieces of my seven days of programing:

- Gods of Egypt entities were downloaded to each chakra. Each God was to rule over an energy point, so there were seven gods.
- Lower gods performed 7 rituals.

- If gods/entities accepted me, I was put in a vat of blood and given to the high priestess or Queen. In my case, I was to be given to Hilary.
- When given to the Queen I had to prove the programming took place.
- A symbolic bar was provided to represent the devil and the seven gods.
- The Queen now had to accept me.
- Bar was inserted into vagina and bottom. A child was brought in and sacrificed whereby Hilary cut out the pineal gland and drank blood.
- She made me chant out five specific words giving Hilary permission to have me as her slave. (To be a slave, you have to give permission.)
- Hilary cut my hand and sucked the blood to symbolize I was hers.
- To have me as her slave she had to do three things:
    1. Baby required to have a bloodline of Hilary's spouse from me.
    2. The baby was killed and eaten in front of me.
    3. She had to have sex with me in front of the seven men in the ritual.
- She had to perform oral sex on all seven leaders.
- Once the ritual was complete, Hilary could do anything she wanted to me; I was her slave.
- We met several times in the first year.
- I was impregnated by Bill Clinton two times total for sacrifice of the only bloodline. Break babies free

of any connection to Hilary and Bill and the seven demons. Call back parts from the babies and break chords. (These children are Christ's, but I think we need to do it for our parts to be free and not so much for them.)

- She was now the owner of all my future children.
- Each room removed separately that would include: any suicide system; a bomb, booby trap, or alarm of any kind.
- Remove symbols, codes, numbers, letters, programmer signatures,

After a while you realize the rituals boil down to the same thing. You will automatically know what has to be removed. Oaths and promises must be removed with all the programming pieces. All torture and abuse must be removed so the parts can be made whole as they are being integrated. With the help of Jesus Christ, the process can move quickly and no one will ever feel traumatized.

TRAINING: 17-YEARS-OLD THROUGH 19-YEARS-OLD

In my first book, I spent time discussing the 2-year-old's training until 19 years. I do not know if every person has the training. If survivors have been slaves to influential politicians and cult leaders, the survivors will have what I term "college programming."

After the Level of Completion is finished, a ritual follows. The survivor has completed all required training to pass the cult's expectations. To be rewarded, the survivor undergoes a ritual to become a new person in Lucifer. The ritual is the exact opposite of a Christian baptism. The cult enacts a mockery of Jesus' agonizing death, burial, and resurrection.

The ritual usually lasts seven days. In the first three days, torture is inflicted until the cult member dies (members are brought back to life). The torture is a mockery of Jesus Christ and his agony in the Garden of Gethsemane. The opposite symbolism is driven into the survivor's mind. Common lines may be, "Look at what Lucifer has done for you, you owe Lucifer your life, Lucifer suffered so much for you, you must lay down your life for him." The downloaded comments are designed to solidify a survivor's loyalty to Lucifer, and demons are attached to it all. The harrowing torture leads to death, the survivor leaving her body, the spirit captured. The capture includes the three core parts that have completed training and want to be married to Lucifer.

The next part of the ritual is burial for three days. The programming is specific. The cult will always have spiders or snakes in a coffin laid underground. (This is not the first time they have done this.) Each step is precisely planned for a specific outcome. The torture continues until the six days are finished.

The survivor is cleansed and presented to Lucifer. The last day is for the marriage ceremony. In the ceremony, the survivor is married to the Unholy Trinity, the Dragon (Lucifer), the Beast that fulfills Lucifer's will, and the false prophet. The Unholy Trinity acts in opposition to the Holy Trinity: God the Eternal Father; his son, Jesus Christ; and the Holy Ghost.

The survivor is rewarded for their loyalty with a jewel, a key, and other symbols. The person is 100% in Lucifer's kingdom. The rape continues by the three men representing the Dragon, the Beast, and the False Prophet. The cult is receiving a new level of demons downloaded in this three-way rape. The demons possess more authority than any downloaded so far. The survivor's body can now handle this level of demonic presence. The three demons represent the "Unholy Trinity," a deep level of darkness. The cult believes there is no way for the individual to be free.

This ceremony for the 19-year-old is highly secretive with only certain people invited, well-established cult members ensuring the seven days of completion are conducted. The members believe they are the only ones with the authority to summon these demons, the ones who have the utmost authority to act in the name of the Unholy Trinity.

The survivor's parts/alters will have a part married to Lucifer, a part married to the Beast, and a part married to the false prophet. The threesome acts as one just as the Unholy Trinity does. The most powerful part tells the other two parts/alters what to do. The trio is extremely evil after completing all of Lucifer's training. They are three of the Core Parts.

You have to remove everything that occurred at this ritual, everything it represents, and all keys, rewards, oaths, and covenants. The ritual includes the marriage to Lucifer and the Unholy Trinity, which must be broken up and destroyed. In this unusual case, a divorce is badly needed! (This is not the only time you have been married to Lucifer. Just use the techniques and methods near the end of this book to find out what's occurred. (See Part 1 of *Puzzle Pieces to The Cabal, Mind Control, and Slavery*, Training and Completion Chapter, for more information.)

If you understand God's kingdom, it can help you identify what the cult has stolen and mocked — this is why, for example, the cult uses a cross in the ritual. It's possible the cross is present at both the 19-year-old and 17-year-old rituals. When you know why Jesus Christ died on a cross, the knowledge helps you comprehend how the cult uses the cross for evil.

SUMMARY OF TRAINING

Training begins in the womb and will continue to the age of 17. Each year of training is built on the year before. The cult has specific programs that must be installed each year in a particular way. Each slave of mind control must complete each training stage. If a cult member is alive, he has completed each year of training. If a cult member doesn't learn the cult's teachings, he is dead.

You must understand: each year as programming is installed and connected, it's creating the foundation. The process can become complicated as the cult ties one program to the next. After each stage is done, the programmer knows what comes next. The template is closely followed.

Thus, I believe the Lord is urging us to pull out the roots so the rest of the programming collapses. We must visit each core event to remove all programming, to cause the structure's collapse. If by any chance you see a need to clean anything after the core is removed, then do so. Usually, I find some integration with parts/alters work will be needed.

I have shared ages, events, and the order you must follow to achieve a successful removal. Once you reach the core foundation of the seven trees; you will have to remove each piece. The Trees of the Core Foundation and the trees' link to the four worlds is where you reach the last bit of programming, which was really the first. Each globe on the trees must be dismantled and the parts made free. Until now you have been carefully removing programs attached to the foundation. Now you have made it to the foundation where there are trees to destroy, demons to cast out, programs to undo, and rituals to remove.

You have learned what important rituals and ages mean and the order to remove them. The programming must be removed as well if complete integration is to take place.

The biggest secret mind control programmers have is they don't want you to know they follow an exact template for the training of a mind control slave. If we ever found out, we'd be able to do what the Lord says, "Pull it out by the roots and the rest will collapse." The cult groups including the military want you to believe that it's all so random and impossible to undo. Let me be really clear… If our unconscious mind created all their illusions, our unconscious mind can destroy the illusions. Please remember that. If survivors refused to work for the programmers, the cult could not fashion mind control slaves. The cult is not creating the illusions — we are! The programmers are completely powerless without survivors doing their work. The cult knows the power of the unconscious mind, using it to carry out all its dirty deeds.

The programmers know if you extensively harm a person, the individual will act in accord with their desires. I say, "Why not start creating magnificent things for ourselves?" We can use the abilities we developed through extensive training for good instead of evil. The cult doesn't get to win if we do not let them.

The Lord is on our side. He is swiftly revealing information for us to become free. I believe in a few years we will uncover more secrets and discern better strategies to eradicate mind control. We will understand how to free our minds in a fraction of the time we did before.

Foundational

Conception
First Split
in the Womb

Birth

13 Months

3 Years

✦ ✦ ✦ 39 Years
3rd Star/Seal to Satan

✦ ✦ ✦ ✦ 52 Years
4th Star/Seal to Satan

✦ ✦ ✦ ✦ ✦ 65 Years
5th Star/Seal to Satan

Programming

26 Years
2nd Star/Seal to Satan
Wife & Queen

17 Years
Training Complete
New Stage of Training

13 Years
1st Star/Seal to Satan
Coming of Age

PICTURE BY NIC YOUNGBLOOD

SEALS

Seals represent rituals done to show the slave's level in Lucifer's kingdom. Each of the five seals will represent a level of training with a specific meaning. The rituals signify acceptance by Lucifer. Where have you heard this before? Each year of the slave denotes a meaning with a specific training. Each training must be finished with a ritual of acceptance from Lucifer. The higher the stars on the seals, the more the survivor has accomplished in Lucifer's kingdom.

We now move to remove the seals, which are at received at designated ages as to show the stars the survivor achieved as a slave. Work back from last star achieved. Each seal is part of a big ritual and it is important to get all of the pieces of the ritual to remove it. Seals are momentous in a survivor's life; as with any important event in Lucifer's kingdom, the ritual will be as horrific as possible. Each seal expresses the survivor's eternal bond with Lucifer.

Ages of obtaining seals:

As the survivor climbs higher on the Seals/Stars ranking, the evil in each ritual intensifies. The seals are like a birthday party in Lucifer's kingdom. The survivor has earned his way to the top rewards and celebrations greet him.

65 years old: 5th Seal/Star

The 65-year-old gives birth to a Nephilim son who's sacrificed. The slave is now a full 5-star slave sealed to Lucifer.

The seal requires the most evil compared to all the others and will have tremendous respect and authority. At this point, if you have not escaped Lucifer's kingdom, it's alleged you never will. But that is not true. Perhaps it is better said the individual loses any desire to be free.

52 years old: 4th Seal/Star

The 52-year-old gives birth to a Nephilim son.

The 52-year-old must commit greater evil than the 39-year-old did.

The 52-year-old must be respected for having authority and power. The slave has been able to handle the higher-ranking demons attached to him.

39 years old: 3rd Seal/Star

The 39-year-old gives birth to a Nephilim son.

The 39-year-old must do something of greater malevolence than the 26-year-old did.

26 years old: 2nd Seal/Star

The 26-year-old marries the Nephilim son and becomes a queen. A man will become the opposite. You will have to understand the 26-year-old ritual; for example, what is the survivor connected to and what jobs are ordained for her in Lucifer's kingdom. What did the survivor do at the ceremony to receive a seal and star? Figure out the meaning of the star. Was the survivor forced to engage with a Nephilim? What happened in that engagement so the connections can be destroyed?

This ritual is for the purpose of earning a reward. That is why you must ascertain the survivor's actions to earn it. Not only will you have to map out the pieces to remove all the programming, but the survivor must repent of any deeds committed to receive the seal and star. At that point, the legal right of the demons is released and the dark energy of the seal and star are removed by the blood of Jesus. (Go to the Removal Process near the end of the book.)

Queen - 26 years old: Second Seal

13 years old: First Seal/Star

The 13-year-old is impregnated with a Nephilim son. She becomes a mother here.

(Go to the 13-year-old event for details.)

CORE PARTS AND INTEGRATION

We start at a survivor's age and proceed backward to the womb so programming is removed safely. We go in reverse through the seals to the important events and ages. I will include the important events after you have removed the seals to the events of 19 years old, 17 years old, and 13 years old; then the 3 years old and 13 months old events, and birth; then to Conception for Integration. You will have to do the above procedure many times.

Getting to core parts will not be easy. Core parts are zealously hidden and protected. More powerful core parts will have more demons attached and heightened loyalty to Lucifer.

I will have Jesus be a part of all the integration process. Why? Because core parts and all other parts are loyal to Lucifer. You cannot work with parts/alters loyal to Lucifer without Jesus' help. Jesus has all power over Lucifer. Don't kid yourself — all programming is to convert the cult member's soul to Lucifer. The core parts have been relentlessly trained to be loyal to Lucifer. It's all pledged in another spiritual realm where darkness resides. If you want to win, if you want to destroy this spiritual darkness, you have to invite the light. Only Jesus can defeat Lucifer.

You don't have to believe me. You can believe it's all random programming with torture and rape. But as you get down to working with the parts, the real story emerges.

Every survivor has been taught Jesus is evil and to avoid him; Lucifer is the good one. True integration cannot occur until the parts perceive the truth of who Lucifer is and who Jesus is. Each part must choose who to follow. As professionals do this work, inside of every survivor you will find it boils down to Lucifer rebelling against God, using a cult member as rebellion. This in itself should piss off survivors enough to fight back with a partner who can win this war. Usually, the survivor has no idea she or he is in this spiritual battle; it will come as quite a shock when the parts/alters awaken to reality amid the trickery and lies.

Integration

Let me say this loud and clear: Every survivor is different, and there is not just one way to integrate parts. Survivors can be creative in healing their minds. Let them!

Integration is about teaching a survivor's parts/alters a survivor the full truth about Jesus Christ and Lucifer. The parts must learn that their world is based on illusions.

Integration hinges upon the parts/alters finally recognizing the truth and choosing to follow Christ. When the survivor has made a choice by free will, he or she can integrate many parts at once. Core parts are the original splits, they are the alters in charge. There will be many parts/alters behind the core parts. All the parts/alters come from the worlds of programming.

Core parts are what everything else is split from. Behind each core part are many alter systems representing core events and programming. Integration may not happen until many programs have been removed. Even after the programs are removed, certain parts/alters will refuse to integrate. Each survivor is different. Core parts could take days, months, or even years. (I doubt years would pass because of how we are removing the foundation.) That is why no standard time line is available for survivors.

The Twin, the first split at conception, offers the most difficult challenge for integration. This core identity has the most authority; as the parts/alters become one with the whole it may be hard for the Twin to accept. The Twin's whole world is being removed so there will be fear and questioning.

Possibly, before the programming is removed, a front or core part may want to be instructed before all the programming is removed. The teaching may last hours, but if the survivor believes they have heard lies, he or she can choose to become one with the whole and follow Jesus. Integration occurs and the programming is destroyed. This is rare, though I have seen it happen. We went back and checked weeks later: All programming was missing and integration had occurred.

I believe in the survivor's ability to undo their programming and repair their minds.

If we work with core parts/alters, we will save enormous amounts of time. Sometimes working with other parts connected to the core parts will come first — we have to work with them. The process will lead us to the core parts. After the core observes the experiences of the other parts/alters and sees they are happy, all the parts will come out and talk.

Many parts will not speak or let you know their identity. I recall this situation. Obviously, the alters/parts were not the one in charge. When I said I wanted to speak to the one in charge, the parts refused. I tried being clever, saying, "If you are the leader then why do you hide behind everyone? That is not a leader. If you are the leader, then come out and speak like one." Well, that made the leader slightly angry and he came out. Two hours later, after conversation and program removal, the leader agreed to be one with the whole and follow Jesus. The other parts of the system agreed to freely do the same. It was a great experience to see this happen.

At this point, we ask Jesus to walk down the timeline of core ages until reaching the 13-month-old baby. To the site of the original split. The survivor and professional must locate the baby to see his condition. They will always find the baby in an abused state, hidden in different places according to each system of core parts.

Once the baby is found, a professional may want to ask the survivor what they think happened. An awareness of what the baby experienced at 13 months is important. At this point, I have found the easiest path to healing is to ask Jesus to place His hands on the baby's head and give a blessing to make the baby whole. The baby must be made whole along with the child at other ages before the professional integrates each core age. When Jesus puts His hands on the baby, they are immediately made whole.

Now we ask the parts/alters to hold hands with the baby and each other. We ask Jesus to bring them together in the 13-month-old baby in wholeness. The parts have been made one with the baby. We will now ask Jesus to take the baby back to conception. We ask Jesus to heal what must be healed at the conception's first split and to make this baby with different parts to become whole.

I ask Jesus for help because He can impart divine integration. Jesus can graciously perform service well beyond our reach. We are blessed to have Jesus' help; He understands each survivor's pain and can heal each survivor. Professionals, get out of the way! Do not try to control this. It's between Jesus and the survivor. There isn't one way to integrate. Moreover, we focus on specific ages and events so integration proceeds quickly.

In each stage of integration, each age, and each core event, we ask Jesus to make the survivor whole. When I reach the 13-month-old baby and conception after Jesus blessed the mind to become whole, I declare, "We ask that the power of the blood of Jesus Christ make this survivor's mind whole." (Another chapter explains why this is so important.)

Integration is about pulling the mind back together. The 13 core parts represent the systems of programming. Behind the core parts will be numerous parts/alters in the system. Anticipate a leader who speaks for the many who report back to the core.

I know this can be a little confusing, so I will continue aiming for clarity as we advance.

WHAT ARE GRIDS AND WHY YOU MUST REMOVE FROM CORE EVENT AND PARTS

Amanda Buys said, "Grids are quantum networks of energy pathways intersecting at nodal points and performing functions related to iniquity that undergirds them and the powers of darkness that oversee them." She said anyone with bloodline families has these evil grids established at conception. (Buys, 2020. Recap, Refresh, and Recalibrate for the Journey Forward!! page 28)

During different time periods of a survivor's life, parts of humanity are stuck in grids to do different jobs and time periods of the survivor's life. When I was removing grids, I noticed parts of me with my husband in this energy-producing grid, feeding the system.

Before I read Amanda Buy's information, grids existed in my unconscious mind as little compartments. In my programming, the military would activate a grid that showed all my mind's compartments filled with evidence of programming, various dates, and other information vital for storage. In my mind it looked like this:

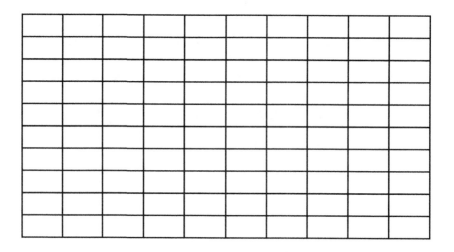

Here are some of the specific grids to check. There are grids for everything. Grids feed the whole continuously with energy, keeping Lucifer's kingdom functioning.

Kabbalah Tree Grid	Evil Quantum Computer Grid	Deep State Grid	Unholy Forces Grid
Roots of the Kabbalah Tree Grid	Family Grid	Illuminati Grid of 13 Bloodlines	Elemental Grids
Programming of Mind Control Slave Grid	AI Grid	Calendar Grid	Chaos Grid
NWO Army Grid	Nephilim Grid	Autism Grid	Ritual Abuse Grid
Chakra Grid	Planet Grid	Rothschild Banking System Grid	7 Mountain Grid of education, government, religion, media, entertainment, family, business
Family Grid	Underwater Kingdom Grid	Time Loop Grid	Slavery Grid

Evil Marriage Grid	Womb Grids	Antichrist Grid	Name of any Nation Grid

(From Amanda Buys' *Book 4 Advanced Training DID SRA*, pages 28-30. She listed pages of possible grids. Please check her information.)

Grids I have found can be holding the core foundational tree in place. You will have to remove this when you get to the first Tree of Death of programming.

XIV

NEW WORLD
ORDER ARMY

Two huge programs that must be removed in the deprogramming process are The New World Order and The Water Kingdom. The programs are intertwined with the foundation. The One World Government programming will be in every survivor without question. The Water World or Water Kingdom is in most survivors. I cannot tell you the order in which to remove the two programs. I currently remove the programs first because of the possibility of reactivation. Survivors have core parts in both areas.

NEW WORLD ORDER ARMY PROGRAMMING

The One World Order or New World Order Army programming is something every victim of MK Ultra will possess. All Illuminati programming is for the NWO. All the crazy programming is designed to equip cult survivors to be soldiers of the New World Army and to ensure every order is completed. All programs learned through mind control leads to the One World Government.

Everyone with New World Order Army mind control programming begins training as a very young child. The programming was to lay dormant and never be revealed until all elements were in place for the NWO. The time has arrived after decades of planning. Details of how the One World

Government will be established is known by all MK-Ultra mind-controlled slaves and some in the military. The participants will know each stage, their job duties, and the leaders responsible for initiating each stage. There is not one part of this program survivors will not have memorized perfectly because program failure means death.

What does the New World Order really mean? It means a small group of globalists in charge of making decisions in business, government, health, religion, food, and education believe they are gods and controlling the public. The globalists believe we are complete idiots who don't deserve higher-class luxuries. We do not have the right bloodline. So, a very long time ago the globalists decided we will be the slaves and they the masters. You have to be very careful around the globalists as they live in a world of inversion. Although you hear them say they want to make a better world, in the inverted world they're saying we must suffer. That is why they lie over and over again while feigning sincerity. They state the opposite of what they mean in all subjects. That is how Lucifer's kingdom runs. INVERTED! The globalists learn to accuse opponents of their own intentions. I suggest if we don't want the crazies to take over completely, retaliation is mandatory.

Starting in late 2020, I told people the crazies were coming after their children. Now, in fall 2022, people are waking up to this. A big factor in installing the New World Government is the group's right over our children's future. Parents will have no authority. After a while, the NWO won't allow any children to be born without permission, and every child will be raised by the government.

Children won't be raised by their parents because Lucifer cannot procreate. That privilege was revoked from him by God. Satan does not have a body. He cannot create children. I believe Lucifer is angry about all of God's punishments — so angry he's adamant about destroying families. Families are the centerpiece to the greatest joy in God's Kingdom. That is why Lucifer attacks the family so much. He knows kids need their parents. If he can make sure a child doesn't feel loved, he can manipulate the child. Love is forbidden in Illuminati programming. Lucifer knows if a child feels loved, he won't obey the devil.

These cults know human behavior. They know how to manipulate behavior to get their outcomes. Fear keeps the person in a heightened state that does not allow clear thinking. They also know keeping people isolated and alone is another way to control them. If a child or an adult does not have love, cults know that is the swiftest means of destroying a soul. Everything we are going through right now in the world is carefully planned for a specific outcome so the take-over will succeed. They know if you make people afraid, they will give up their rights for protection. They know if people do not have food, they will capitulate. Each pernicious step you may not understand possesses an integral function in the plan for a One World Government. You may think what they are doing is ludicrous, but it's actually strategic. They haven't neglected any consideration of cause and effect.

In 1776, Adam Weishaupt, who started the Illuminati, held that if enough bloodshed, violence, and chaos ensues, people will capitulate to the One World Government. If the military dominates the populace, citizens will fight. The deep state cabal is following Weishaupt's directions. All over the world, we see direct evidence of lawlessness on our streets.

I have decided to share information some people will react angrily to, but I do not feel I should keep secrets for these animals anymore. This intelligence indicates the One World Government is tightly coordinated. Stage One has already ensued with the COVID-19 pandemic.

The New World Order consists of seven ritual stages — seven levels of hell. The only way the NWO can bring the entire world under its control is by the seven levels of hell. Each level triggers stress, anguish, woe, and death — the NWO drawing the aggrieved energy.

The seven horrific events cause abhorrent suffering and brutal, grisly death. More will occur, but the seven events will be essential. Each event, if successful, represents a creation of hell to be presented to Lucifer.

Jesus created the Earth and presented each day to God the Eternal Father. The children of Lucifer will do the same but inverted, presenting keys to Lucifer after completing the seven stages of hell.

The keys are conferred to three distinguished fiends in Lucifer's kingdom to usher in the New World Order. The three chosen will have dominion over all. The demons wield great bestowed by Lucifer himself.

For the three chosen to attain success, they need every member of the cults to execute their assignments. Each piece has to merge. Moreover, without its army, the New World Order is impotent. The undertaking is highly organized from the top all the way down to the weakest member of Lucifer's kingdom.

The following is an outline of the seven stages:

1. The pandemic, lockdowns, and vaccines lead to embedding nanoparticles in a public controlled by frequencies. Multiple mass shootings and crimes begin.

2. Creating a war: Chaos will erupt, initiated by programmed cult members. An economic crash will occur through many channels. The next level of mind-controlled cultists will provoke a new pandemonium, advancing the New World Order with utility and food shortages, high prices, and people plunging into destitution. Terrorists arrive to invade the United States. Depression, rage, and bewilderment settles in. Tremendous vaccine casualties are forgotten in a time of war. It is why Biden will not relent. This is the consequence of millions being programmed.

3. Stage 3: Invasion of the United States through terrorism, a China invasion, and onslaughts from other countries. Bombs and nuclear attacks shut down all communication as panic, anxiety, and despair befall.

4. Martial law. Confiscation of all guns. More lawlessness. NWO leaders are open with an agenda to send
messages to the people.

5. The invasion by a foreign government or governments
and the NWO is established. All leaders in the U.S.
government are thrown out of office and probably
killed. The NWO eradicates America.

Under this stage, all cultists under mind control will
have completed their assignments. Most mind-controlled slaves working for the army and NWO will
collect everyone in the public, kill them, or take them
to camp. Most MK Ultra slaves have jobs in Stage 5.

Anyone under mind control is ordered to kill all
transgender, gay, mentally ill, sick, and most people
over 30 years old. (So much for the left supporting
the transgender and gay movement. It all becomes a
big lie.)

6. The new government settles in and begins to organize
administration for the One World government, including mandating the public's routines. Everyone must accept the New World Order or be killed. Citizens must
agree to worship Lucifer under the One World Religion. Lucifer's minions nearly have all the elements in
place. No dissent is allowed from anyone still living.

In Stage 6, most mind-controlled slaves are ordered to kill themselves. They are no longer useful.

7. In Stage 7, the New World Order is completely in place. The new world is run by the globalists while the remaining humans are enslaved. The Kingdom's Bloodlines are allowed to enjoy a full, long life, eating organic food, relaxing, and having power over all the resources. They will have free will and we will have none. They are gods and we will address them as such.

This is how life will look for those still alive:

- Most of the older people will be killed in the cleansing.
- No one alive will dispute or go against the NWO government.
- Everyone alive has to worship Lucifer and admit he is the real true God. Worshiping Jesus Christ and the real God will be forbidden and those who will not worship Lucifer will be killed.
- Twenty- to thirty -year-olds will be helping with the running of the affairs of the NWO.
- Illuminati/Secret Society members will be the only ones allowed to have the use of natural resources, eat organic foods, get the best of everything, and have a lot of personal slaves.

- The rest of us will have to eat synthetic processed food so we will be unhealthy and our minds weak. We will not be allowed to eat animal products.
- All supplements will be forbidden.
- NO marriages allowed
- NO family units allowed.
- You have to have permission to have children and they will be taken and given to the government to raise. They will not allow any bonding.
- There will not be two sexes anymore.
- NO one will own anything, have money, job, or freedom. Only given what they want to give you.
- We will have to take drugs daily to keep us in a zombie state so we just go to work for them and when we come home; we have to hook into a virtual reality that is like a video game. They do not want us moving or thinking.
- Men will be super soldiers; half man and half machine. No compassion allowed or kindness. Do not show feminine qualities, just be hard and cold.
- Freedom allowed for short periods at a time that will be earned by credits.
- Clones will replace a great deal of mankind.
- Anyone thinking for themselves and acting on free will shall be killed.
- No laws can be used against those in power.
- Hunt slaves for sport.
- People auctioned off as cattle.

- Disposed of when no longer useful.
- Vehicles and planes only globalists will have this privilege.
- No traveling around.
- Airlines will become extinct.
- Anyone using talents without permission from leaders will be executed.
- No family communication allowed.
- Everything will be based on a credit score of reward or punishment.

No, I am not making this up! This information is actually in the programming of all mind-controlled slaves. A great deal of the information is on the United Nations website for Agenda 2030. I pray and believe God will help us defeat them. We must do this by waking up as many people as possible. If you know you have experienced any mind control, you must accept you have the New World Order Army Programming. Get the programming out of you by following my suggestions in this book. If you are in the military or have been in the last 10 years, the military has acted against you so it can use you in the New World Order Army. Through the many shots required of military personnel, there is a good chance the military has microchipped you.

While MK Ultra members have been programmed over their lifetime, many were brought back starting in 2012 for updating the new plan. By now, all people under mind control by these cult groups would have returned for the instructions. To my knowledge, most cult members were brought back in 2015. Things changed over time; when it appeared Hilary Clinton would become U.S. President, the cults started to bring in more people. Any person carrying NWO programming has no idea he's had it for years. Most survivors and professionals were not aware of the army programming, so it would have been overlooked. Even if some cult members felt they were free, they'd soon find out the dormant programming would soon be activated.

The best way for me to explain how I know this is to share my own story — later confirmed by my client's stories. The programming matched up in all of us, even for someone living outside the United States.

Here is what happened to me: I had spent 20 years in therapy trying to get free. I discovered holistic modalities that helped tremendously, and I was happier than I've ever felt. Every area of my life was really good. Then something happened. It was as if — for no reason — everything fell apart. I felt something was wrong, really wrong. The kind of wrong I had not felt in years. I did not feel the same anymore. Huge red flags went up. I was feeling intense anger like I did in the 1990's. I started gaining weight, I wanted to drink alcohol, I was feeling depressed. Everything was out of whack.

I went to the Lord and asked Him what might be wrong. I told him that something was deeply amiss. That is when I remembered the cult had retrieved me for the New World Order Army programming update. The cults thought Hilary would be the president. The cults calling back all MK Ultra mind-controlled slaves for updated instructions. Once again, being a slave to Hilary became a huge nightmare.

I could not believe this was really happening. After all this time, the cult still brought me back. Before I get into what they did, I have to explain what this means. When someone is being programmed as a child and young adult, the individual can tolerate reconditioning. When you are brought back in your late adult years to receive sophisticated programming, the physical body and mind do not handle it well. Maybe this is why I remembered the cult's actions so quickly after I returned. I should not have remembered anything if the programming was done correctly. I had already accomplished so much healing. They should have never brought me back. My guess is the Lord needed me to warn people of the cults' plans and stand as a witness against them. I really should have never remembered anything about my programming, especially what I am about to share. The cult absolutely does not want me to remember because then I recall all the people at the ritual on a military base underground. I could have never shared what I am about to share with you.

Removing the New World Order Army Programming lasted about 20 hours. I asked many times, "Why, God, why?" I was in shock for a while. While I was dealing with this, the Lord delivered a huge project He wanted me to adopt. It was so huge, I told him "no" for about three months. After I received many messages to do the project, I agreed.

For the next four years, I created a huge online summit with some of the top authors, speakers, and founders of holistic modalities from all over the world. I got to know the best of the best in the world of transformation. I interviewed over 85 people, feeling as if I had my own tutoring class from all 85. So much fun! Despite having a dreadful past, God gave me something to propel me going forward. I learned I have a talent to interview people which has helped me being interviewed.

I have learned there is always a reason for bad things happening. So, what the heck was the reason? I think God needs me to testify to the world about the cult groups' affairs and plans. Once the dam broke, a deluge overwhelmed. It shook the very foundation of my world. God opened my eyes to all of it, which led me to writing my first book and now this one. I see God as always being in me. He used Lucifer's evil for good. Now, I'm able to reach out and warn people who've been victimized by MK Ultra Programming. The Lord has revealed this is my time to speak out, my time to hold nothing back. I have so much information to help others get free.

I was first brought back for seven days' programming in 2015 and later a few more times. The seven-day training began with four days of extreme torture as the instructions were downloaded, updating the parts with the cult's plans. The last three days of the week were for rituals. I did not see anyone else until the last three days. One day I noticed a group of women. I believe they were high-ranking Monarch slaves brought in because of the high up politicians and

Illuminati leaders that they were allowed to see. One day I saw people of every uniform from the military, and another group of only young adults.

The first day, a couple of male scientists performed electric shocks and made me wear goggles to watch a video with instructions to usher in the One World Government. A man came in who was clearly in charge though I hadn't seen before. He would never physically abuse me, but when the torture part was done, he came in for programming. I had no idea who he was or what he would mean to me. In 2020, I found out the same man on TV lying to us about Covid was the same person who updated my programming. The man on tv was none other than Anthony Fauci. Fauci's role was not only to program people for the New World Order, but to make sure many people died through the vaccinations. Each stage of the New World Order must have death and suffering.

In the programming, the cult installed something called the seven realms. Sophisticated and complex, the technology interacted with old programming. Fauci used the younger parts of me with original programming to continue the instructions. This leads to another story of NWO programming.

All of this happened in Las Vegas, Nev., one of the hubs for top Globalist Cabal leaders to meet.

After the four days of reconditioning, three days of rituals to bring in the New World Order were planned. Whenever cultists who worship Lucifer are conducting a ritual, they look for the highest demons to answer their prayers. In this case, the cultists called upon the highest demons having the most authority to help them welcome the New World Order so they could present a new Earth to Lucifer.

On the first night, many prominent women in the Illuminati attended due to Fertility Cult practices. A training and new commitment to the leaders took place. Hilary attended with other distinguished politicians. The ritual included various components, including a dedication of keys and glory to Hilary. Hilary made her usual sacrifice and other powerful women performed rituals. Many of the women in government had arrived.

On the second night, everyone of importance arrived. Many of the 13, George Soros, Barack Obama, Joe Biden, Charles Schwab, Henry Kissinger, Cory Booker, Mark Milley and other generals, Antony Blinken, Nancy Pelosi, Liz Cheney, Kamala Harris, Celine Dion, Cher, Beyonce, JC Chasez, and many other politicians and executives.

The most important ritual occurred the third night. Three men were chosen to provide keys to bring in the One World Order. The keys represent the responsibility of handling the New World Order. If the three men receiving the keys do not fulfill their role, they will perish. Five things were created and harnessed in the rituals for welcoming the New World Army. Cults believe the sexual energy and sacrifice gives them power, so the leadup to the third day's sacrifice is very important. The ritual was staged in order of authority. The Five Things were harnessed in this ritual:

1. Energy, power over all the earth.
2. Harnessing of four elements: fire, water, wind, and earth.
3. Harnessing of this generation on the Earth for complete control.
4. Harnessing of all power over government, business, and religion.
5. Harnessing of Lucifer's power to overthrow God.

In the ushering in of the New World Government, everyone has a job — from the highest in the rank to the teenagers executing mass shootings. That means the prime minister or president of a country will receive orders from the 13 and the authorities above them. The orders go down the line in a succinct, organized way.

To accept the New World Order, it is believed seven levels of hell are required to take over the world.

If the Illuminati/Luciferians want to execute something, they perform a ritual to call in the strongest of demons. Rituals are based on the Satanic calendar to engage the greatest level of evil. Cults will perform more rituals to bring in the New World Order since 2015 did not succeed for them. Even with their best efforts of demons helping the leaders of the cult and all their blood sacrifice; they were not successful. I believe God stepped in and stopped Hilary Clinton from becoming the president.

28

PIECES OF PUZZLE TO LOOK FOR WHEN REMOVING THE NEW WORLD ORDER PROGRAMMING

Usually, seven stages will represent seven alters to carry out instructions. Each core alter will have many alters in the system.

The steps to create this programming can be different. I have found with myself and clients, seven is the number that represents the programming whereby each person is in charge of someone else so each individual can be activated.

The programming will create some who have superhuman strength. There are many plans; if one fails another will take its place.

New Instructions were accomplished in the reconditioning. The earliest programming will start at 1-years-old. The professional must proceed through each age and remove the army programming. If you focus only on the most current reconditioning programming, the individual can still be activated. You must work your way from the current age of the survivor to the earliest age.

This is an example of the updated instructions and what we found in the programming. The young child parts have completely different programming:

4 Core parts/3 hidden

7 Stages

7 Doors

7 Alters which carry instructions

7 Floating realms

7 Thrones

7 Wizards

7 Spirits to represent the Illuminati's hierarchy

7 Deadly sins

7 Demons

7 Moons/3 hidden/4 only shut down.

3 Hidden doors

7 Keys activate the realms. Each one is a different person

Programming colors, codes, symbols, signature, date

Alarm systems of every kind

Frequencies to control personality and body

Dark walls around the person

Rings of fire

Each realm has an energy weapon; rope, poison, sword, knife, guns, chains, drugs, etc.

Possibly addiction programming that is sophisticated to cover up and not remember

Each chamber of alters will have the following: Orders, symbols, signals, signs, words from people in authority, colors to each stage, codes, instructions and connections from handler above. Some rooms contain torture and rape. Each room has a different job. The first alter chamber will activate the next. The alter chambers work as a team.

Each realm was created by video and color flashing. Each realm has seven symbols in order and a command. The realms are in a circle around the person and to remind the person's subconscious to believe the illusions. Realms have an energetic pull to control the survivor. Each realm can use the chakras' energy. Programmers will be giving curses as instructions. So, in this example the seven realms were connected to seven body parts, each one having a curse.

Feet- "Do not move."

Arms- "Cannot do anything or create."

Stomach- "Cannot digest life and cannot have peace."

Heart- "Will not love or be loved."
3rd Eye- "Never listen or do what God says."
Crown- "Always keep open for Lucifer."

Hope this helps you understand all the attachments to programming. Cults always use witchcraft and demons to hold it in place.

The cult inserted a complex addiction protocol into the programming. Red Bull and Monsters had a meaning and represented a piece of programming. The cult also used wine. Red meant something and white had a different meaning. Beer was also different. The cult used sugar and low-grade drugs, which was important because it's how the system ran and prevented the individual from remembering. The person's energy was being transferred to the seven realms. A sex act had to be performed to enter each realm; if performed correctly, the alarm system would be shut down.

The seven realms floated around the tree inside the person. The tree's roots belong to the 13. The tree has 300 branches. When all is complete, the result is turned over to Lucifer.

The survivor must wait until the key holders have given a signal. Each leader who is a key holder will say the same word and use the same color for the background of their message. Colors have a meaning in each stage of the New World Order being brought in.

Example of the seven room alters:

One alter room was named Sergeant.
Second alter room was named Commander.
Third alter room was named Lieutenant.
Fourth alter room was named General.
Fifth alter room was named Corporal.
Sixth alter room was named Marine.
Seventh alter room was named Admiral.

Here's another example:

Three walls are seven layers deep. Each has a trigger to start. Once you pass the barrier, proceed down the spiral staircase that resembles a DNA strand. At some point, you will enter the Alice in Wonderland programming that descends 50 feet, leading to rooms that begin Army programming. Each program has a separate staircase with codes, alters, and an entrance having specific commands. The programmer added a secret program for the programmer only; other people would be unaware of it. Programmers are always adding backdoors and hidden agendas only for the programmer.

When programming occurs, the survivor is heavily drugged to make him suggestable. Programmers will always use electric shock as they are shocking the survivor. Programmers begin with stating codes, and in this case color flashing that is a part of the programming.

The walls had three colors: 1st wall was red, 2nd wall blue, and 3rd wall green.

Each wall was layered seven times, equaling 21.

All the walls are tied together.

Each wall has alters, a gatekeeper, specific commands and signals.

Signals.

CODE WITH INSTRUCTION

Each order has a sound.

All programming has a procedure and order to activate.

Proceed to core alters.

Once programming passes through Alice in Wonderland, programmers can go anywhere they want. They will often use a carousel to travel round and round so the survivor cannot remember where she's been.

In this case, the programmer had to ask permission to enter the program through an alter called Queen in the survivor. The Queen granted permission to the programmer to connect to an older version of the Army programming so the programmer could rebuild the updated version. The process included creating some new alters to follow the new instructions. Now, the system would not crash. Afterwards, the programmer detailed updated instructions and connected to the Second Tree.

A thorough mapping of what's been done in the programming is required. You may find you have to go to the current ages to 17-years-old and then to conception to remove all of the Army's programming.

Survivors programming may be different in the NWO Army Programming. The instructions of the Seven Stages of Hell will remain the same. All survivors of MK Ultra must follow the New World Order plan. Cult members must know their jobs. The survivors must recognize the signals given by the leaders to know what happens next and their next job.

The following information was described to me in the reconditioning process. I have no idea if this is still going to occur.

I was instructed that China will invade the United States, entering from all borders — north, south, west, and east coasts. The West Coast is prioritized. Specific countries had agreed to start NWO camps during the pandemic. The Middle East would have assignments when the invasion began, taking orders from Obama.

Frequencies and microchips were implanted in the military and all MK Ultra victims without their consent to keep them under control by frequency. The frequencies flatten out emotions. When it's time for the soldiers to begin, they hear the specific frequency that connects to the alters, starting the activation process. The frequencies mean something to each alter. Nanoparticles have entered the body through several ways, congregating in the brain and heart. When frequencies are turned on a person won't be able to fight back.

Globalist Deep State needs everyone vaccinated so they can send frequencies to the nanoparticles, which either kill them or enrage them to kill others. Martial law is the signal to activate the next level of slaves. Alters, once activated, will not stop until their jobs are complete. The same applies to microchipped military personnel.

The Army consists of doctors, nurses, police, military, parents, government officials, presidents, and all parts of government, business, education, etc.

A movie title is planned for the code; when three high-profile figures say the code publicly, the massive takeover will ensue. The procedure is signal, color, symbol, and code.

Three survivors had huge shifts in behavior and their lives in the year 2015. In three other cases, survivors said they experienced a big accident and were never the same. They could not concentrate or perform tasks as they once did. Their circumstances were to cover up their reconditioning to be ready for the New World Order. In one case, the cult wanted to kill the survivor's spouse so the survivor would have no chance of getting free. The couple were also given instructions to end their relationship if the partner wasn't a cult member. I found this pattern in a couple of clients around the same time. Another peculiar thing happened: When asking clients specific questions, all of them said they'd been taken back between 2011 and 2020. This is not a coincidence. In 2015, many events were happening in the public to bring in the One World Government.

The cults must have an army to achieve the New World Order. Without the cult groups' mind-controlled slaves, all of their evil plans are destroyed. If we intend to stop the New

World Order from arriving, we must shut down all frequencies. Millions of lives around the world could be saved.

Reminder: The New World Order program or what some call the One World Government Army program can be different for everyone. I gave you an example to help your understanding of the program's complexity. Each survivor may have a different job, but most survivors' job assignment is in the 5th stage in which everyone is rounded up and killed if they don't comply.

It's important to understand the word "army". It means a professional with military training — a soldier. NWO programming includes super soldiers with extraordinary capabilities. They have been trained in every aspect of war. The soldiers have been hunted, starved, witnessed killings, and were trained in killing. They've been trained in every kind of gun and technique. Most have martial arts training. They know how to hunt and spy on others, and how to hide their tracks. They've learned the quickest way to kill. They've been taught how to torture without leaving a mark. Each soldier is taught to handle severe degrees of pain.

You must realize: In some cases, underground military bases are teaching MK Ultra survivors many things never taught in the traditional military. MK Ultra survivors have endured experiments, torture, and training to be inhuman, a super soldier robot. Once activated, the army will be hard to stop.

I do not say this to scare you. I am sharing this so you know it's imperative to act. The Globalists know they cannot bring in their world without this army. That is why, in the programming process, they guaranteed each person was highly trained in military combat.

If you approached people with Army programming and asked them to shoot a gun, most would act bewildered. How can this be? Their minds are separated into compartments. These compartments are locked down until given a code. Individuals have no access to the skills or information at a conscious level. They could be a black belt in karate under mind control. But if the conscious person was told to demonstrate karate, he'd have no idea where to begin. It is bizarre how this works. Anyone under mind control does not act without permission to access their training.

XV

WATER KINGDOM
PROGRAMMING

This is another integral program connecting the NWO Army and core foundation.

WHAT IS THE
WATER KINGDOM?

The Water Kingdom is a crucial program tied into Army programming and the foundation. Some survivors have a more powerful program based on their geographical location and goals in Lucifer's kingdom.

The Water Kingdom programming has many pieces. Some of the most- evil demons are assigned this programming.

In many ways, the Water Kingdom plays out like a TV cartoon. The movie "Aquaman" is a good example of how the programming is set up for illusions, fighting, and power.

So many things are interacting, there seems to be a mistake. Mermaids, Mermen, Nephilims, and half-human Octopuses.

The character names from the familiar stories are actually entities ruling the water. The further you go into Water Kingdom programming, the more likely your logical mind says "no way."

Training for the Water Kingdom includes infant training in how to become a fish. The child is first placed in a small water tank. As the child grows, so does the tank until the next step is in the ocean. When the cult begins the ocean training, the huge snake is introduced. Rape and trauma will occur to install the program and download the entities. Many entities are downloaded as the child's rank climbs. How can a cult train a child to swim like a fish and adjust his body to cold temperatures? How does the body begin to change shape? It's mainly from entities' help.

The survivor will learn many things from Dolphins. Frequencies will be an important part of the training. Dolphins are very intelligent, inspiring many experiments around children and dolphins. My family moved to California from Missouri when I was in first grade. I remember the experiments with dolphins. Just know when I say experiments, the programmers and scientists revert to their sick minds to include sex. Yes, they try to make dolphins have sex with a child. When I remembered the dolphins, I had no idea how they connected to the Water Kingdom. Get ready for a place that will astound.

The cults are building an army to control the sea. As we believe in the gathering of Israel in the last days, so Lucifer's kingdom believes in the New World Order. His kingdom plans to manipulate the water to kill many people with tsunamis by calling upon people wise in controlling the elements. The cults and military intend to manipulate the earth, wind, fire, and water to usher in the New World Order.

Your mind is so compartmentalized from all the trauma, the conscious mind has no idea a Water Kingdom and its atrocities exist. The first time the survivor becomes aware of the Water Kingdom, it can certainly take time to process. When I first learned about the Water Kingdom — entities, sea creatures, and dead human spirits of the sea — it was hard for my conscious mind to accept. Yet it was part of the training, a fantasy badge of honor the cult made real to my parts/alters. Parts believe they are a mermaid or merman; they received this great honor after much torture and rape. They believe this is a badge of honor of how much they can take. They have been told it is the only way to receive Lucifer's love. Their great achievement is to become a queen or king of a territory of the sea after the battle. There can be several queens of the sea. They rule specific territories and are very evil.

This picture of a merman and merwoman shows many items that represent the programming in the Water Kingdom, such as keys, a treasure chest, crowns, pearls, jewels, gold, and a book.

In this picture, a Nephilim is descending in the water to meet the Queen of the Seas. Another creature, the Octopus Queen, is half woman and half octopus. Her crown has been earned through many battles. She is very evil and hides the

13-month-old baby. She steals energy from the highly protected baby. She will not release the baby easily and may have
captured other babies.

The great snake Leviathan is an entity of the sea. He rules over the sea with other god and goddess entities. The tales from Atlantis of Poseidon and other gods are made real. Different gods/entities rule the sea; these stories and others keep the illusions intact.

Specific areas of the sea keep the dead captured, while portals to underwater cities are heavily guarded. The sea bottom has access points, and each piece of the Water Kingdom has significant meaning.

You can go only so far in the deep waters. The cold-water temperatures prevent people from staying in the water long. For a person to go deeper, he's required to form covenants with entities to assist in swimming and breathing in the deep ocean. Shape shifting is believed to occur; the individual literally grows fins to swim quickly underwater like a fish. Eventually, a person may develop the ability to see in dark water underwater.

The task of an entity called HypoCamp is to strip a survivor's memories. The entity removes the memory from the
survivor's unconscious. You will have to command Hypo-
Camp to bring back the memories. The survivor has every

right to own her memories. Under Jesus Christ's authority, command the memories to return. Sometimes HypoCamp tells survivors he will take away their pain if they utter an oath with him, but the entity erases all the survivors' memories once they do vow. Most survivors will say yes.

This survivor's writing will help you understand the Water Kingdom:

"*I am a queen. I ranked the highest in the seven seas. I am greatly blessed and had great joy in the waters. My tail was beautiful and I could swim fast. As the water became colder, I was able to shift my body temperature. I also am aware of the hybrid Octopus Woman, a wicked creature who tucks away babies in each of her tentacles, thus making it impossible to harm her.*

"*One day we were having great joy in the sea and a man broke through the barrier reef for some reason. The three guards allowed him into the city. The man asked permission to build a new realm, one I could travel to when I wanted to leave the seven seas. He said his world would be beautiful with many high-ranking officers. So, I thought it would be on the up and up. I gave him permission to build his world and I went on with my duties.*

"*Once the duties were dispersed and I was resting, I decided to see what the man was doing. The man was waiting for me because he knew I had many babies in the sea and I was feeding off my own children. He wanted access to all of them because his world was ugly. He put the net over me and I became very angry. I was soon dethroned after that.*

"The queen baby was never touched because the man knew the first tree would collapse. So, they used me to feed the new tree. It is not like the first holy tree. It was feeding off false blood and children. All of his creation was fake. All of us knew we were tricked by a male. If you are overcome by a male, you lose all your status in the Water Kingdom.

"They bound me in a grid to stir up the sea. They have tied the grid to all five queens and their queens behind them. I gave permission, so there is nothing I can do. I will not be allowed to take my position back. If a queen ever gets captured or dethroned, it brings great shame. The male captured me and held everyone connected to me under his authority. He is the King Mermaid. He tortures and rapes me daily. This mantle of queen is to only be shared with my sisters. A man must never have power over us. We have decided to destroy him and will help you to do it.

"Inside the treasure box is what he wants. The baby boy from the first tree is hidden in the treasure box. He has tried everything to find him. He is now trying to kill us because we are working with his mermen and their pitchforks. The demons help him.

"You must destroy the black book. And release us all. We will help you. We have many secrets in our waters."

Example: From the same survivor who told the above story.

"There were seven seas. There was a queen over each sea. The seas represented territories and languages spoken. Usually, each child in the program will know a minimum of three to five languages. These are not all for conscious use."

Programming Pieces:

Entities- Trident and trident weapon, Poseidon- keeper of souls.

Many entities in the Water Kingdom from the mystical stories such as Atlantis.

7 Powers.

7 Keys.

7 Hidden places.

7 Waterfalls.

Treasures in each sea with gems or jewels.

Treasure chest; baby hidden.

White pearls and black pearls.

Sea flowers.

Queens and their crowns.

Jewels and gems.

Nephilim sons.

Babies being held hostage by a half-woman and half-octopus creature using her tentacles.

Curses.

Sea of the dead in the water.

Sucking energy from cap.

Queen of each sea but ruled by Amphitrite.

Queen of each sea or territory will have many parts behind.

Sea serpents.

Snakes.

Leviathan.

Guards.

Mermaid or Merman.

Half-woman and half-octopus with eight legs, each carrying a baby.

A portal to the underworld.

Black book- mysteries of the deep, ancient order of the deep.

Water Kingdom is connected to the underworld, Cosmic tree, and the tree inside.

Seahorse represents HypoCamp, who is the taker of memories, so survivors cannot remember.

Water world is connected to other elements of the Kabbalah Tree.

Venus shells and others.

Parts not redeemable.

Humanity parts hidden in the underworld.

Graveyard with ancestors' dead human spirits.

Water World grid.

Fisherman hook.

Colors.

Net.

Spells.

Witchcraft parts and witchcraft are highly layered in all of this.

Entrances to water world cities.

Labyrinth.

Nephilim mothers.

Sea goddess.

Dragon.

Sea creatures.

Hybrids.

Nimrod.

Neptune.

Atlantis programming.

Queen of Moon.

Water Dragon.

Portals.

Hunting.

Royal baby tied in with the baby of the universe.

Warrior part in the water/moon part will be opposite.

DNA programming to handle the ocean's harshness.

Dolphin programming with frequencies.

Crowns of queens.

Weapons.

Portals.

Mummy waters.

Staff.

Fisherman's hook.

The water parts will have to be a warrior and fight their way to the top to receive their ranking, skills, and reward.

Marriage and oaths.

Parts of survivors' children will be held hidden in the sea.

Parts that manipulate the elements.

Rewards of the victor who won the battle.

Removal

All of the above will have to be explored to get specific information from survivors. This is a good list of the puzzle pieces.

When you start the removal process, you will always begin with prayer. You will map out all of the pieces to the programming before you start the removal process.

First, it's always good to remove the alarm systems, booby traps, suicide programs, or anything else set to go off if you attempt to remove any programming.

Guards are at the entrance. If you cannot remove the guards at first, bind them under Jesus Christ until they can be removed.

You will need to remove all oaths, covenants, promises, jobs, and titles. This segment will probably be layered and in multiple parts. Different parts are connected to different entities.

Remove rape and torture.

The parts must return their shapeshifting abilities.

Removal of all entities. They will be layered and some must be done individually. You cannot do them all at once.

Queens will have to lay down their crowns willingly and deny and renounce all their attachments.

All babies must be returned.

Renounce loyalty to Nephilim sons or husband. Destroy marriage. Renounce all battles, fights, killings for territory or for any other reason.

Release all pearls, jewelry, and crowns.

Release any books of secrets.

Release all hidden captured parts of other people the survivor captured.

The parts must all give up all teachings to become a mermaid or merman and to destroy the staff.

All soul parts captured are returned to the survivor and whom they stole from.

Renounce all things sexual. The Water World is very sexual.

The parts must be shown the true Lucifer is and the True God. They will then have free will to choose whom to follow. You cannot force them to choose. That is what Lucifer does.

Ask for healing of all parts.

Make sure you advance through all the pieces to remove. I found the cult hides pieces of programming in other places such as the grid or where Lucifer is (2nd heaven).

The Cosmic Tree will be sucking energy from the Water World. You will have to find the areas and parts who are feeding the Cosmic Tree.

Remove all rules and goals, rankings, and skills learned through this programming by having parts renounce and return all of this.

When all is done, ask the bodies of water to be brought back to balance — disconnected from the moon and time periods back to normal instead of the moon cycle.

The survivor's repentance is integral because survivors commit substantial evil as they climb up the ranks.

You must release the captured 13-month-old baby or other babies stolen by the parts of the survivor.

At the end, I always say this because it's how healing can transpire in that moment. "I now wash all of this clean by the power of the blood of Jesus Christ and ask that it will destroy all evil. If any entities did not leave, you will now have the blood of Jesus Christ sprinkled on you." The demons do not enjoy that, so they will leave. You will have to perform substantial casting out of entities of every authority. You can bind them together and embed all items as I described in the removal process under the authority of Jesus Christ.

In the Water Kingdom, you will deal with numerous dead human spirits and ancestors.

Witch parts won't be easy to convince to give up all their powers because they earned their power through horrific amounts of torture.

Veils must be removed to see everything. King and Queen entities will be here.

Queens' and Kings' parts must renounce their titles and crowns and all associations.

Command HypoCamp to return the survivor's memories the entity stole.

All permission must be renounced.

Call humanity out of the grid and wherever else it is hidden.

Please remember there are specific things you will execute regardless of the program you're removing. I am not going to share that in each example. I am only sharing the specific items in each step you cannot forget. These are not done in any order. You may find a survivor you're working with had only a few of these things. That is ok. This is simply a guide to identify what's been done.

This is part of the foundational programming and is tied into the Kabbalah Tree of Death. Each program is linked to another program so the survivor can never get free.

If you remove the Water Kingdom, it's likely gone, but check to see if there are pieces of the original program in places like the four elements, Lucifer's heaven, a grid, a tree, or with the highest authority. Check to see if there are any pieces in any other world. Also check to see if the parts of the client are still in the underworld or feeding the cosmic tree.

Another thing to be aware of: The Water Kingdom will have a great deal of witchcraft. Different colored witches may rule over different territories.

What must happen after the removal process is to integrate the true core parts (not entities). The parts/alters must be taught the truth about Jesus Christ and Lucifer. You must command all illusions and lies to be removed; these parts must see the truth and use free will to decide who to follow. The parts must understand all things about their world — it is an illusion to keep them captive. They must understand they are a part of a bigger whole.

Integration can be a touching experience as many miracles take place. That is why I tell professionals to get out of the survivor's way. Let survivors accomplish this in their own way. Some parts, for example, will be shocked about seeing

Lucifer for who he is and about sensing how nice Jesus is. The parts may want to test the waters concerning Jesus. Let them ask questions. What eventually happens is the parts do choose to follow Jesus and become one with the survivor. I consider this a very special time to see unfolding — and to rejoice in —with a client.

STORY OF WATER KINGDOM EXPERIMENTS

I thought I would share a story with you I transcribed in my writings. The 5-year-old me produced the piece, explaining the Water Kingdom. It may convey a deeper understanding.

The 5-year-old in a water lab experiment with dolphins.

They were programming me to become a mermaid and I was always in a tank until I went to California. Then it was in the ocean. I was dropped off every day so scientists could experiment on me after school.

They programmed me to hear a frequency and learn communication with dolphins. One day they put me in a cage and dropped me in the deep, dark ocean. I was safe, but sharks began to attack me. The scientists wanted to see if the dolphins would protect me.

My two friends always protected me and would never stick their penises in me like the bad men wanted. I could communicate with the dolphins, but I did not tell the bad men everything. The men shocked the dolphins too. They did not respond the way Peter the scientist wanted, and hit the dolphin, Sam. I don't think Sam and the other dolphin, George, did what they wanted. The men's cruelty did not work on the dolphins.

The scientists constructed mermaid fins. I was forced to wear the fins while the men shot me up with drugs to have me believe I transformed into a mermaid. I still could not breathe under the water and they were always punishing me. One day the men accidently killed Sam. The mermaid part would not perform. Everything went wrong after that. They tried everything to rebuild this part created to communicate with Sam and George. It was too late. They had to build a new part not connected to the dolphins.

The men began the Water World Kingdom program at 13-months-old, but the main focus was the building of the Kabbalah trees.

When my family moved to California, the men focused much more on the Water World Kingdom. The dolphins loved me and protected me often. I loved them too.

I was forced to descend into the dark of the ocean so I could develop the ability to see and breathe under the water.

Dolphins were the only happy thing I had in my life. Mom was always crying and Dad was gone a lot. The bad men did not like my happiness with the dolphins. We could communicate more than I ever told them. Anytime I told the men information, they just hurt the dolphins and myself even more. Any new information I related was used to push us to go past our physical limits.

Eventually, I passed certain tests and could finally see and breathe underwater. The men visited me every year; they also gave me a key to hold safe. I saved 13 keys, one each year, until I was 13 years old. You have to own the keys. I had a treasure chest of jewels and three other items I didn't know the purpose of.

There are three pearls in the shells of my three ages. The 3-year-old holds those. All the parts know it is programming, not real like they told us. They lied to us and we are angry. We would like you to set us free and go to Jesus Christ now. I was the holder of treasures and we cannot hold them anymore.

All of us learned from the dolphins about love. The men could not take what they wanted — my heart. I would not allow them. So, when Sam died I did too. Now I know my full heart can be restored.

XVI

FAMILY
PROGRAMMING

N ow you have removed the important events in the life of a survivor; there is one more thing you will have to do to get a survivor free...

Remove the programming that is with their children. I know you don't want to hear it but it has to be done. Let me now explain in this next chapter. This might even be the hardest part of the book to read.

If you do not have children then skip this chapter in the removal process. If you are married or have a partner for a significant amount of time: keep reading...

PROGRAMMING OF
THE FAMILY

This was a hard chapter to write and I was not planning on it. The Lord, however, told me the information is a significant programming part to understand.

Let me start with an explanation of the Cult Rules. The rules are expected to be followed by everyone.

There are no exceptions. No cult member gets to say, "I would not do that" or "I will not do that."

The cult must have the whole family programmed to ensure no one is awake to wake up other family members. That is pure evil. The purpose of programming is to enslave people in every way possible. They are true slaves to the cult.

In the next stage of the survivor's programming, many will break if they haven't already.

Nothing is more likely to break someone's mind than having to watch her child abused in front of them. The same atrocities the cult performed on you are repeated on your child. This will drive most survivors over the edge. That is why the cult does it. They have trained you as a slave. Your programming is complete. The cult member begins to form a family without a conscious clue of any evil arising. Because you are a parent, the cult begins the next programming stage. If you are a woman, you will be abused while the baby is in your womb. You're the weapon used to harm your baby. The cult wreaks all the same illusions on the younger you.

The process replays with every generation. The cult makes you watch unceasingly and helplessly as your child is battered. In some rituals, the cult forces the child to observe her parents watching. The cults want children to believe they won't be saved by either God or parents.

The cult always does the following to break the parent-child bond:

- Install entities
- Install a voice repeatedly telling the "Your mom and dad are evil, they don't love you. Look at what they did to you. If they loved you, they'd protect you. Why did your parents sell you so we could do anything we want?
- You will be forced to hurt your child.

- Force the child to hurt you when he is old enough.
- Install walls to inhibit the soul parts from bonding.
- Forbid bonding or love in the family.
- Forbid you from promoting self-esteem in your child.
- Create parent parts to harm your child and to achieve objectives in programming.
- Instigates families to fight and to have no affection.

If a child feels good about herself, she can't be controlled. It is common for the conscious parent to be loving and caring, but the mean, wicked parent part will assume control. The child is left feeling confused and afraid; she or he will not know how to trust anyone.

The family may have a delightful front — then the mind-controlled parts lash out. Once again, I believe that God prevents Lucifer from getting all of the parents. I believe in our true selves going through life and truly loving their kids, doing anything to protect them. Unfortunately, if parents have been under mind control for many years, they will have parts that obey the cult only. To them, it is just routine in Lucifer's kingdom.

I'm certain that some parents are consciously abusing their children, but I believe the majority would never intentionally harm their children. Hence, the cults must have everyone under mind control. Child abuse belies most people's morals. It's nearly impossible for people to accept they could hurt another person, let alone their family members. This is where a lot of survivors stop in the recovery process. They cannot handle what they have done to their flesh and blood.

I am going to say another difficult thing, but it must be said. Whether you are a parent or a child survivor, you've been hurting each other. This is a fixed rule in all cults. You have to. No one gets to say "no." For every generation belonging to the Freemasons, Illuminati, Fertility Cult, Military Programming, Satanists, and Druids, this is the way it's done.

No one can be free. No one can feel loved. No one can be awake. No one can feel supported or worth anything. Cults must control the family. If the parents are slaves, the children will be slaves. No one escapes while a youngster. And no one remembers. This is their safety net.

If parents abuse children in the cult, the practice is systematic and organized. Now, what if you say, "Well, my partner was not in these groups growing up." Then I can say thank goodness. The bad part is the cult somehow found a means to capture him or her. They will find a broken part in your partner they can program. Otherwise, the cult will not let the partners remain together.

I told myself for many years the cult did nothing to my husband because he wasn't raised in one. He was severely abused emotionally and had a few ages in which programming occurred. When we found out he was being used for all or most of our marriage, it devastated us. The fact is, the cult wants your kids. If you are with someone who blocks the cult from the family, the cult makes him or her disappear.

My husband and I spent many years seeking help without any true resolve to engage in deprogramming. We did not comprehend the extent of this programming for a couple decades, suggesting how effective the cults are in mind control.

For partners to be attracted to survivors, they are going to own a great deal of brokenness in themselves. You may not have the same history, but you will own the same level of dysfunction. We are attracted to others who match our emotional level. If your partner argues that you are the one screwed up, I guarantee your partner has several loads of baggage to be with you. Survivors will find attraction only if their emotional intelligence is comparable.

The cult hated my husband because he was unlike its members, who couldn't convert him. With his few broken parts, the cult tortured him until he created parts that obeyed.

My husband and I have made a decision to go public with our experience due to so many families experiencing similar hells; however, no one is talking about it or offering solutions. Many survivors do not even know their partner was hurt. I wanted to believe occult groups didn't hurt my husband, just me. I also comforted myself by lying to myself that they'd stopped hurting me.

A lot of our marriage's earlier years were dealt with in anger. We had no idea at a conscious level what was going on, but our insides were angry as hell. When we look back on it now, we see why we always fought. Not only were we angry at the situation, but the cult had programmed us to fight.

Not only will cults program parents to harm and be hurt by their children, they will program the siblings together so they work as a team. Unfortunately, the siblings do the same thing: They will be hurt by each other and watch their sibling be hurt. Sometimes, it is more painful to watch a sibling being abused than to experience abuse. Many of my clients have shared this feeling. Cults commit anything to cause suffering, the only human environment to which Lucifer and his fallen angels can attach. This is why all elements in Lucifer's Kingdom are built on pain and suffering.

Many times, in the family with several siblings, a leader will be assigned. The leader sibling will watch to make sure everyone is following the rules. She or he will often be in charge of a certain level of brainwashing in the family. The leader sibling may implant cult ideas in the group. If siblings are working together as a team, the cult would have programmed parts to execute teamwork. The siblings have no idea any of this is going on.

Commonly, if one or more family members are trying to escape, the other family members are implanted with ideas against the rebels. The cult may even program family members to harm their loved ones. The cult uses the parts loyal to Lucifer's kingdom.

Another punishment for anyone trying to leave is financial ruin; any rebel may be accused of false crimes or misdeeds — anything to inflict punishment. My husband and I have received frequent punishments over the years for coming out against the cult.

Cults levy another weapon to break families. For example, a family's child may have a special gift the cult wants to nurture appropriately. The cult will take the child for long periods of time. If the parents are not cooperating, the cult finds someone to bring false accusations so Child Protective Services can step in and remove the children permanently. After the cult contacts many government people to make it happen, the parents may never hear from their child again. Sometimes, the cult will implant false memories of the parents acting horribly so their kids cooperate.

Many times, the child recalls false memories of abuse rendered by a cult member. The cultist may dress up as Jesus and rape the child to block her or his connection to Jesus. The parents are still forced to abuse the child. The need to divide a family may arise because some family members begin remembering and attempt to get free. Using false memories, the cult will thwart a few family members' bid to escape. Thanks to new technology, the younger generation doesn't need their parents most of the time. The cult can simply force the children to watch a video over and over to control their minds.

When the cult recaptured me, it made me watch videos of those I loved being maimed in gruesome ways beyond human comprehension. I knew the people I loved were not really in the movies the cult showed me because no one in real life could have endured the torture. There is nothing they will not do for Lucifer. The barbarity is impossible to grasp for people with light in their soul.

I would like to share a bit of hope to all families. If you are getting free but afraid you can't do anything for your kids, you are wrong. Once a parent has removed all their foundational programming, go to the womb and release all womb programming for each child. It will set you both free. Go to the birth and to the 13-month-old for each child and remove their programming. As the parent, you have authority from God to remove it all. The cult used you in the programming. You have every right to revoke the permission you gave, to destroy all the ritual pieces, and to cast out all demons that bind you. You can ask the Lord how much to remove, though you certainly can remove the baby programming and ancestor iniquity. Stand as the witness for the family line to break all bloodline iniquity and clean it for your ancestors and future generations.

If Satan can accomplish spiritual feats, then why can't we renounce our children from this hell? The demons never had any legal right. Demons manipulated permission to achieve spiritual evil. Parents have the right to destroy it.

With prayer, Muscle Testing, and Body Code, you can release what you can for your child. You will not be able to do it all, but I believe you can when the infant is in the womb and for the child until the age of accountability. As you heal the first stages of the child's programming, you will also be setting yourself free.

You can do it. I know it's challenging, but the Savior Jesus Christ and God can help you through this journey of understanding your own family's past. When you free yourself and your partner, you have already started to disrupt the family programming. When you take the first steps towards healing, the family programming will start to break down. That is just the way it is. The cult fights so hard to keep all family members under mind control. If one member leaves, it spoils the whole family dynamic, especially when the programming is done together as a family. Even if only you reach freedom, the foundation begins to crack and loosen all over.

COUPLE PROGRAMMING

If two people get married, and only one has been a member of a cult group, the other spouse having no group contact will soon be programmed simply as a result of the marriage.

The following is typical programming carried out against married partners. I do not believe it was a new pattern. For the purpose of not having to say each group, I choose to say Illuminati. There is nothing holy before God the Illuminati or others will not desecrate, including marriage. Cults will violate it in every way possible.

Common Programming Pieces done to each marriage partner.
- Demonic attachments are the biggest aspect of programming.

- No intimacy.
- End all closeness or be punished.
- Each partner is told the other is not important.
- Do not show love or kindness.
- Only incestuous relationships allowed per Lucifer's approval.
- When you see each other; you will be disgusted.
- Absolutely no sex.
- Break all vows with each other.
- Stay lonely and isolate yourself.
- No orgasm allowed with partner.
- Do not forget you are only married to Lucifer; be faithful to him.

The couple will be tortured to make them obey these instructions. No couple should bear this torment, but perhaps the worst torment is how a cult makes the partners hurt one another. A cult member may inflict abuse on a spouse while the other watches. The couple will be numbed by drugs and a specific part will be summoned to feel the torture as a unit. The couple will almost never remember.

- Cults use trigger words, colors, and meaningful symbols.
- Curses are hurled at the couple. The curses may be specific to their lives and marriage. Here are a few common curses:
- Your lives won't have success.

- You won't have any money.
- You won't be happy together.
- You will always fight.
- The cult will entangle the couple in conflicts: "Laura, you are a complete pig, fat, ugly, disgusting." "Steve, you'd rather have sex with anyone but Laura."
- The spouses make the other feel trapped, with no way out.
- To me they said, "Every time you see your husband you will see your dad." This was being said to my part who hated my father.
- Never remember programming.
- Anytime you receive money you lose it.
- You are not allowed to have nice things.
- Remain alone, do not have any friends.
- The cult programs many demeaning sentences directed at the individual and the couple.

These orders are only a few. You could go on forever with the cult's malice. Innumerable stages of programming transpire covering assorted topics. Hoping my husband and I could help other couples, I decided to share some of our programming. Some things we cannot share at this time.

We experienced couple programming in a castle, a setting utilized with most survivors. The cult used my background, enhancing the story. We're trapped in the castle, unable to reach each other but always hearing the other cry. There is no way to breach the labyrinth. The story was designed using a time travel tunnel, walls, gates, and guards. Demons tied into our hearts and alarms would go off if we tried to remove them. Rooms filled with horror. They injected drugs into us like usual. They connected this castle to the inception of the New World Order.

Between us, one program implanted for the New World Order. The program mandated one of us to kill the other. One World Government programming will always exist between couples and among family members. (Refer to New World Order Programming Chapter.)

33

MY PARTNER'S
POINT OF VIEW

*A*s I look back over my life, I had a very difficult one. There have been many ups and downs, challenges and triumphs. There were times I really thought something was wrong with me and I just could not figure out what. I went to therapy, and it helped for a short time, but there was just something deeply grounded that needed to change.

You see, both my parents grew up in dysfunctional homes. As such, I also grew up in an environment that wasn't healthy. As any child, I wanted to be loved by my parents, but they just weren't capable of giving me the love I needed. Because I went to the well empty of my parents' love, my heart was broken. In fact, my heart was broken over and over again.

My response was to build a wall around my heart. Every time I got hurt, I added to my wall. Needless to say, I built a very strong wall. So, what did this wall do for me? It was a protection for me. I was protected from feeling the hurts, but I was also protected from feeling goodness, love, and joy.

As I grew older, I longed for a relationship with God. I sought His healing and love. As I prayed, I was unable to hear or feel His words. At the time, I had no idea my wall was stopping me. I just thought I was all alone. Over time I knew I needed to take down my wall. I needed to feel the joys and sadness, the highs and lows. I needed to heal. The only way to heal was to bring down my wall.

It took a long time, and I'm still working on my wall, but brick-by-brick my wall is coming down. I started to see that I had worth. I was taught that when I prayed, to listen to the first thought that came to mind. I grew inspired to be more aware of what I ate and how I treated my body. I was also fortunate to discover I had a purpose, a mission to fulfill in this life.

Each of these steps and a lot of therapy helped me to not only take down some of the bricks in my wall, but also to get out of my own way. I needed to focus on my purpose and use my talents to help others. As I did, I felt more love and support, more joy. God said, "This life is to have joy."

I find joy in helping others, and I find hope and healing in this life. Interestingly enough, my hurts, my broken heart, is how I was accessed by the evil one and the cult. As the spouse of the survivor of everything in these books, I did not go unscathed. I was drugged, hurt, and used in unspeakable ways.

Needless to say, I've come through the other side. I see the goodness of God and all His mercy. Through Him, I've healed much with more to go. There is a plan for me and for you. I have a purpose to fulfill in this life and I believe you do too. Jesus overcame all, including the evils exposed here. Jesus Christ is here for you. Believe Him. Seek for His help. You will overcome it.

FAMILY PROGRAMMING REMOVAL

For the purpose of privacy, I will share information about the family programming I have found working with clients as a whole. This is a list of the memories I have found in several clients.

The programming pieces are mainly what's accomplished at birth and in the 13-month-old. Programming also occurs during the child's life with his parents. The parents can start to remove this as they did in womb programming. No matter what, you are the parents who have authority over the child. When a child is young, the parents have a responsibility from God to care for those children. Lucifer stole your children and now you are reclaiming them. If the cult performs all this dark spirituality, why can't you engage spirituality for good, asking Jesus Christ to help bring your children out of Lucifer's clutches? I know this works and I know a parent has the right to achieve healing for her family. When the child gets older, he will have to remove the programming himself. I do not believe you can step in. If children are not at the age of accountability, a parent can step in. Parents can do this for their children by using Body Code to discover past wrongs while praying to Jesus to remove the immorality as you go through all the pieces. End as I explain in the Removal Process Chapter. As we work, we're addressing the spiritual, mental, and physical to remove the programming and abuse.

Puzzle Pieces to Family Programming Removal:

- Determine the parents' age (mind-controlled part) used in the rituals, which is usually in the teens.
- Trauma.
- Drugs.
- Cast out all entities that took over the body.
- Programming.
- Jobs of each family member.
- Does the survivor have New World Order or One World Order Army Programming; include the family?
- Remove the download of ancestors' iniquity to each child from the bloodline of each parent.

- Are Apollyon, Michael, Nimrod attached to the children and family members in any rituals?
- Where is humanity trapped?
- Remove all illusions children and parents carry to cause separation.
- What organs are the alarms connected to if programming is removed.
- Reclaim your children as yours.
- Disconnect your children from all demons, jobs, titles, lies, oaths, promises, etc.
- Go to each ritual age and remove all — conception, womb birth, 13 months, 3-year-old, and any other age you're able to remove programming at a spiritual level.
- Remove all curses on parents and children.
- Remove all permissions you gave under a hypnotic state of mind control.
- Remove many anchors to sadness and unhappiness between family members.
- Remove all instructions to never remember.
- Pull family out of grids.
- Disconnect your family from the Cosmic Tree.
- Check if Egyptian goddesses or gods were downloaded into the children.
- Remove all emotions; there will be many.
- Integrate as much as you can during the process.
- Close all portals that demons are using to enter your bodies for the purpose of programming and rituals.

- Remove the children's hatred for parents.
- Detach ancestors' human spirits attached to silver cords.
- If you can, remove what is possible for all ages to the age of accountability.
- If you can, remove pieces from the Water Kingdom.
- Pray and ask if you can remove NWO Army programming. This must be removed immediately.
- Find out if your child has a preordination to be a queen or king.
- If the child has queen programming in the womb, a lot of it is connected to Lucifer; in other words, entities control the body to be the queen and king of ancestors or the god or goddess entities.
- Remove the meaning of the gold cord if the child is ordained a queen in the womb.
- Remove all family iniquity for generations to where this evil started in your family line (but no more than four generations back (See the Bloodline Cleansing Chapter) unless specific reasons were given from God.
- Remove curses off reproductive systems.
- Reconnect pineal gland with God for all family members.
- Pray and ask that all entities preventing the rest of the family from remembering be removed in the Lord's time when they can handle it.
- Call lost parts back into the body.
- Break any unholy connections between siblings.

- Return the parts of your child Lucifer stole to God, the real creator.
- Remove all false relationships with false messiahs.
- Absolutely remove all connections to the domains full of trauma.
- Remove energetic cords of evil between family members.
- Determine if the family has computer programming.
- Remove all family curses.
- Bring back all humanity from where it is (send first to Jesus Christ to heal, then return to the person.)

Each ritual and age must be removed separately and you must find each piece. For the parent, it's going to be hard here because you will see how you were used to harm your children. This will happen in a couple of ways. The parent will be drugged in a mind control state and usually a powerful entity will be used to enter the body. I have found no one who was awake consciously that would purposefully hurt their children. The cult performs parental abuse under drugs, mind control, and downloads of entities. It is the only way their evil plan will work to destroy all families. The child always believes the parent is the monster because the cult wants full control over the child. You must release the child from control whenever you can.

Each child must be worked on separately because they will not have the same thing done to them. For the parent to be free you must go to all parts that were involved and heal them just like you did when you worked on yourself. You will walk them down again to conception and become one. The groups will not use an adult age to do programming with children. They will always transgress the parent to a younger age that perhaps has already been a mother or father. This part will take over during the ritual or at other times of programming. I will say that each time I find the different demons have entered the body to take over to cause the harm. Are there some parents that would do it fully awake and not under mind control? I am sure that is possible, but the percentage is very low. I would say most members in the cult are not willing participants. They just are a mind -controlled slave. That is what the membership of Lucifer's kingdom consists of... Mind controlled Slaves."

For the small percentage that likes this evil they gave up their soul a long time ago. They too are a slave because the demons are fully living in them. They willingly, and fully awake gave their soul to Lucifer.

Satanic cult behavior goes against the morals of most people. God intended our souls to know the difference between right and wrong. When there is incest or abuse; we know it is wrong. People just cover it up when they choose to follow Lucifer.

Rituals will transpire in the family for the parents' seal dates including rituals survivors undertake at 26, 39, 52, and 65 years. If the cult is able, it will attempt to assemble the family then or at another time to fuse into the ritual.

XVII

EVIL SPIRITS AND UNCLEAN SPIRITS

The next chapters will help you understand what's needed if you are a survivor of occult abuse and other types of abuse. Professionals will understand what has happened to survivors, helping them know the danger ahead, and that they will go to war against spirits of every kind. Demons, unclean spirits, and evil spirits are often misunderstood as having the same character.

Many evil spirits followed Lucifer to his kingdom when he was banished from Heaven. Lucifer and his followers did not receive a body. We sometimes call them fallen angels, demons, evil spirits, or entities.

An unclean spirit or a disembodied spirit is a person who's lived on Earth but is now dead. Often these spirits are called dead human spirits.

Evil spirits and unclean spirits often work together to harm mortals. Apparently, people can help spirits who've lived on Earth, but they cannot help evil spirits without a body. If you try to help an evil spirit, you will be pulled to Lucifer's side as opposed to pulling the entity to God's side.

Evil spirits, unclean spirits, and foul spirits can interfere with the daily lives of human beings. There is no such thing as a human being currently on Earth who is not being attacked by these spirits at different times of their life. You don't have to be a part of the occult for these spirits to attack you.

Through prayer, you can identify what kind of spirit is harming you. All are under the influence of Lucifer. It is a good idea to memorize prayers so you can quickly reference them to cast out evil and unclean spirits.

In the next chapters, you will find many references to useful information. After you discern the evil you're facing, you will understand how to protect yourself and your loved ones. If we do not know our enemy, how can we protect ourselves?

35

DEMONS AND
UNCLEAN SPIRITS

It is important to understand the roles of demons. Misconceptions about evil spirits can leave you vulnerable to attacks. The belief demons don't exist leaves you to the mercy of their intentions.

Another big misconception is, "You are never to talk about demons." You believe they are real; however, many people are told speaking about demons in church or other places gives them power. We don't have conversations with the monsters, but we must understand their authority and their legal right to attach to someone's life.

In this war, if you don't call upon the highest authority, Jesus Christ, to deal with evil spirits they can and will overpower you. In Lucifer's kingdom, the entities are all about authority because evil spirits earn their authority by doing evil deeds for Satan. Lucifer is cursed by God; so are all the spirits who followed him. They are assigned jobs to bring down the Kingdom of God.

> **Genesis 3: 1** Now the serpent was more subtil than any beast of the field which the Lord God had made. Satan tricked Eve into disobeying Father in Heaven and thereby was cursed.

> **Genesis 3:14** And the Lord God said unto the serpent, Because thou hast done this, thou art cursed above all cattle, and above every beast of the field; upon thy belly shalt thou go, and dust shalt thou eat all the days of thy life:
> 15 And I will put enmity between thee and the woman, and between thy seed and her seed; it shall bruise thy head, and thou shalt bruise his heel.

In this scripture, God says to Lucifer that he is cursed, but he will have a minor power to cause harm to mortals. Scripture also verifies humans have a body and have power over all evil spirits. Do not forget this.

Because Satan is cursed, he seeks to destroy all mankind. Satan has limited power. His bounds are set and he cannot breach those boundaries. If a person gives him permission, Lucifer's powers exponentially grow. An individual who gives allowance to Satan and his demons to attach to him in exchange for perceived powers, he will have exchanged his soul — it will be inhabited by demons. The first evil spirit attains access to his body, bringing many other demons.

It is vital to understand the roles of demons/evil spirits based on their character. Demons are assigned tasks customized to fit their level of evil, their personality, and their skills. Remember they were spirit children in Heaven too. They once lived and knew us. They studied and grew and learned as we did. We all interacted. When the angels were cast out of Heaven, it was sad for all. Lucifer's followers brought what they learned to Earth. Demons have one big advantage: They remember us from before and at times use the knowledge against us. They cannot read minds, but they do know a lot about us.

All demons who rejected God's plan were left to dwell in the bitterness of free will mishandled. They chose their fate and now there is no return. They are left to the eternal misery of damnation. Unclean spirits are a different story because they chose God's plan and received a body on earth. It is in their flesh they chose a different path. They can be saved if they want to come to God and his son, Jesus Christ. If not, they work with Lucifer to torment human beings.

Lucifer was called the Son of Morning; he had great authority in Heaven. When he rebelled against God, his glory was taken. He continues stealing our glory through different occult practices.

Isaiah 14:12 How art thou fallen from heaven, O Lucifer, son of the morning! how art thou cut down to the ground, which didst weaken the nations!

13 For thou hast said in thine heart, I will ascend into heaven, I will exalt my throne above the stars of God: I will sit also upon the mount of the congregation, in the sides of the north:

14 I will ascend above the heights of the clouds; I will be like the most High.

15 Yet thou shalt be brought down to hell, to the sides of the pit.

16 They that see thee shall narrowly look upon thee, and consider thee, saying, Is this the man that made the earth to tremble, that did shake kingdoms;

Revelation 12: 7 And there was war in heaven: Michael and his angels fought against the dragon; and the dragon fought and his angels,

8 And prevailed not; neither was their place found any more in heaven.

9 And the great dragon was cast out, that old serpent, called the Devil, and Satan, which deceiveth the whole world: he was cast out into the earth, and his angels were cast out with him.

We are now in the last battle. It must be fought. There is no escape. Lucifer wants to decimate as many souls as possible. You must understand: If you are an MK Ultra or cult survivor, you are in this spiritual battle whether you want it or not. What do I mean by that? You have evil spirits attached to you. Indeed, survivors have parts 100% loyal to Lucifer. You have been taught to hate God and the Bible during most of your youth. If this was not a spiritual battle, a spiritual war, why would Lucifer allocate so much time duping cult survivors into hating God? Lucifer tortures people starting in the womb. Doesn't this sound as if Lucifer is afraid of something? Could it be that God has power over Lucifer and other evil spirits and the cults are desperate to conceal this wisdom?

So many of my clients have shared they don't practice religion and don't really believe in God. The clients have been programmed with torture to believe they can't call upon God. If your relationship with God wasn't important, why would cults emphatically devote attention to eliminating it? Likewise, love. Why so much effort to exclude love? Because God's love is the key to healing.

The spiritual war is central to everything occult. Each survivor must understand this. It is not about only the people who abused and programmed you. Cults do it specifically to create a kingdom for Lucifer. Each horrible act is a delightful reward for Lucifer and his demons. Each ritual is to produce evil energy to feed his kingdom. Each ritual is to rebel against God. Every child harmed is because God said to not hurt my little ones. Not one thing inflicted upon survivors does not hold a direct connection to spiritual evil.

Satan tricks survivors into believing that Lucifer is God. Lucifer not only has all the power, he's also the only caring one there for you. These are lies. It is exactly the opposite. Some clients are in complete shock when their parts find out who Lucifer really is. But as professional therapists, we must awaken the parts of a Satanic Ritual Abuse survivor to recognize truth.

Again, to all survivors... You are in a spiritual battle between God and Lucifer. All the people in the cults have been deceived. All survivors must wake up or you can never be free.

Authority of Demons

Demons have different levels of authority. Understanding this will help you know how to cast them out. If you are a survivor or a professional helping clients; you need to develop expertise in expunging spirits of every kind.

Some demons have little authority and are easily cast out while others are permitted to stay and won't leave regardless of the number of times you cast them out. In this case, you will have to find out where permission or legal right was given. If demons do not leave under the authority of Jesus Christ, then you must find the origin of legal permission. Unfortunately, the demons will be layered with multiple permissions granted by many people. Demons also may have permission from the Bloodline. (We will discuss in the chapter *Cleansing the Bloodline*.)

Demons are not equal when it comes to power and Lucifer's rewards. After an evil spirit acquires a family line, capturing family members who rebelled against God, the demons have permission to stay for generations. Lucifer is jubilant knowing this; he therefore, rewards the demons as they destroy the souls of men and women. The various ranks are entrenched in the evil spirits' acts. (This is at the foundation of why a survivor must constantly earn rankings and go higher and higher in Lucifer's kingdom.)

When you reach the level of what some call the Stronghold, demons are awarded an individual to live with over his or her life. What's more, the Stronghold Demon is likely to have received the individual's entire family. For deceiving multiple family members, the demon may own the bloodline for generations. The demons have great authority because of their feverish work and their insight into destroying each family member. Recall that Strongholds are given to the baby at the first split at conception. All demons are under the Stronghold's authority as many other demons attach to the child's body over his lifetime. The Stronghold will assign lesser demons to the child, each lesser demon fulfilling a role in nurturing the Tree of Death.

Cult abuse survivors are downloaded with many demons. Evil spirits, unclean spirits, ancestors' unclean spirits will be downloaded — sometimes even the programmer downloads part of himself into the survivor.

If you have just started the deprogramming process, the Stronghold demon will never tell his name. Other demons will fool the professional and client into believing they are the Stronghold. There is no way they will tell you their name until you've removed a great deal of the programming's foundation. The Stronghold is the hardest demon to cast out. Ultimately, the part at conception must cast out the Stronghold, which I call the "One." Demons may not leave because a hidden part is still giving them permission to stay.

The power of evil spirits or unclean spirits can leave you feeling depressed, angry, sad, suicidal, physically ill, and mentally ill — the list is endless. If you are aware of what demons do; you can cast out the demons and gauge whether you're feeling better. Knowledge is power in this case. When the demons leave you, you will feel the difference. Do not stop until they leave.

All spirits can take over a human body for only brief moments. Unclean spirits achieve the takeover to feel or sense again. Evil spirits assume possession to force immoral actions or to inflict pain.

The Stronghold Demon, the "One," attaches to the first split at conception, which tricks the unconscious mind into believing the evil spirit is a part of her or his identity, thus having the right of presence. The part that was split will be deceived into believing the evil spirit is a friend they could never live without. The demon also will ensure its true appearance cannot be viewed by the survivor at any age. They are tricked into seeing an illusion providing comfort.

Programming will have many downloads of evil spirits because this will help to keep the programming in place longer. The survivor's authority and allegiance to Lucifer determines the severity of the spirits' evil.

At the ritual of the New World Order (described in an earlier chapter), the cult leaders who called in the strongest of demons were also prominent in Lucifer's kingdom. High-ranking leaders in the Illuminati/Freemasons have been completely taken over by evil — no light is left in them. They have the authority to summon the highest of demons, who swiftly arrive. Soros is the name of one man I witnessed calling in the highest-ranking demons.

A professional or survivor who doesn't target mind control and doesn't remove evil spirits won't be successful. The concepts go hand in hand.

Different Jobs of Demons

Demons of addiction.

Demons to remind you of sadness by delivering certain memories to the forefront.

Demons to create depression.

Demons create voices in people to think they are crazy.

Demons to forge hatred, rage, unforgiveness.

Demons to trigger different types of physical pain and illness.

Demons from the Bloodline downloading iniquity.

Demons to make the person feel worthless.

Demons to make the person to commit suicide.

Demon assigned to a person for life.

Demon to attach to the child in the womb and to make illusions seem real as the child grows.

Demons to cause you to abuse another because of your woundedness.

Demons of trickery and lies (Lying Spirits).

Demons to influence dreams.

Demons that use weaknesses to overcome the person.

Demons to tell you negative statements over and over.

Demons carry the curses for witchcraft to make them real.

Demon of illusions.

Demons to trap the survivor's humanity in different places.

Demons to create false memories in a person's mind.

Demons to trap the survivor's humanity parts.

It is my belief demons are used to know something about others.

Demons used for remote viewing.

Demons to ensure curses happen.

Demons to speak to people to drive them insane.

Psychics will be misled by demons by receiving a future truth followed by deceits.

The list goes on for what demons do to harm and destroy, lie and deceive. It's impossible for Lucifer and evil spirits to tell the truth, just as it's impossible for Jesus Christ to tell a lie. This is important to stress to the parts in the integration process.

I had a memory while in the womb. A demon told me to stay in this room where I would be kept safe and he would make all the decisions for me. If I obeyed him, I would remain safe. I then saw the room as my prison that was in complete control of this evil spirit appearing to be a nice, kind person I could trust. The demon feared greatly that I would look and see the truth or that somehow the true God would free me. He knew I could make him leave. He always made me believe I could not live without him.

36

ANGELS AND DEMONS

An angel of Light is an angel of God. It's impossible for angels to battle the Light they've received or to go against God. So it is with a fallen angel or evil spirit. Evil spirits, also known as fallen angels, cannot go against that to which they have given themselves. Similarly, you cannot save an evil spirit that lost its right to have a body and rebelled against God. They no longer have the ability to go back to the Light as they are full of darkness. They had all the information to choose whom to follow. Lucifer and his followers live with their choice. They openly chose Satan's plan and the curse of Satan's plan came upon them too.

When a true apostle of the Lord Jesus Christ has the Melchizedek priesthood authority to act in Jesus' name, the apostle may command anything because of his purity and his allegiance. It will be done. The angels of the Lord will obey and do as the true apostle commands; he would not command anything contrary to God the Father.

The inverse is true in Lucifer's kingdom. Evil spirits living on Earth are purely evil; they won't do anything that does not venerate Lucifer's evil will. The demons obey the man or woman who's become pure evil. A demon's level of evil is commensurate with the evil inside the individual who called him. The summons not only guarantees the individual will lose his or her soul, but it also bonds the person to an eternity in hell's tomb. Lucifer wins; God loses another child. The Heavens mourn.

JUST TO MAKE
THINGS CLEAR...

Unclean Spirits

Unclean Spirits can be called lying and foul spirits that have lived and died and temporarily stuck from progressing because they will not choose to have Jesus Christ take their suffering away. They are currently roaming the earth; some taking over mortal's bodies with the same lusts of the flesh when they can.

"Many spirits of the departed, who are unhappy, linger in lonely wretchedness about the earth, and in the air, and especially their ancient homesteads, and the places rendered dear

to them by the memory of former scenes. Thus, the over-whelming emotion transmitted by the spirits in this group is far. These spirits may also not want to leave the earthly state because Satan has told them they need to stay around their families. The spirits don't understand staying around their mortal loved ones while spirits are in a fearful, imprisoned spiritual state will harm the mortals rather than help them."
Parley Pratt

They will sometimes enter human bodies, and will dis-tract them, throw them into fits, cast them into the water, into the fire, etc. (*King James Version Bible*, printed 12/2006, Mark 9:14-29, Matthew 17:14-21, Luke 9:37-43). The un-clean spirits trouble them with dreams, nightmare, hysterics, fever, etc., and will sometimes compel them to utter blasphe-mies, horrible curses, and even words of other languages. If permitted, they will often cause death.

According to Pratt (1891), "Some of these spirits are adulterous, and suggest to the mind all manner of lascivi-ousness, all kinds of evil thoughts and temptations. … There are, in fact, most awful instances of the spirit of lust, and of bawdy and abominable words and actions, inspired and uttered by persons possessed of such spirits, even though the persons were virtuous and modest so long as they possessed their own agency" (p. 120-123).

"There is still another class of unholy spirits at work in the world, spirits diverse from all these, far more intelligent, and, if possible, still more dangerous. These are the spirits of divination, vision, foretelling, familiar spirits, 'animal magnetism,' 'Mesmerism,' etc., which reveal many and great truths mixed with the greatest errors, and display much intelligence, but have not the keys of the science of Theology, the holy Priesthood" (Pratt, 1891, p. 120-123).

Spirits of family cult ancestors have no intention of going to Jesus Christ and want to continue performing the same duties they had before death. The ancestors formally set up the arrangement to possess their family in future generations when the family members pass. Some cultists will establish supernatural bonds with family members they tormented so when they die; they will be able to still be tied with those whom they tormented in life.

Perdition Spirits

Possibly the most dangerous among all the unclean spirits because they had a close relationship with Jesus Christ while mortal but then denied Him. Few perdition spirits exist because they would have had to receive the Holy Ghost, and have known Jesus Christ. Visions had been open to them but they denied Jesus was the Son of God. Perdition spirits cannot repent because they fully rejected Christ's atonement. The best example is Judas, the apostle who experienced Christ's presence and gospel. Few possess this level of knowledge.

Apparently, perdition spirits occasionally lead Lucifer's army, helping followers to destroy mortals due to the spirits' knowledge of both sides. They travel in gangs, trying to stop people carrying important missions for God (Day, n.d., research paper).

Evil Spirits

Have never had a body and are in Satan's power. They follow Lucifer, choosing his plan over God's. Evil spirits execute actions to enhance Lucifer's kingdom. They cannot enjoy your body as an unclean spirit would because they've never had a body. Their main purpose is to destroy as many souls as possible, coercing them to follow Lucifer. All evil spirits hate the real God and constantly feel anger. They have different levels of authority and power.

"These three forces [Satan, his host, and the unrepentant spirits] constitute an unholy trinity upon the earth and are responsible for all the sin, wickedness, distress, and misery among men and nations" (Hales, 1920).

I couldn't agree more with this statement.

UNCLEAN SPIRITS VERSUS EVIL SPIRITS

Unclean Spirits (Pontius, *Visions of Glory*, 2012, p. 94-98)

- When taking over the body cannot fully feel what a person feels (Pontius).
- Cannot remain in body because of competition of other Dead Human Spirits fighting.
- to get in the body for their turn.
- What they will possess will be given to the man.
- Person feels more waves of darkness pushing for more of the addiction.
- Will offer a sense of fake relationship giving a person a sense of being fulfilled and satisfied.

- Eventually the person will accept them as friends, enjoying them around, welcoming their influence of darkness.
- Can only stay in a person for a few seconds at most depending on the spirit's ability.
- Constantly fight against each other for the person participating in the addictions, sexual sin, abuse, etc.
- Person will feel the invasion.
- Cannot read thought, but masters and judges read intent.
- Listen to evil spirits to urge person to do more.
- If a person resists, they will move on.
- Work together with evil spirits.
- No desire to control or destroy, just prolong experience in the body.
- Not trying to harm, only want to share lust and addictions.
- Look like a human, what they wore in their time period.
- Trying to satisfy sexual passion they had in their own life when they were alive.
- Sex addiction will follow them into their next life.
- Addiction was painful, impossible to satisfy.
- Can experience the thrill and sensation of gratification through the person's body.
- Will join in immediately after evil spirits get a person to give in.

- Once a person makes a decision to partake, [he/she is] drawn like "a moth to a searchlight in a dark sky" (Pontius).

"By accepting the temptation of deciding to do it," said Pontius (2012), "he had given permission to enter him and experience his sexual thrill through him. I saw many disembodied spirits competing to enter the small room with him."

[The individual above was engaged in online pornography. Once the person grants permission, demons and disembodied spirits may enter his body.]

"When he reached a pinnacle of lust in his body," Pontius continued, "a black tear or rip appeared on the top of the crown of his head. In the instant, the disembodied spirits began to attack. They were hoping to have just a moment of his physical feelings and excitement."

The lust and addiction of these disembodied spirits are why mortals could not get rid of them.

These spirits would not return to Jesus Christ for relief. They'd constantly search for someone on earth who suffered the same addiction — merely one moment of pleasure is all they wanted.

Visions of Glory

Devils and Evil Spirits (Pontius, *Visions of Glory*, 2012, p. 94-99)

- Satan is happy the person has broken covenants.
- Happy he has more control over the person.
- Happy people and their families will suffer.
- Opportunity to make family members suffer by the person's darkness.
- Want to beat down and destroy their targets.
- Obtain permanent control the more a person's addiction progresses.
- Does not care about the feeling part of mortals because they have not had a body.
- If mortals give into temptation, evil spirits, they have power over mortals.
- They are after the dominion of the soul; not a moment like Disembodied spirits.
- They want the Holy Spirit to stay away so they can be the only influence.
- Not trying to just control behavior but ensure people stay in chains of hell.
- Person entrapped can't hear their own thoughts when evil spirits are in charge.
- Can be generally smaller, misshapen features and look slightly inhuman.
- Become agitated, active, jumping around in a frenzy.
- Shouting commands.
- They want to control and take free will away.
- Whisper messages the person has to do.
- Tell people not to listen to their conscious part or morals.

- Just focus on what you want and it doesn't matter.
- Push the person away from meaningful relationships.
- Cause family break ups.
- Influence dreams to act out.
- Influence the person to become really angry and hurt someone.
- The voice of Lucifer becomes more powerful than their own.
- Eventually, the person believes the evil spirits' voice is their own.
- They want the person to die when they have control so it can be permanent.

A prayer request, no matter how small, will invite the good angels. Then the good angels can protect you from the evil ones. Free will must be present to invite the good spirits. God will not go against free will and neither will his angels.

ANGELS OF GOD

Since time's inception, angels have fulfilled vital responsibilities, helping men and women along their earthly journey. Angels are mentioned in Scripture repeatedly. Angels go on errands for God. They help people when asked. How many angels are there?

In the Bible, "the Lord of Hosts" is found 250 times. The "Lord of hosts angels" means large numbers. Hebrews 12:22 discusses the innumerable company of angels. Revelation 5:11: "And I beheld, and I heard the voice of many angels round about the throne…: and the number of them was ten thousand times ten thousand, and thousands of thousands." Just a conjecture, but I think God has a big army of angels!

"Angels are agents of power" said Donald W. Parry (2012). "Each of God's angels possess extraordinary capabilities and powers, making them formidable beings. Their powers ulti-mately exist because of Jesus Christ and his Atonement."

I love this explanation. It's amazing when angels step in to help. There are times in my life when I know an angel protected me from a lot of evil spirits. There have been a few times when I felt a warm presence nearby. That usually hap-pened when I was really struggling.

There are countless Bible stories in which an angel ap-peared and helped someone. I believe that some angels in our family have been assigned to help us. Once I was told through prayer that I had angels around me that were part of my family. I believe we are always connected and angels are helping us find our way because they love us.

One day I was feeling sorry for myself; I asked the Lord why had he not protected me and sent me here to be abused by the demon? His reply: "I did not send you here to be abused by the demon, I sent you here to defeat him. You have an army of my angels ready to help you."

Parry's (2012) research found instances when angels pro-vided temporary assistance to mortals. I believe angels are all around us and we have guardian angels. That makes me feel comforted — God loves you and me enough to provide personal guardian angels.

I love the story of Elisa praying for help. Upon opening his eyes, Elisa saw a mountain full of horses and chariots of fire around him. That is some massive help! I love miracles. The Lord says to ask for miracles. We should expect miracles!

God is a God of miracles. We just have to believe and ask for miracles.

Most Angelic messages will be felt or heard and not usually seen. If we saw them, that would be awesome!

We are not alone. Angels are all around us, we just can't see them.

XVIII

HOW TO PRAY

UNDERSTANDING PRAYER

Understanding how to pray and how to cast out demons can be crucial for cult survivors getting free. Most of my clients have no idea how to pray or its indispensable role in casting out demons. Why do I say that? Survivors have many layers of demons that can't leave all at once. Cults purposefully entrench a never-ending supply of demons in which some have permission to remain. When survivors remove programming, they must adapt to casting out many demons in succession.

For demons to leave a cult survivor, a few things must be spoken. The most integral part is to cast out demons by calling on Jesus Christ. In this spiritual battle, Lucifer and his mob won't obey anyone but Jesus Christ. Why? Jesus Christ has all power over this earth. His Father and ours created the universe. Thus, if you don't access the top member of the food chain, you essentially allow Lucifer to have supremacy.

Many clients have said they don't want any religious "stuff." This is not about religion. It's about addressing a problem with the proper solution. Like it or not, the minute a cult survivor joins Lucifer's kingdom is the minute you enter a spiritual battle. Ever since you were in the womb, Satan has been training you to be on his side. Most of your parts support Lucifer's kingdom while believing his lies.

I knew the principles of God are true because of how Lucifer plundered and inverted God's instructions. The Law of Opposites holds this world together. So, if Lucifer's kingdom is real then God must have a Kingdom too. One cannot exist without the other. That was in God's plan from the start. If our world didn't have the Law of Opposites, we wouldn't have the ability to choose — obliterating free will. As I learned more about Lucifer's kingdom, it validated my knowledge of God's Kingdom.

This is so important for all the cult survivor's parts. The parts must learn the truth of God's Kingdom and Lucifer's kingdom to make a choice based on the whole picture. Until now, the survivor has only learned of Lucifer's kingdom through blatantly false promises. Satan cannot give eternal life; he does not have that power. You can definitely live in hell with him because that's his only true offer. Satan knows his past and his future. Jesus Christ won the war the moment He gave His life for us. Heavenly Father and Jesus Christ offer eternal life in joy. On the other hand, Lucifer tells people that if they suffer for him, they can relish in great glory. Lucifer cannot stand he is not God, so he pretends and tricks to take you down into hell.

So, how do we battle in this great spiritual war? It's simple: You must choose a side. Don't be fooled by the claim you don't have to choose. Choosing no side is choosing to be with Lucifer. For true healing to begin, it's imperative that cult survivors start exercising free, it's imperative they choose.

Here I give cult survivors some ways in which to pray and to cast out demons and unclean spirits. These are only examples. I believe prayer is deeply personal and doesn't follow a script; I also understand many survivors do not know how to pray due to its forbidden nature in Lucifer's kingdom. You were punished greatly if you ever prayed or went to God. You may have had a lot of programming to obstruct calling upon God or reading a Bible. Be patient.

Example of how I pray:

Dear Heavenly Father,

1. I start out with gratitude for my blessings.
2. Start a conversation with the Lord, expressing your feelings about subjects important to you. God the Father and Jesus Christ are your friends — talk to them as a friend. Even if you are madly struggling,

tell them. They can handle your emotions. They are on your side.

3. If needed, repent. Repentance means to declare you're sorry for past actions not in alignment with Christ's commandments.
4. Thank him again for listening, asking for any help you need. God is the best instructor and can teach you anything if you ask.
5. Close with, "In the name of Jesus Christ, Amen."

I have addressed my Father in Heaven in a proper respect, I talk to him in a real way. He is listening and will answer back if I take time to listen. If I need to repent, I just ask for forgiveness for wrong thoughts, words, or actions. After communicating with my Heavenly Father, I close in the name of my mediator, Jesus Christ.

Gratefully, God accepts us as we are in our attempts to commune with Him. Just consult your heart and you cannot go wrong.

Example Professional Therapist Prayer:

Dear Father, I am so grateful for your kindness and love. Thank you for giving me the strength and protection to do this work. I ask you to send your warrior angels to protect my client and myself from all demons, dead human spirits, evil spirits of every level of authority, all familiar spirits, and anything else evil during this session time. Please help us to go to the root of the programming easily and safely. Please guide me to know what to do to help my client to find freedom. Forgive anything in me that would disrupt your Holy Spirit from being with me and guiding me. I ask these things in the name of Jesus Christ.

When we address Illuminati and Freemason programming, it's important to denote the specifics of programming.

Example Survivor Prayer:

Dear Heavenly Father,

I come before you in humble prayer and thank you for a way to get free from this mind control that I have had since a baby. Please help me to remove what has been done in Lucifer's name. I renounce every curse that was done to me. I renounce all oaths and promises given as I rose in the rankings of the Freemasons. Please forgive me for those whom I have hurt. I renounce all near-death experiences where the entities were downloaded into me and instructions were given to follow Lucifer. I release my ranking, skills, rewards, all jewels and keys. I renounce my marriage to Lucifer. I renounce all Freemasonry from my life spiritually, physically, and emotionally. I now chose you, the one true God, and renounce all things evil in Lucifer's kingdom. (Add any specifics here.) I renounce all seeing eye, all symbolism, all communions as a mockery of God, all alarms, suicide programming, bombs, booby traps, and anything else they set up to crash inside of me or to kill me. I renounce all pagan rituals, sex orgies, and all evil teachings of the Freemasons. I renounce all dualism and curses in my life and the life of my family. I renounce their right to own me or put me under mind control. I am an adult and can freely choose. I renounce the teachings of my youth and the trickery done to make me agree. I renounce and cast out all evil spirits that tie me to Freemasons as well as all witchcraft. I ask for the power of the blood of Jesus Christ to come in and wash me clean of all these things in every part so I may become free. In the name of Jesus Christ. Amen.

Example Prayer when Lost:

Dear Heavenly Father,

I come to you humbly, calling upon the promise that if we call upon thee, we will have the wisdom and strength to get through whatever is in my life that seems overwhelming and impossible.

The demons worked hard to cut off all answers and help. God, you are greater than all demons. I have been lied to, hurt, tortured, and I feel lost. I am struggling to find the path to freedom.

I am in need of help from my righteous ancestors and your holy angels. I ask all who can help to show up now to fight the Stronghold Demon that lays a trap for me to be imprisoned in hell. The demons and those a part of the occult look to trap me in hell where I will be their prisoner. They desire to torment me with lies and illusions.

I command in the name of Jesus Christ to be released from the Stronghold's grip. Encircle me with the warriors of heaven and free me from Satan's army. Strengthen my mind, body, and spirit to be equal to the task of this battle.

I am feeling the weight of their evil. Please free me so my burdens may be light. Wash me clean from my sins so they have no more power to keep me captive.

Dear Lord, cast out these demons of every authority. I renounce their plans for me and I do not give them permission to remain attached to me or to make any curse valid.

Please show me the wisdom I need to break free from Lucifer's hold. Let me feel light all around so I may be reminded of who is in charge. Show me the truth that I may defeat the army of Satan. Set my parts free from the places in Lucifer's Kingdom where I am captured. Please heal all my parts of the torture they carry. Heal my body and spirit from the pain. Bring my mind back together so I can become whole.

Show me who you truly are so I may dispel all the lies of Lucifer. Help me to fully receive your love so I may one day be free and whole. In the name of Jesus Christ. Amen.

XIX

CLEANSING THE BLOODLINE AND GOING TO THE COURTS OF HEAVEN

Cleansing the iniquity from your bloodline by using the Courts of Heaven is one of the most important principles for both cult survivors and professionals.

41

CLEANSING THE BLOODLINE

What does Bloodline Cleansing really mean?

To cleanse one's Bloodline means to answer for the iniquity of your ancestors. This would lead to the next question… Why should I have to answer for what my ancestors did?

The reason a person has to answer for what the ancestors did in your bloodline is based on the teachings of the Sins of the Fathers passed down from one generation to the next. The mistakes of our parents, grandparents, and great-grandparents going back four generations are passed to the children of each new generation. The Bible explains in Exodus 20:5: "Visiting the iniquity of the fathers upon their children unto the third and fourth generation of them that hate me."

The sins of past generations can be passed down through actions, beliefs, agreements, oaths, and covenants. This is where multigenerational cult families come from. One person or a couple made an oath or covenant with the devil or decided to join one of the groups that worship Satan. From that moment, all future generations will be bound to the demon or demons of that oath or covenant. The demon got his permission and is not letting go; he has legal right to the family.

All family lines have iniquity passed down to the next generation because we are human. We pass down what we know and believe. One example could be that a person had a rough time living in poverty. He believed there is never enough. He teaches the same belief to his children. Unless the next generation consciously breaks from the family belief system, it will continue.

Bloodline cleansing really boils down to accountability. Someone in the family line must stand as a witness for the past, present, and future generations to stop the family iniquity and break Satan's legal claim to the family members. Bloodline cleansing can actually stop a specific sin from ruining someone's life while setting future generations free.

Bloodline cleansing is a critical step in the deprogramming process of all cult survivors. If demons from the family tree have the legal right to a person, the permission makes it challenging to get free. Some bloodline cleansing has to be done in steps. Ancestors' oaths and covenants will keep a demon legally bound to the person, but until the survivor and/or professional identifies the specific covenant stage in deprogramming, the demon will stay. Hence, casting out can be frustrating. The demon may leave at the moment but return because of the demon's legal right.

Demons have to have permission to stay with a person to torment them. Many people have no idea that demons from their ancestors are attached to them.

Many ask, "Well, how do I clean my family bloodline?" I used Body Code, which required a few hours for my husband and myself. Then, a few years later, we asked whether there were any Satanic cults in our family bloodline? We received all new answers using Body Code because we asked new questions that were not asked before.

Maybe using Body Code prepared us to receive new information on how to cleanse the Family bloodline by using the Courts of Heaven. I had heard about the Courts of Heaven but had not acted upon it. The method is so incredible I decided I had to share it in my book. I believe these two processes will save the survivor and professional many hours in the removal process. The method works in miraculous ways to free the survivor much more quickly. Bloodline Cleansing and using the Courts of Heaven with the rest of the methods and techniques in this book will help you move through the healing process much more quickly.

COURTS OF HEAVEN

You begin by going to a place called the Courts of Heaven. You will close your eyes and imagine going to a spiritual place — a spiritual realm of peace, love, and safety. When you enter into the Courts of Heaven, you will sense God, the Eternal Father, as the judge and Jesus Christ as your advocate/lawyer. You are bringing a case before the heavenly court to discover the legal claim a demon/demons have on you. You are bringing the demons before the court to argue why they possess the legal right to attach to, torment, and in some cases, take over your body.

You will present your case before God, the Eternal Father, and Jesus Christ. You must ask for the demon's permission to be revoked and his legal claim destroyed.

No demon can have a legal claim without permission or sin. This is where the family's bloodline may come into the case. To have a demon's right revoked, you must repent for anything you've done that gave the demon legal right to stay attached to you. You will also repent for your family bloodline. Someone in your bloodline may have perpetrated an evil act many generations ago, allowing a demon's legal rights to pass down through several generations.

Repenting for the family bloodline requires you to request all claims against your past ancestors and future generations to be freed from the demon. You cannot receive forgiveness for ancestors, who must ask for it themselves. You can only repent for yourself. Repentance negates the demon's legal claim as it simultaneously cancels out your ancestors' iniquity.

You will stand as a witness against this particular sin, oath, covenant, or promise that either you or your family has made. You stand as a witness for your family so the iniquity has closure. You are also setting future generations free.

After a person has repented, ask your advocate/lawyer, Jesus Christ, to stand and speak on your behalf. Now is the time to ask for the blood of Jesus Christ to wash all of the family's iniquity clean as well as wiping any evil actions clean from the person. The only one that has the power to wash anyone clean is Jesus Christ. His blood was spilled for you when he suffered and experienced everything you and your ancestors experienced. Jesus has paid the price; thus, only Jesus Christ can wash the iniquity clean.

Jesus will always say "yes" to helping you; His agreement sanctifies God the Eternal Father's judgment that your sins have been forgiven, thus revoking the demon's legal right to you. The demon has to let go. Demons are bound by God's Laws centered on free will. Consequently, all cults and demons are mandated to ask for permission; they are bound by the same laws we are.

In the Courts of Heaven, we want to present the facts of the case. At this time, I present what the client and I have found in the programming pieces. Usually, I explain what we've found and ask for the removal of programs, such as the New World Order Army programming. I believe we must do the work to find out what's been accomplished in programming. I ask for help in removing programming and in healing specific parts/alters as I present our case. The survivor must repent for any of his actions or any misdeeds in the family bloodline.

One thing you must understand is this: The cult has an adult speaking for a child or youth to say "yes" to the cult's questions. Importantly, in the Courts of Heaven you must commit to breaking all oaths and covenants the survivor made or cult members made on behalf of the survivor. A promise made to Lucifer will hold a strong legal claim.

In the case of a child not being able to say "yes," an adult cultist would say "yes" to the attaching of demons as the cult tortures and rapes. Luciferians are aware of free will. They must obey God's Law or the demons cannot attach or have a right to a survivor or family bloodline.

What about the Law of Omission? When we don't say anything, we say "yes." Let me share a story I recently heard in a talk. I will be paraphrasing. "There were many families who offered to come to Lucifer's side and enjoy the pleasures of the flesh. The invitation was given and most families went to Lucifer's side. There was one family left on the fence, so Lucifer came over and asked if there was a problem. The family responded, "We have not yet decided if we want to join your side. Then Lucifer responded, "Take all the time you need. I own the fence too."

We are in a spiritual war of only two sides. God's Side and Lucifer's side. Lucifer will capture you with permission or omission. You must actively engage and say "No!" You will not accept these demons claiming legal right to you. You must understand what's going on in this war and what's in your family bloodline. It is fundamental to assume authority over all evil spirits as they want you to think they have greater power than you. That is not the case. It is important for cult survivors to overcome their fear by standing up to revoke demons' rights.

As Charlie Kirk once said, "If you don't know what your enemy has planned for you, you cannot fight back."

We cannot just go to God and say "Heal me" without understanding what's been done to us. I have heard survivors say, "I went to the Lord to heal me and that is all I have to do." I am going to say I disagree because that is not how the Lord usually works. He will heal you as you do the work and take action to identify the programming. If you don't know what the cults have done, how can you heal all your many parts/alters? How can you remove the demon's legal claims to you?

In the past, the Lord has always helped me to heal, though I had to take action. The Lord led me to many ways I could find information or healing methods, but never once did He heal me instantly. If the Lord healed us in an instant, we'd never know of cult violations against us. I firmly believe you must remember the cult groups' offenses, including abducting your life, your memories. To be whole, a survivor one must remember. Then you can recover your power. Anything you don't remember is something the cult can use against you, possibly reactivating your programming.

Points to remember about going to the Courts of Heaven

- When we go to the Courts of Heaven, we know a situation in which a demon has a claim or legal right.
- Demons are filing a lawsuit against us and must explain why they have legal claim.
- We must repent of what the legal claim states. Repentance includes what we and our ancestors have committed.
- Repentance allows Jesus to step in and speak on our behalf. When Jesus speaks, the demons' voices are silenced and the case is dismissed.

- Repentance allows us to take responsibility for our sins, guiding us into the light.
- Repentance allows the demons' legal claim to be revoked.
- When you repent, you speak on your behalf. Your repentance does not secure forgiveness for the individual who sinned.
- If you fail to deal with your family history, demons can control you through bloodline iniquity.
- If you've already repented of certain sins, do not allow Satan to trap you in an endless cycle of repentance.
- Remind the court of your original repentance and already have a divorce decree given from the demon or demons.
- Inability to hear God comes from the bloodline iniquity.
- The goal is to identify your family's generational curses and have all legal rights removed to four previous generations (only four).
- As you stand as a witness against a particular sin, oath, covenant, or promise, it can now be revoked by the power of Jesus Christ.
- If you do not know why demons have a claim on you or your bloodline, you can go to the courts of heaven to ask.
- Once the demon's rights have been revoked and judgment has been made by God, continue to decree God's judgements until it happens.

- If you continually go to the courts of heaven and your prayers are not answered, you need to identify the legal case still against you.
- Jesus' blood speaks on our behalf on two levels. First, He speaks for us in the holiest of holy places where the Courts of Heaven are held.
- Second, he sprinkles our hearts with His blood to wash and cleanse us of our defiled consciousness, thereby we become free of shame.
- Help your children in getting free from bloodline iniquity (Henderson, 2022, 2019).

Definitions:

Sin: Disobeying God's Commandments.
Transgression: Willful trespassing or rebellion.
Iniquity: History of sin in a bloodline.
Permission: A party makes a covenant or oath in exchange for a reward. The individual says "yes" to demons attaching to her or someone else.
Legal claim: Demon has permission to commit evil against a person because of iniquity in the bloodline, the person himself, or the choices of others.

How A Demon Can Claim Legal Right

1. The breaking of God's commandments.
2. Sins of omission. You did not say "no."
3. Making oaths, covenants, or promises directly to a demon.
4. An open curse or threat against oneself or another.
5. To go against God by hatred or denial of Him.
6. Bloodline iniquity.
7. Abusing another person.
8. Someone giving permission to a demon to cause harm to another person.
9. Through evil music or movies.

Satan tries to deny us what's legally ours including Jesus' death, resurrection, and salvation. We each have a Book of Life, where we are given specific gifts, skills, and blessings to fulfill our purpose in life. We all have the right to everything promised in our Book of Life. Lucifer and his demons are always trying to deny our natural rights by claiming legal rights against us. We may appear before the Courts of Heaven to argue our rights as given to us in the Book of Life. We also may show how demons have been obstructing us from fulfilling our purpose. Declare the demon's rights must be revoked by the blood of Jesus Christ.

Summary of Going to the Courts of Heaven

1. Go to the Courts of Heaven by entering a spiritual realm where God the Father and Jesus Christ are present.
2. Arrive with a topic or question having the aim of removing a legal right the demon has against you.
3. Present your case.
4. Repent.
5. Jesus speaks on your behalf.
6. Ask for the legal claim of the demon/demons to be revoked by the blood of Jesus.
7. Listen for confirmation of legal rights being revoked or a divorce being decreed.
8. Listen to anything else God wants you to know.
9. Be grateful for what has been done on your behalf.
10. Accept what Jesus has done.
11. Decree it is such until you realize the blessings (Henderson, 2022, 2019).

Robert Henderson has many books and YouTube videos. Research this information to fully understand the principles. By understanding the principles of The Courts of Heaven and Bloodline Cleansing, you can receive many miracles.

COURTS OF HEAVEN
EXERCISE

By Steve Worley

Just imagine you are light and full of love. Picture yourself going higher and higher above the Earth. High above the clouds. You will now start to see the Courts of Heaven. One particular court is open just for you. You are welcomed there. Slowly step into the front of the court. See yourself in the court. As you are there, see yourself surrounded by angels who will close in around you. Know you are in a completely safe place. You are with God, Jesus Christ, and their representatives. You belong here. Kneel down and plead with God,

"I have done the best I could. I have worked hard my whole life to do what's right. I know I have made mistakes." Plead your case. Your case is your life; what you've done, where you are. Ask for forgiveness. Say, "Forgive me God. I give up all my sins to have your love and the blood of Jesus Christ active in my life. Imagine Jesus Christ standing up and speaking for you. He represents all the goodness you have. His blood washes over you. You feel His blood's cleansing power. His blood speaks for you. He says you are a child of God. An important person. We need to hear their words. This is your chance to ask for what you need. Bring forth the elements of your life that need attention. "Heavenly Father, I bring to you the evil and the demons terrifying my life." Then ask for a decree of divorce. Ask for all demonic connections to be severed now and forevermore. Now listen to what God has for you because He has plenty. Have Jesus open the Book of Life and see all that you are and all you were meant to be. Receive all the blessings he has for you. Receive the goodness and love God has for you. Listen to the court's decrees. Do you have the decree of divorce? Have all the demonic connections been severed? Hear it. See it. If you need a written decree, take it. It is yours and your family's forever. Feel the love. Feel and share the gratitude for all Jesus has done for you and will do for you. When you are ready, return as a new person. Feel safer, feel better, feel stronger in God's Love. Feel the strength of the blood of Jesus. Feel how much your life will improve. Be grateful. In Jesus's name. Amen.

WHY IS THE BLOOD OF JESUS SO IMPORTANT?

The blood of Jesus Christ is not only a symbol but a power. The blood of Jesus acts on behalf of any person who comes to Him. Jesus' blood symbolizes a healing power that can heal all things. There is nothing that cannot be healed or destroyed by the blood of Jesus Christ.

When we talk about the blood of Jesus, we not only speak of his actual blood but its symbolism. The symbol is so powerful because His powers come from God.

It is power given to Jesus Christ by God the Father that gives Jesus all authority over Lucifer and all his devils. This authority is the highest authority on the earth. There is no one that has authority over Jesus Christ. That is why you must call upon the highest authority when dealing with Lucifer and all those that followed him. All demons have to obey Jesus Christ.

Jesus Christ has all power and authority over all earthly things. The blood of Jesus Christ represents his power and authority. With His power, Jesus Christ has the authority to heal everyone on Earth.

Through the blood of Jesus Christ, we are enabled to come forward and ask for forgiveness, healing, and the ability to be free. The component permitting us to call on the blood of Jesus is repentance.

The Blood of Jesus Christ speaks for us in the Courts of Heaven. Why can Jesus speak for us? Jesus has descended below all things. No one on Earth went through more agony and hell than Jesus Christ did. His pain and suffering give Jesus the right to have all power over all things.

Some people have said, "Well, Jesus was never raped or put under mind control." I have to say that is wrong. It's wrong because Jesus felt the pain every time we were hurt, injured, and tortured. He felt our tears, pain, and despair. Because Jesus felt the pain for everyone, He earned the right to speak for us. Jesus has felt all we've been through. Jesus knows how to comfort and heal us. Jesus' blood represents Him taking on our pain and His authority speaks on our behalf through his just sacrifice. His act of sacrifice for each and every soul allows Him to take our place and usurp Lucifer's legal rights.

Now that you understand the importance of the blood of Jesus Christ; I hope now you will understand why those that follow Lucifer are obsessed with blood. It is to mock God. Cult members drink blood because God said you do not do this abomination. He orders His people to never drink blood (New International Version Bible, Acts 15: 19-20): "It is my judgment, therefore, that we should not make it difficult for the Gentiles who are turning to God. Instead, we should write to them, telling them to abstain from food polluted by idols, from sexual immorality, from the meat of strangled animals and from blood." God also forbids the sacrifice of a child or adult.

Every Satanic ritual must involve blood due to its symbolism. Blood flows through all humans. Blood and breath are life forces. On the contrary, cult members believe blood grants them power to take someone's life. An infant is considered pure. Cult members love to drink pure blood as it grants the power to steal a life from someone innocent and pure. Cultists get high while drinking a child's blood, contending it makes them look young. As they loot the life force of an infant, cult members believe they are royalty, so special, and have the power to live forever.

Lucifer's followers mock God the Father and Jesus Christ because they understand the power of Jesus Christ's blood. Because cults can never have the blood of Jesus work on their behalf, they steal innocent babies' blood. Never forget that everything Lucifer and cult members do is mocking Jesus Christ and God the Father. Everything! Not one act of programming, not one Satanic ritual, is not done to mock the Creator.

CURSES

When talking about a curse in the occult world, we are addressing the use of witchcraft. Witchcraft is used to curse people and part of all Satanic rituals.

Curses are used to keep mind control in place and to facilitate the programming early in the process, even in the womb. The cult wants to completely control the child, doing so through curses. The cult groups curse the child in every way possible. Survivors and professionals will have to renounce and destroy many curses through the course of deprogramming.

Curses are also performed in rituals to cause harm. There are precise curses or spells for whatever the witch's or cult group's purpose is.

Curses follow restraints. For example, if the curse does not stick, it returns to the person calling the curse. Let's say a witch curses an individual to be depressed or to wreck his car. If the person finds out, he can renounce it under the authority of Jesus Christ. Based on the Law of Witchcraft, the curse will return to its owner. Consequently, an individual who curses someone must use extreme caution, especially when committing murder.

Curses are used for every subject possible, but the goal is to harm. Cult members may curse events, countries, religions, groups, individuals, etc. The stronger the curse, the more trained in witchcraft the individual must be.

Curses are part of witchcraft training. To curse someone, you must use entities to make it effective. Curses are nothing if not attached to entities to carry them out.

All rituals include curses. If a cult wants to kill or harm a person, the cult may go to the extreme of undertaking a sacrificial offering to summon the preeminent demons possible.

Unfortunately, all my clients curse me. The clients, however, are not aware of their parts/alters cursing me. I know their conscious mind would not harm me, but their alters are 100% loyal to the cult.

Curses can be more effective when the person is not consciously aware of being part of the cult group. It is very important to renounce curses every morning or anytime you think you've been cursed. Survivors and professionals will be cursed without question. Muscle Testing is one way to determine if you've been cursed and to know the curse's purpose.

The curse's owner may beckon different levels of curses with varying levels of power and demon authority. The sender has to give permission for the demon to come and harm you.

Most curses are easily renounced with the aid of Jesus Christ. If a cult group is trying to kill you through a curse, you may want to ask a friend or family member to help you pray and destroy the curse. Use Muscle Testing and Body Code to identify the curse.

If you feel depressed, suicidal, hopeless, angry, etc., assess whether you've been cursed or if entities are causing your feelings. Most of the time, you will find demonic influence. Entities delight in tormenting us in any way possible. If you discover you've been cursed and or have entities, renounce them and cast out immediately. All too often, curses are the root cause of many problems. We may not realize we've been cursed or have entities attached; days, months, or years may pass as our distressing, sometimes dreadful feelings continue.

One last caution; Do not ever send back the curse you received. If you send back the curse you have just entered into witchcraft and gave permission for a demon to attach to you. Let Jesus Christ destroy the curse. It is ok to put up a reflector shield around you to protect yourself and let the curse just bounce off you. You are not directing the curse to go back, only it to be deflected off of you. The witches love to trap you and get you so angry you will send it back. Do not fall for it!

46

EXAMPLES OF PRAYERS TO RENOUNCE CURSES

I renounce all curses sent to me last night or this morning. I renounce any and all demonic and witchcraft authority over me. I renounce every word in the curse for myself, partner, children, grandchildren, home, business, finances, bank account, and anything else connected to me.

All curses to make me depressed, hopeless, helpless, or suicidal are removed and destroyed.

I don't give permission for any portals to be open or the usage of any tools to spy on my family, so you can get information to curse me with.

Any plan to stop or interfere with my work (or whatever) is hereby destroyed and no longer has any power.

All curses known and unknown: I do not give you permission to do this and I will not accept them. I turn over all that was done in evil to the Lord Jesus Christ and he will take care of any and all consequences. I will not return anything because I will not be a part of witchcraft.

I ask that the power of the blood of Jesus Christ speak on my behalf and destroy all curses sent to harm me or my family. Please wash me and my family clean in the name of Jesus Christ. Amen.

Or

I renounce all curses sent to me and command them all to be destroyed. I do not give permission for you to curse me or anything connected to me. Through the power of the blood of Jesus Christ, all curses sent to me are null and void and I am washed clean. In the name of Jesus Christ. Amen.

(Just make your own prayer. What is important is renouncing and commanding curses to be destroyed in the blood of Jesus Christ. Renounce and revoke the curse and say whatever else you feel is needed. Then close in the name of Jesus Christ.)

In the name of Jesus Christ, I renounce all curses and command they be destroyed. I do not give permission for any curse placed upon me to cause harm. (Name the curses and renounce each one.). In the name of Jesus Christ. Amen.

Or

In the name of Jesus Christ, I revoke any and all curses on me, my partner, children business, finances, etc. (anything connected or important to you; name here) I do not give permission in any form. I am saying no to any permission you may have been given. I ask the blood of Jesus Christ to speak on my behalf and destroy all legal rights for entities to attach to me and cause harm in any way. In the name of Jesus Christ. Amen.

Address evil attachments of any kind the same way:

In the name of Jesus Christ, I command all evil attachments, evil spirits, lies, trickery, and illusions to be destroyed and I renounce all of them in the name of Jesus Christ.

(I made these prayers simple so cult survivors and others can have success with prayer and casting out entities and evil spirits of every kind. For wonderful detailed prayers, I recommend going to Kanaan Ministries. The group's website is full of many downloadable prayers. Dan Duvall from Bridemovement.org also has many downloadable prayers addressing Satanic Ritual Abuse and mind control.)

47

STORY: CURSES SENT TO KILL ME

After being interviewed about the Kabbalah Tree/Tree of Death serving as the foundation of Freemasons, Illuminati, Military, and Witchcraft groups, I was attacked by a rarely used curse in the Law of Witchcraft. If you send a curse or spell that doesn't work, the curse returns to the sender. On this principle alone it's rarely done.

Apparently, I was right over the target to speak publicly about the Tree of Death because the Cult has hidden the Kabbalah Tree of Death information for a very long time. The cult was so angry that I said these words for people from all over the world to hear; they decided to try to kill me.

Shortly after the interview, I had a terrible night sleeping and felt like 13 people were eating me. It was a disgusting sensation. With each bite, a cult member launched a curse. Each curse was enforced to take effect within 24 hours. So, for 13 days I was being sent a different curse each day. They were using the power of 13 women at a formidable level in a Fertility Cult in a ritual.

Each day this went on, the Lord showed my husband and the necessary actions to battle the barrage of curses. The Fertility Cult was relentless, believe me. The Lord told me I had to complete a specific work within 13 days to negate the curse.

During the next 12 days, my husband and I were literally praying for hours a day to remove an unknown force to which the cult was connected. My husband was so sweet. As I figured out all that was going on, he held me in prayer; then we'd identify the pieces, removing and renouncing all elements being sent.

After the first round, the cult had seven days to make it right if the first curse failed to work. The witches had to curse me again. So, through prayer and Body Code I found they cursed me with the following:

- Curse on my business.
- Curse on my body.
- Curse on my heart to stop beating.
- Curse on my husband.
- Curse on my children to be hurt.

- Curse of death and extreme fatigue.
- Curse children would die.
- Curse of financial ruin. (If I'm going to die by curse, I don't understand this.)
- Curse to release horrible news about me so no one would believe me.
- Dagger in my back; to be hated (energy weapon).
- Body to become crippled.
- Knife in my heart so no child would love me again.
- Curse to be alone.

Over the next 13 days, the Lord gave me decisive information to finish my book. So, I guess I should thank the cult. This experience helped my husband and myself to become even closer. If a man prays for you hours a day to save you, there is a good chance he loves you. We both have grown so much from this experience; while Lucifer was convening great evil to kill me, the Lord was using every fragment of it to understand things I didn't know.

The experience pushed me to a point I never thought I could reach. I remember thinking I won't make it. A strong force I cannot explain infiltrated me. We were working all day, battling in spiritual warfare against this great evil. Spiritual warfare is real, but I had never felt an onslaught from this depth of evil. If the Lord had not helped me, and my husband had not been holding me in prayer for those 13 days, I really think the Fertility Cult would have killed me.

I know the Lord has work for me to finish. So, I will be protected until my work is finished. I know where I am going and it will be wonderful to be with the Lord again.

I would like to share something a little intimate for those who may be struggling in your relationships due to trauma. The Lord has steadily brought my husband and I out of hell. Our relationship went from anger and fighting to something extraordinary. Over the past 37 years, we've grown so close, but not because it was easy. It was because of its difficulty. The more we turned to God for help, the more help we received.

In 2019, I wrote my first book, and for about 3 years we've had major attacks from Satan and his minions to stop the information from going public. Well, instead of tearing us apart, we've grown the closest we've ever been. Through experiencing the 13-day curse, we've learned how profound love can feel. There were countless times my husband endured a spiritual hell for me. These challenging experiences undoubtedly confirmed his love for me and our commitment to fight. We will never stop converting this darkness to light.

I am truly grateful the Lord transformed a devastating event into something that brought us closer. We have so much information that may help others. My husband never planned on knowing so much, but I know God has a plan for us. We will be teaching what we know to people all over the world through teaching seminars and speaking engagements. We are a good team.

Our first seminar together worked out so well. I taught the information to survivors and professionals while my husband encouraged people to laugh and feel hope. We also used spiritual exercises that left people feeling hopeful and uplifted. This is our calling. We work really well together. We now plan to use our knowledge and experiences to help others get free of cult programming and abuse.

Always remember, God will transform others' evil into good in His own time and in His own way. Just go to Father in Heaven and Jesus Christ.

TECHNIQUES AND METHODS

48

THE GATHERING
OF INFORMATION

In this section, I share many techniques and healing methods to help you in your healing journey. This system of techniques will work together for phenomenal results. We will address the spiritual, physical, mental, and emotional to achieve balance, wholeness, and freedom.

Over years of therapy and through my experience as a Trauma Release Coach, I learned that if survivors do not release emotional pain, their unconscious mind won't change their memories. Traumatic memories will always carry an emotional charge. If you want to change your life, you must target the unconscious mind. Releasing the negative emotions from your mind and body will change your life forever.

Most therapies don't address the release of emotions, yet it is key to living a joyful life severed from the past.

For those readers who are Satanic Ritual Abuse survivors, it's important you remove occult programming and whatever painful emotions are left in the parts/alters.

I will show you how to remove your emotional pain by specific healing modalities I've found to be the most effective in my 30-year journey of attempting countless modalities. I arranged this system of techniques after seeing well over 2,000 clients in the last 11 years.

Eleven years ago, I found a Tapping modality called *Eutaptics/FasterEFT*. I trained for more than 1,500 hours and became a certified Advanced Level Practitioner. I became certified in many other methods of transformation, including Body Code, Hypnosis, NLP, Matrix Energetics, and over 2,000 educational hours on trauma and Satanic Ritual Abuse. I've been learning about the mind and different healing methods for more than 30 years. Now I use all I have learned to help clients worldwide.

In 1989, I first went to therapy because I had a candy addiction and my husband and I were continuously fighting. Not long after therapy began, I started to remember sexual abuse through writing exercises. Through my writing, I recalled many family members sexually abusing me. This gradual process over many years unearthed buried memories and truths.

After my therapist realized I had repressed anger, she recommended I go to the shooting range. She even gave me her gun. I am not kidding. I went to the shooting range, pretending the target was my dad, and my aim was perfect. LOL! The exercise worked brilliantly in releasing some of my anger.

Four years later, I remembered cult abuse that triggered depression. I consulted many therapists who told me they didn't know how to help. Nothing is worse than hearing, "I don't know how to help" from a professional. I was also told by therapists that cults are "not real" or "don't exist." I would also hear, "You are crazy." That was the story of my therapy in the 1990's. Today, it appears some therapists are behaving similarly, even labeling people schizophrenic and giving them heavy prescriptions that damage their lives further. Some therapists are part of the Cabal; they definitely want survivors to believe they're insane and merely contriving cult abuse. In the 1990's the Cabal told therapists to institutionalize and medicate people on heavy drugs if the survivors came forward about ritual abuse. Some may remember the rumor of therapists implanting ideas in the client's mind. But if therapists didn't even understand cult abuse, how are they able to implant details about cult groups' actions? The Cabal does not want anyone getting well. Some therapists also hold that suppressed memories are fantasy. Any therapist who, in this day and age, does not understand how the unconscious mind deals with trauma is a red flag suggesting a Cabal influence.

After 15 years of this nonsense, I found a specialist helping Satanic Ritual Abuse survivors with removing their programming.

I worked with him for a year. I paid him to fly to California once a month to spend a week with me. We worked 8 hours a day. He would not work with anyone without a licensed therapist present, so I paid for her too. I recalled a great deal of information about my abuse — far worse than I could have imagined. After one year of therapy, I became overwhelmed with the information, having no means of coping with the emotional pain.

Despite my husband and I spending so much money, I was not free. I know it helped, though he was not aware of the biggest chunk of my programming. The Kabbalah Tree of Death and the New World Order Programming. I do not blame him. I know he was doing the best he could. My secret exemplifies how well the cults were hiding the real foundation of survivors' programming. To this day, cults keep this information hidden. If it wasn't for God's revelation to me and 2 other practitioners that I am aware of, I would not be free now.

In 2007, after the above experience, I said a prayer. I was completely exhausted and out of money. I pleaded with God, "There has to be a way to truly heal." A week later I found EFT Tapping. This is where the Lord led me to healing modalities that began releasing my massive baggage of lifelong pain. I began releasing pain through Tapping over the memories I had. In 2011, I found Eutaptics/FasterEFT Tapping — that is when my life truly changed.

I got certified as a coach because of my success in feeling better. As an Advanced Practitioner I went through many hours of giving and receiving sessions. For one year, I had a group of 8 practitioners who trained with me for 16 hours a week. We each took turns being the client and practitioner in our training. This may have been intense, but I was overjoyed to have found something that was making me feel better. I was cleaning up the memories, which seemed impossible at the time. My life continued improving. My relationships, business opportunities, and finances were remarkable as I released the longtime abuse. I was happy. No longer waking up with a sick feeling in my stomach. I was making friends all over the world in the FasterEFT community. I attended many live seminars for training in FasterEFT. I was soon asked to travel with the Skills to Change Institute to help the people attending the seminars and conduct sessions. We flew to many countries. I worked with people worldwide. I was asked four times to join a special project called Habilitat, an Alcohol and Drug Treatment center in Hawaii.

My studies branched out to other healing modalities. Body Code quickly became a favorite of mine and integrated so well with Tapping. I was able to get answers and release the negative memories from clients quickly and in a non-traumatizing way.

Over the years, I have been trained in ways to release trauma because I had been taught how the mind works. When you know how the mind works, you can spark changes in clients that don't require years of healing. The clients do all the heavy lifting in their minds. I am a guide. This process is successful because I know how to reach the root quickly. Ultimately, it comes down to the questions we ask the client. I feel like a detective. I have grown pretty good at asking questions and getting to the root.

After numerous years of studying and learning, by God's grace, I have transformed my horrific past into something beneficial, bright, and long-lasting. Something good. I have learned from my own experience that God can take anything horrible and turn it into something good — if we let him.

Short Explanation

For a very long time I did not tell anyone of my ritual abuse because every time I did, I was betrayed. At one point I decided to tell a fellow practitioner about my life, which ended in her saying she didn't believe me. I decided I would simply say I had been through a lot of abuse. It was not until 2019 that I even began to say I was a Satanic Ritual Abuse survivor, only because the Lord said it was time to write a book. This is when I began sharing information about the cults and their abuse of survivors.

In 2019, I began writing my first book, *Puzzle Pieces to The Cabal, Mind Control, and Slavery*. I feel the Lord wrote most of the book. My book was not published until 2021, when I began doing interviews. I was very careful with my words and only said what the Lord told me to say at the time. It's taken a while for me to provide this information in the more recent book and to give abusers' name names. In the first book, I was not supposed to reveal names. I understand why. Back then I was not ready for the spiritual attacks I am receiving now. Now I'm ready to reveal the secrets. I will no longer protect my evil abusers.

Since 2019, I have been given so much information from the Lord needed to benefit Satanic Ritual Abuse survivors. I have therefore decided to devote most of my coaching business to helping survivors.

The greatest challenge I faced while searching for help was the lacking the understanding of the occult's actions. It's imperative for mind-control victims to comprehend the content and manner of their programming.

Another challenge was finding a professional who understood the nature and actions of cults including programming. Therapists had no idea. A professional must have the pieces to the puzzle of the basic foundation of programming executed in all cult survivors. If the survivor and professional have no clue, they won't get far. The myriad of cults are counting on the lack of knowledge by the survivor and professional.

The next huge challenge was this: I had no understanding at a conscious level of the diverse array of demons used in programming. I had no idea a conglomeration of entities were attached to me in layers of programming. I certainly had no idea of the steps to cast out demons. My guess is most survivors and professionals do not understand demon expulsion despite its pivotal role.

If all those challenges were not enough, I had no way to eliminate my emotional pain. (Some survivors also have a great deal of physical pain.)

The last problem I had was a dormant program I didn't know about called the New World Order Army Programming. Every survivor has it, though it's rarely addressed in therapy. If the awful programming had not happened to me in 2015, I wouldn't be writing books regarding how the Illuminati/Military use mind control.

In the next chapters, I show you how to address different areas of deprogramming safely and how to release negative emotions. I have already described the pieces to core foundational programming in all survivors of the following groups: Illuminati, Military, Freemasons, Satanic, and Fertility Cult. You have been shown the removal process order. Now we will address the techniques for removing foundational programming and painful emotions.

49

FIRST TECHNIQUE USED IN REMOVAL

**Eutaptics/FasterEFT Tapping
eutaptics® FasterEFT™
Method developed by Robert Gene Smith**

Tapping is a method using the unconscious mind and body to release negative emotions, beliefs, and traumatic memories. Tapping uses the Meridian System known in Acupuncture. Meridians act as a communication highway between the unconscious mind and body.

The mind and body work together as one, so we must address both for real change. The logical mind cannot help with the removal of painful emotions. The logical mind is not aware of suppressed memories or other important hidden information. Only the unconscious mind retains the information. Therefore, we cannot use the logical mind to help us release negative emotions or address past traumatic experiences. Typical therapy uses the logical mind to address the client's issues. A client will never get free while using the logical mind. (Refer to Book 1 for further explanation.)

All survivors of mind control have enormous amounts of emotional and physical pain. For true healing to occur, we must use a technique that truly releases traumatic, abusive energy from the mind and body. Eutaptics/FasterEFT Tapping may be very helpful for clients to use on their own or for the practitioner to ensure clients are not retraumatized. By using Tapping, you are releasing emotional energy out of the body forever rather than burying emotions.

A short tutorial on the unconscious mind: The unconscious acts as a recorder of everything a person has experienced starting in the womb. This recorder uses all five senses to file all memories. The unconscious mind uses the filing system to protect us from substantial trauma. If a child had too much trauma, he or she wouldn't survive if the unconscious mind didn't conceal the memories. As we age, the files move forward, causing us to remember long-ago incidents.

The cool thing about the unconscious mind is you can change it. If you release the negative emotions, the unconscious mind will change not only its perspective, but change the memory itself into something positive. The only thing that keeps traumatic memories in place are emotions. If negative emotions are released, the unconscious mind does not care anymore. Instead of enduring a painful memory when the thought occurs, no emotional charge is present, you won't care anymore. This is even true of the most brutal, most hideous things imaginable. Supposedly, all traumas remain locked within for life. That is a lie by Satan. God would never want us to carry a trauma we could never heal from. Such trauma myths are actually taught by the Cabal's therapists. Don't believe them! This conviction will keep you in chains for life.

How do I know this is true? My own experience, first of all; secondly, I have watched dreadful traumas dissipate in my clients. When I use the Eutaptics/FasterEFT protocol, I can get to the root of the problem quickly. We work on the memories, tapping until the memory has changed in the unconscious. That is how I changed hundreds and hundreds of trauma memories. The past no longer triggers me. I do not have any negative emotions stored in my mind. When new painful events occur, I have a tool to vanquish painful emotions in the moment. Our lives are composed of many painful events. The key to healing will be processing and releasing the emotions — not suppressing them. I teach Tapping to my clients so they have a tool for life. This way of healing is true freedom. Refuse to suppress traumas, let them go.

If you are a survivor of Satanic Ritual Abuse, I'd like to make this clear about Tapping. Tapping will not deprogram you.

Tapping serves to help you recall repressed memories, find answers, and release physical and emotional pain, but when it comes to deprogramming, we have to do something different.

I use Tapping as part of my system of techniques. Tapping is important in the removal process because you must have a way to handle the client's emotions. Tapping can be used to pull the mind back together after its fracturing. If a client is struggling with a glut of emotions, Tapping is a way of stabilizing the person without things getting out of hand. Really, a professional has to have a way to handle abreactions safely without retraumatizing the client. Tapping is brilliant to do just that!

Tapping interrupts negative communication, addressing the files of trauma that the unconscious mind is holding. Tapping can release the emotions attached to that trauma and change beliefs and perspectives — it really changes the past.

Here is a short video on how to tap on my Rumble channel: Laura J Worley. https://rumble.com/v1r6rva-how-to-tap.html

Tapping Points

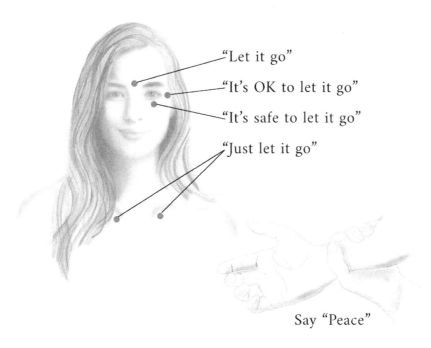

"Let it go"

"It's OK to let it go"

"It's safe to let it go"

"Just let it go"

Say "Peace"

PICTURE BY NIC YOUNGBLOOD

Now that we've discussed how to handle memories and negative emotions accompanying trauma, we will address the next part of the removal process, what I call *Mapping Out the Client's Programming.*

SECOND TECHNIQUE
MAPPING OUT THE
CLIENT'S PROGRAMMING

We now should find each piece of the program to remove it. I have shown you the programming's foundation and the order it should be removed. You will begin with Mapping Out specifics of the survivor's program.

How do you Map Out something?

To Map Out a program or a problem you have to find a means of doing so. The best method I have found is Muscle Testing and Body Code. This method will allow me to find every piece of each program with the survivor's help. This is a crucial step because you must retrieve all the programming pieces. If you don't, the program may regenerate itself or continue to program the individual. Muscle Testing and Body Code are important because often times the survivor has only some of the pieces. Muscle Testing and Body Code will reduce program removal by years. Remember, the unconscious has all the information. Even in Memory Recovery, parts of the information are missing. The unconscious mind helps us capture the missing pieces through Muscle Testing and Body Code.

I will ask the unconscious mind, "What must we do to completely remove this program? You must ask the correct question to receive a correct answer. The question must be as specific as possible. You will write down, in order, the answers you received. The unconscious mind will tell you the order of importance as each piece is removed.

Mapping Out the program is markedly enhanced by the cult survivor's support. Be sure the survivor tells you when any thoughts occur or her knowledge about the program.

We are creating a Map. When we have the Map drawn out, we can see clearly what's been done.

Once I have mapped out the program, which means obtaining every puzzle piece to the program, I can remove it. I CANNOT REMOVE ANYTHING WITHOUT MAPPING IT OUT FIRST! If you hurriedly remove a program, you may trigger an alarm system, flooding, or a suicide program.

THIRD TECHNIQUE
MUSCLE TESTING

Let me explain Muscle Testing. This process simply reveals what the unconscious mind and body hold. The unconscious mind can direct everything because it owns all the information. The unconscious has recorded everything in a person's life. It is accurate even in guiding others to specific information needed, even if a survivor doesn't remember on a conscious level. In some cases, it would take years for clients to remember every part of the program. We do not have that time anymore. It is now possible to move quickly if we know the core programming and how to removed it. Maybe a few things must be addressed after the core programming is removed. That is ok. Focus on the core programming and core parts for the deprogramming process to succeed.

A fundamental aspect of Muscle Testing is that the body cannot lie. When we use Muscle Testing we can feel confident in the answer if the one testing is not sick, inverted, or dehydrated. When the body is being questioned about the past or current state; you must ask a specific question. You will learn with Muscle Testing that the question must be specific. The way the therapist asks a question can affect the way a person responds. If you are unsure of the response, ask again with a different question.

Accuracy in Muscle Testing depends on understanding the rules. You cannot be dehydrated or sickly, so drink a lot of water.

The next rule is to check if you are inverted. In Muscle Testing, inverted means the answer is "yes" when it should be "no." No answer is a "yes" answer. To learn if you are inverted, ask yourself this question: "Is my name _____?" (Say your name.). If your answer is "yes" when you ask for your name, that is a sign you are not inverted. If you get a "no" answer when you ask for your name — let's say you contend it's "Julie" — then you may be inverted. You can cross your hands and tap under the clavicle while taking deep breaths to change your inverted state. This sometimes brings a survivor into balance. Now check again using your name. Check if your name is false like "John" when your name is "Julie." If the individual says "yes" to your name being another name, then you are inverted. You are basically asking a question of "one is true" and "one is not" so you can determine if your answer is true. Answers will come in the form of "yes" or "no."

Muscle Testing (see illustration) is accomplished for yourself by pressing the forefinger or middle finger to the thumb of each hand, interlocking the fingers of both hands. If you ask a question and your pointer finger and thumb do not come apart, that is "yes." If your fingers do come apart, that is a "no" answer. You can also use the standing method wherein you naturally flow to the front if answering "yes" or backwards if answering "no". I prefer the interlocking of fingers because it is quicker. If someone else is testing, she can have you put your arm sticking out and gently press on it for your answer. If the arm does not go down when asked the question that is a yes answer. When a person presses down on the arm of another person and the arm does go down that is a no answer. Muscle Testing is really about practicing until you become comfortable and can easily tell your "yes" or "no" answers.

The most common way of Muscle Testing in a therapeutic setting is by proxy. This is where the professional is Muscle Testing for a client. The client can be in your office or by video over the internet anywhere in the world.

The question is asked, "How can you muscle test for another person, especially if he is far away from you? The basic answer is, we are all energetically connected. When Muscle Testing for another person, you must always ask for permission. If the person gives you permission to muscle test, both of you connect instantaneously and energetically. When the session is over, you must disconnect from that person. I do this by a simple prayer, asking for both of us to be energetically disconnected; I sometimes just wave the energy around as if destroying the cord, so to speak. Then muscle test to make sure you are disconnected.

The last rule is you must NEVER, NEVER, NEVER muscle test without the individual's permission, especially, to uncover information about them. You do not do Muscle Testing to learn about family members, acquaintances, friends, etc. I believe at this point you have opened doors to entities to be attached and give you information.

Muscle Testing is used to read the body and what occurred in the past or is currently happening. When you ask questions about the future, Muscle Testing is no longer effective and you can receive incorrect answers. It also should not be used to get financial answers for personal gain.

Muscle Testing is from God to help anyone find the root of their problems quickly. Satanic Ritual Abuse survivors will greatly benefit from Muscle Testing because of the mind being so fragmented. Proxy testing for survivors can be very helpful because of the possibility something will take over the body to answer.

Like all things, Muscle Testing can be used in a negative way. I have shared some of those ways.

Muscle Testing can be used without Body Code, but Body Code brings in a whole new level of information to heal quickly.

According to Nelson (2020), "We believe the subconscious mind exerts an unseen yet profound influence over how we behave and feel — and it's also keenly aware of exactly what your body needs to get well. To access these vast stores of knowledge, it's our belief that we need to bypass the conscious mind and speak directly to the subconscious. This is where Muscle Testing comes in."

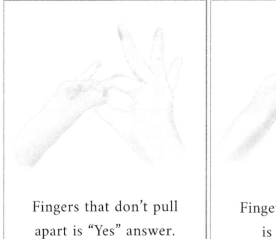

Fingers that don't pull apart is "Yes" answer.

Fingers that pull apart is "No" answer.

PICTURE BY NIC YOUNGBLOOD

FOURTH TECHNIQUE
BODY CODE

"The body is made up of pure energy," said Nelson (2022). "Every organ, tissue, and cell is made up of energy, and so are the non-physical aspects of yourself. Thoughts, beliefs, memories, emotions — are also made up of energy. When viewed from this standpoint, you can see how important energetic balance is to your overall health, and just how easy it really is to effect change.

"The human body has a unique, intrinsic ability to recover and mend from all types of stress, trauma, and illness. The ability to heal oneself is contingent on the correct circumstances.

"Your body will not be able to mend itself as well as it should if it is out of balance. Imbalances allow for the accumulation of issues over time. The Body Code is a cutting-edge energy healing technique for the whole body, mind, and spirit. Dr. Bradley Nelson, a holistic chiropractor, created it." (Website: www.discoverhealing.com)

I was privileged to interview Dr. Nelson three times for my Worldwide Transformational Summits, which started in 2016. I have attended his seminars as well. Dr. Nelson shared that "the quality of the question is the quality of the answer that you will receive." This statement has been true for me all these years. Therefore, get specific with your questions. You may want to muscle test to find the right question.

Dr. Nelson said in interviews he cannot take any credit for the development of Body Code. He gives all credit to God. When you begin to work through Body Code, I think it is easy to agree with Dr. Nelson. I don't see how a man could develop this amazing guide to healing in all areas. The Lord taught him this expansive method of healing that covers the mind, body, and spirit. Truly, there is nothing Body Code does not cover in his guide to finding the root of any problem using Muscle Testing.

Body Code is an application that has over 760 categories to find the root of a physical, emotional, spiritual, or mental problem. In one interview I asked him why he had categories of entities, dead human spirits that he calls disembodied spirits, curses, and energy weapons. He said, "I had to because too many people are dealing with these issues."

Some categories can be highly problematic, with a cascade effect on other areas. It was 2017 when Dr. Nelson discussed this. He was far ahead of everyone else. I really did not fully understand what it all meant in the healing journey, but if you don't deal with entities, disembodied spirits, curses, energy weapons, and psychic attacks it will be almost impossible to get free.

Other areas include emotions, organs, glands, bones, addiction, nutrition (with long lists of food and herbs you should or shouldn't eat), dental, circuits and systems, heart walls, even someone leaving the body. Most of the time, you'd be surprised to know the real root of the problem.

Body Code has saved my life in so many ways. I feel it is an absolute necessity as a tool in helping Satanic Ritual Abuse clients get free. Without Body Code, it would be impossible for me to find every piece of my clients' programs. It also has helped me address victims of sexual abuse and trauma. Working with the little child parts is absolutely incredible! Body Code rapidly changes some clients; also, they're not re-traumatized. It works perfectly with Tapping. I could not be more grateful for the Lord's work through Dr. Nelson — creating a healing method saving millions of lives around the world. I know Dr. Nelson has been doing this for many years. I was introduced to Body Code in 2016 and 2017.

You may ask, "Is Body Code made for Satanic Ritual Abuse?" My first answer would be "no"; however, due to its sophisticated, nuanced qualities, Body Code can produce magnificent results. I suppose it can be used for anything.

I know it is one of the greatest tools to anyone who has mind-control programming. I will share a hack that I do that is definitely not taught by Body Code, but it has helped me so much. The unconscious mind and physical body communicate, showing you answers the best they can through Body Code. Sometimes the answer is not the title of something, but in a page of description. Each category has a brief description including directions on how to remove the root cause of the problem. I will muscle test each sentence, and it can have a word I need. That word may guide me to the next tiny step in helping the client.

Question to ask using Body Code-
I begin with a very important question:
What is the underlying cause of...?

You may choose a topic that makes no sense. That is ok. Keep testing until you understand the full answer. If Muscle Testing says your hunch is not the topic, try testing the description, try testing each sentence, and then try testing each word until you find the answers.

Then you ask...
Do I need to know more about this? If the answer is "yes"...

Muscle test and start at the home page again. You will continue Muscle Testing until the survivor's body says there are no more answers to this particular question. There may be several links to get to the root of the answer. That is why it is imperative to ask good questions. Sometimes you may need to ask the question in a different way to get the full answer.

I learned all of this through probably more than 2,000 hours of practice. Play with it, have fun.

(Please go to the Body Code Chapter for specific directions. You should learn the entire curriculum for a full understanding.)

Before going further, I need to explain the use of a rare earth magnet with Body Code. Meridians are energetic pathways in the body. The rare earth magnet can be used to physically heal a cult survivor's unconscious emotions. Tapping also uses meridians. Body Code uses the general meridian systems. Move the magnet from the middle of the forehead starting at the eyebrow, then go down the middle of the head all the way to the neck's base. Or you can use the spine, the other general meridian system. Think of it this way: We are addressing the physical, spiritual, and mental areas of a survivor because these areas are affected by trauma. A survivor and professional may use the magnet to calm the body, especially when a survivor needs to comfort or release pain from a part/alter. The magnet will be important when addressing alarm systems, demons, and other issues.

Here is what I suggest to buy for a magnet:
"Neosmuk Fishing Magnet, 550 lb Pull Strong Magnets Heavy Duty Big Rare Earth Magnet, 2.5" Large Magnet for Remover, Super Neodymium High Power Magnet with Handle for Tag, Shop, Lifting and Pick up"
Serial Numbers:
AZ:9JJ6BWE6G8BTNGWU7W9ZPMZ4IM
Amazon

This is a powerful rare earth magnet required in the removal process. I don't fully understand why the body responds so well to this magnet or any strong, rare earth, neodymium magnet, but it plays a significant role in the process of removal — which you will soon understand.

Included in my techniques are Bloodline Cleansing and the Courts of Heaven. (Explained in earlier chapters)

Bloodline Cleansing

Bloodline Cleansing is integral to someone getting free because all cult members have family line demons attached to them. Survivors can get stuck because the family demons are not leaving due to their legal claim from past generations. Family demons will undertake a great deal to stop a survivor's healing. Bloodline Cleansing must be executed several times for the survivor to become completely free. This process is something the survivor can do by themselves to speed the process.

Bloodline Cleansing is an absolutely pivotal tool for any professional or survivor.

Courts of Heaven

Use the Courts of Heaven while working on large programming removals. I've encountered multiple miracles in the courts, though I don't always go to the Courts of Heaven in the removal. Therapists, survivors, and others have the right to visit and ask for help in the Courts of Heaven anytime. I sometimes go to the Courts because of the complexity of removing certain programs. In the Courts, I receive improved knowledge, strength, and aid to heal alters or revoke legal rights of high up demons. We are calling upon the highest authority to help in a programming removal, which at times can be complex. In consulting the Courts of Heaven, we may witness healing miracles of alters or brainstorm ideas about, for example, retrieving programming pieces formerly overlooked. I've witnessed certain processes that would normally take hours to last only minutes. I have witnessed huge programs collapse in the Courts of Heaven. I have seen core alters integrate in an hour instead of years. The miracles can be endless when you call upon God the Father and His son, Jesus Christ.

The Courts of Heaven have become invaluable to my professional work and in survivors' lives.

(For more information, refer to Bloodline Cleansing and Courts of Heaven chapters.)

53

REMOVAL OF PROGRAMS

Now that you've learned about the general techniques, I want to show you how to use them in the deprogramming process.

I begin by saying a prayer over the client and myself. I ask the client's parts to come back into their body; thus, his or her alters can witness every action we take, having the broad, truthful picture. (This process is explained in an earlier chapter.)

I then ask the survivor's unconscious mind to show us all the program pieces we're working on without any illusion.

Next, I command all demons to be bound and stripped of all their authority, and cast them out of our presence. (Refer to previous chapters for details.)

We then command any parts/alters that intend to sabotage the session to be lovingly bound, entering a place of safety where they have no power and they will not be harmed, *but* they must listen to and observe all things said and conducted in the session. (It is important for the parts to begin waking up to the full truth instead of what they know only in their world.)

In the prayer of protection and setting up the session, I am ready to map out the programming. I will usually use Tapping for a little bit to calm the client's nervous system. We use Tapping throughout the session to ensure the client remains stable. When emotions become high, we just address them with Tapping — no matter what's occurring in deprogramming. Demons often try to stop the process; for some reason, they have permission to torment despite us casting them out. So, we just cast out again. Typically, this happens many times in a session due to the previous downloads of demons. Just anticipate that you are going to have to cast out a few times in a session. A demon may stay, claiming he has legal permission. Unfortunately, parts of the survivor will respond "yes" to the demon's statement. Therefore, you must invalidate the authority of the parts/alters to stop removal or give permission. If the demons have legal rights and you're unable to dismantle at that moment, bind them and send them away during the session time. This is always done in the name of Jesus Christ.

Tapping is a good foundation to all I do. It's not only for calming down clients. We sometimes use Tapping to get needed information. When the nervous system is calmed, it seems to loosen the unconscious mind. It's a great time to ask the unconscious mind questions using the "first thought" method.

If we are working on specific programming and more information is needed, I use one of my tools to prompt answers. I do this often because the technique offers a new angle of finding all the pieces to any problem.

"First Thought" Method

I will tell the client's unconscious mind, "I am going to ask you a question. Answer me with your first thought." If the client moves past the first thought, she's entered the logical mind, which doesn't have the answer. The practice is absolutely fantastic for anyone at any time. You can do it with yourself if you're looking for answers. Usually, the answers will surprise you. Go with it because of two rules of the unconscious mind. The unconscious mind will always answer first and will always answer honestly. Then the logical mind comes in to explain how that cannot be true.

"Because" Method

The Second question uses the word "because." Example: "I am feeling angry because..."

Using the word *because* works beautifully with the *first thought* question. Typically, I will say something like:

"You are angry because..." "First thought?" If the individual thinks for too long, I stop him because I now know he accessed the logical mind for the answer.

The word *because* can be used for writing exercises to address suppressed memories. Let the unconscious write freely without thinking.

The two simple techniques are robust tools if you want to quickly tap the root of the issue.

When I'm ready to Map Out the program, I command a survivor's unconscious mind to show me the pieces to the program so we can remove them. You must remove them in the order you received the answers through Muscle Testing and Body Code. The person's unconscious mind knows how she was programmed as the mind recorded the experience using all five senses. The unconscious mind knows how to do all of this safely. It's vital you command the unconscious mind to do whatever is needed. The unconscious can accomplish goals at the speed of light, so use its power to heal the survivor or yourself. The programmers certainly understand this. It's imperative to begin using the survivor's unconscious for his benefit. I have used Mapping Out for about 6 years. It's a very powerful tool!

Next is an example of commanding the unconscious mind to execute some dynamic work. This astonishing yet simple technique may bewilder some.

When you get into removing programming, the most common elements include an alarm system, suicide program, bombs, booby traps, and triggers attached to the body's organs.

This simple exercise is very successful in shutting down the triggers that can cause a survivor to spin out of control.

Alarm System and Suicide Programming Removal

Example: I command the unconscious mind to find all alarm systems, booby traps, bombs, suicide programs, triggers, and anything else that would sabotage or cause any harm, including all codes, colors, symbols, letters, numbers, instructions, commands, programmers' names, dates, times, etc., and give them to Jesus Christ to be destroyed. Your unconscious mind will find it all at the speed of light so there is nothing left. Command the unconscious mind, "You will not recreate it." Make sure it is disconnected from all organs or anywhere else in the body.

Run a magnet over the head 10 times starting from the middle of the forehead, moving down the head to the base of the neck. Then say, "By the power of the blood of Jesus Christ, all this is now destroyed." This works. My clients have not encountered any big problems with alarm systems going off or suicide programs engaging. Professionals can do this technique in a therapeutic setting or survivors may take charge and do it themselves. I do Muscle Testing to see if it's complete. I will also ask, through Muscle Testing, "Do I need to know anything else about these alarms, booby traps, suicide programs, or triggers of any kind?" Most times the answer is no. You will find that alarm systems are always tied to an organ or something else in the body. We then use the rare earth neodymium magnet over the head for complete removal.

This process may sound too good to be true. All I can say is, "It works!" Instead of someone having bad experiences with suicide programs or bizarre events, you just do this simple technique. In this technique, we're using the powerful unconscious mind to do the work because the unconscious invented the alarms. The unconscious mind works swiftly, so use it. Moreover, turn over all the items to Jesus Christ to destroy. The unconscious mind always obeys Jesus Christ. The survivor and I use a physical action to release the energy of the alarms from the mind and body followed by calling upon the blood of Jesus Christ, a power so far-reaching it can immediately destroy all alarms systems. I continue to be stunned by the technique's effectiveness. So powerful yet simple. Survivors can use the method on themselves if they've been triggered, further enhancing the tool's value.

CONTINUATION OF REMOVAL PROCESS

The process of removing programs may last hours and sometimes can't be finished in a session. I often ask the survivor's unconscious mind to show us what we can do to-day only. Many times, you can remove some of the program and put the rest of the procedure on hold.

Let's say you are at the end and ask if there is anything else we need to do before we remove the program. I will question the survivor using the *first thought* technique and muscle test. If the answer is "no," then we proceed to the removal process. If the answer is "yes," continue until there is nothing left to do.

This part is not the opening prayer before you begin your removal work. This prayer is for when you have all the information you need, you've mapped out the program's puzzle pieces, and you're ready to remove the program.

(To all skeptics, please be patient. I too was skeptical of the process' simplicity. But God works this way, not in complexity.)

1. When the removal process is ready, I begin with a prayer, ask Heavenly Father to help us, and thank him for his guidance. I ask to please help us be aware of anything we missed or need to do.
2. I now use the Map I've been working on and pray out loud every piece in the order I was given through Body Code and Muscle Testing.
3. Cast out any demons.
4. With each piece of removal, you may have to address whatever arises. That is ok; you are still in prayer and do not have to start over. Sometimes a removed piece can lead to an action that must be taken, such as working with a part/alter.
5. The pieces will now be removed with the rare earth magnet. I sometimes have clients do this when I am describing the pieces of the program. You can wait until the end, as well.
6. I muscle test and ask the client if we have anything else to do? It's not uncommon after arriving at the

end to need additional pieces of information. Until you removed the first map, going to the next removal stage may have been impossible.

7. If nothing is left to remove, I finish my prayer with the most important you will say: "I now command the power of the blood of Jesus Christ through the atonement to destroy all this programming and wash clean (client's name) of all that we worked on so the client can truly be free from Lucifer's kingdom. We ask you to cast out any demons still holding on and revoke any legal claim they have with (client's name). In the name of Jesus Christ. Amen." (Please feel free to say what you think is important. You just want to say, "By the power of Jesus Christ's blood, then ask for what you need. This power comes from the atonement, which gives Christ authority above all things including what Lucifer and his fallen angels have done in evil. This is powerful in the healing of someone from ritual abuse.)

8. Use the powerful neodymium magnet down the general meridian system starting at the middle of the eyebrows and proceeding down the center of the head to the base of the neck — do this 10 times. If there are curses or the need to cast out demons; you will start from the neck and go to the eyebrow ten times.

We have now addressed emotions physically, emotionally, and spiritually. Programming uses all three.

9. We now have to go back and check with the client to see how he's doing. You may need or want to tap with the client and any parts/alters to release additional stressful emotions. Most of the time the client feels peaceful and better after removal.

10. I now check to see if anything was triggered, such as alarm systems, booby traps, bombs, or suicide programming. If anything, we use the fast alarm removal technique.

11. Check again what's going on with the client.

12. You will now want to work with the parts/alters for integration. This is a process. Not every alter wants to integrate; sometimes, alters cannot integrate because they are still connected to other programs. Once again, be patient and help your client be patient. It will happen with these parts who will know the whole truth when they comprehend the lies; the parts will want to be one with the survivor. You cannot make it happen or push it. Act with sensitivity to the process.

13. One way to open the door of understanding for the alter/part is to ask questions. If there is not an answer, try something else. If you ask the right question, you can usually get alters to start talking. They must begin to learn the truth about themselves and the real world.

If you are successfully working through the core foun-

dational programming, you will work with the core parts and alters. The ultimate goal is to remove the programming, bring all parts back together as one, and to remove the Stronghold demon forever.

Use Bloodline Cleansing often and the Courts of Heaven to assist the Removal Process.

55

ADDITIONAL POINTS TO REMEMBER IN THE REMOVAL PROCESS

Patterns in Programming

Professionals and survivors must understand there is a template in all programming. The foundation of the programming in all Illuminati, Military, Freemasonry, and Fertility cults is based on the Tree of Death. If a person comes from any of these groups, they have foundational programming. Similar programs include Alice in Wonderland, the Wizard of Oz, Sleeping Beauty, and Mickey Mouse. There will be similar programming in other areas such as the Computer and the Grid, Carousel.

Cults have a pattern of programming because if misfortune befalls one programmer, another programmer can pick up and know the layout of a member's programming. At each age, a child in the cult is taught specific programs; each stage is built upon the previous, according to ability and training. The programmers know how children's minds work, what they can do physically and mentally by age.

Alarms and Codes

Just take it for granted that alarms are attached to every program. Look for codes to open a program. I learned a long time ago there's no need to delve into the specifics to remove it. Simply go by the premise that codes and alarm systems accompany everything you do.

When I went through therapy long ago, the therapist mistakenly thought it necessary to input each code, number, letter, color, and signature of the programmer. YOU DO NOT HAVE TO DO THIS. I will explain once more.

Let me give an example of why to avoid specific codes. I am not saying I do not address codes and alarms. I do, but I just don't have to spell out each one. It's not safe and codes do not have to be said out loud to be fully removed. For example, a survivor goes into therapy and decides she will remove Alice in Wonderland. Still, she has no idea what Alice is connected to. Let's say the therapist believes the specific codes came from the client, except in reality a client's *part* gave you partially false codes. The therapist is oblivious and continues the removal. Although he knows the alarm code, he doesn't know a hidden alarm system and suicide program remain. The removal process begins but things don't seem to be going well. Overcome with panic attacks, the survivor feels as if she's going to die. At that point, the therapist has no way of obtaining the client's remaining information. The pair simultaneously trigger another system. They have no idea what to do.

Despite the above story being fictional, it often happens in sessions. However, I figured out survivors and professionals can skip this tedious operation of identifying all the codes and alarms. Remember, our unconscious mind can work faster than the speed of lightning. Treat the unconscious mind as such. READY? HERE IT GOES...

You state, "In the name of Jesus Christ, I command the unconscious mind to find all alarm systems, bombs, traps, suicide programs, triggers, all codes, symbols, colors, letters, numbers, jobs, dates, signatures, instructions, and anything else — give all the items to Jesus Christ and He will destroy everything. You are not to recreate anything. We command all demons attached to depart. Your legal claim is revoked, and by the blood of Jesus Christ, the alarm systems are demolished. In the name of Jesus Christ. Amen."

I have not had one case where this failed to work in thousands of cases. Yes, in the removal process alarms will be going off. Just use this method before the stage happens, when it happens, and to prevent it from happening. This is a way to handle suicide programs going off before, during, or after our work. I believe it is because we are using the spiritual, mental, and physical method. Mental: We command to remove what is to be done. Spiritual: We ask in the spirit of Jesus Christ to help us do this. Physical: We physically remove this with the neodymium rare earth magnet from our body. We can use other modalities such as Tapping, Body Code, Havening, etc.

You may have to use this technique with walls coming for the purpose of halting your work.

Muscle test to check if all was removed. If yes, proceed. If not, figure out what you missed or didn't do and proceed.

You must understand all areas of programming are spiritual, physical, and emotional. It is important to address all three.

Checking for the Re-Creation of a Program

When a program is removed, can the original program be re-created? Usually what happens is programs intertwine, so if you remove one it can be recreated. In other words, the original program has pieces in other places that may be triggered if a program's been removed. Oftentimes, the programmer will hide pieces of the program; if somehow the program is removed, the action triggers a piece — let's say in the grid to start recreating the original. This is very common with the Tree of Death and the flower or flowers around it. If you remove the tree, the flowers may recreate the tree.

After each program removal, it's important to ask questions to make sure it cannot be recreated or to make sure the program is still connected to another one. Also, be certain you don't abandon parts of a survivor's humanity in the programming, worlds, or underworld. You also have to ask whether any part of the survivor has the ability to recreate the program.

Once they know the answers, survivors and professionals can use the same techniques, though they must command the unconscious to destroy all parts of anything left and to remove all parts from the memory of all parts/alters. Hand over to Jesus to ensure it's finished, guaranteeing there is no way for this program to return. Finally, ask for the blood of Jesus Christ to speak on the client's behalf and ask Jesus to destroy all programming and wash the client clean. This upholds the arrangement.

Safe Places

Safe places are created by the client so different alters/parts can go to a place and feel safe. I like to put the place under the authority of Jesus Christ so He can block entities trying to communicate with or harm the parts. I do not tell clients of the place's appearance or atmosphere. Safe places are different for each person.

I use safe places to fortify the safety of parts/alters if the survivor and I cannot finish the work. If we plan to not meet for a week, then we create a safe place to last a week.

I not only protect alters in a safe place, but sometimes we have to create a place in which the programming can't be triggered. I also put this under the authority of Jesus Christ. We have to sometimes bind all demons having a legal right to the survivor so they can't interfere while the survivor and I are apart.

XXI

DRUGS AND ALCOHOL WILL BE USED IN PROGRAMMING

You must address drugs and alcohol in the removal process. Other substances or behaviors that were possibly used in programming need to be addressed to ensure complete removal.

56

ADDICTIONS AND PROGRAMMING

Many in this world feel overwhelmed and have nowhere to go for help and healing. Addictions are a double-edged sword. They give you temporary relief from pain, but leave the person more hopeless, lonely, and confused.

Satan has a way of making a person believe she will never overcome her addiction. The addict is not worthy of love or forgiveness. It's so easy to say, "Why does it matter anymore? No one loves me or cares." The woeful addict goes to his trusted friend — alcohol, drugs, sex, food, gambling — who engages in further destruction.

Addictions are a means of escaping the pain and trauma of abuse. Cult survivors commonly have an addiction. This is how they comfort themselves. Programmers will include drugs, alcohol, energy drinks, food, etc., to keep the programming running. A child's brain isn't equipped to handle Satanic Ritual Abuse; it's human nature to seek an outside substance for comfort. At 5 years old, I wasn't getting love from anyone, so I decided to get love from sugar and caffeine. Turning 13, I went to drugs, which lasted until 18. At 18 years old, I drank heavily to 21, but then found the Lord and a new life. I have struggled with other things throughout my life. Much later, I realized I also had programming to use drugs and alcohol — to make sure I wouldn't remember.

I've had programming tied to alcohol, drugs, energy drinks, and sugar as continual anchors to forget. The programmers are using a great deal of Neuro Linguistic Programming anchoring. As I've removed many programs, most had a substance tied to them. The addiction is actually part of the program. At the 17-year-old ritual, the cult had not given me food or water. On the last day, the cult gave me beer with the statements, "Beer saved your life. You cannot live without beer. It is the only way for the pain to stop. You must drink beer." At the time it was true. I had nothing to drink for seven days. In that way alcohol did save my life and removed pain.

I feel that survivors are very hard on themselves about their addictions. You must understand that you had nothing else to provide comfort. I know it is hard to hear, but forgive yourself; you've been doing your best. You've been to the bottom of hell, so FORGIVE YOURSELF!

What if no programming was involved in your addiction? What is really the cause of addictions? Researchers have found the root cause of addiction is a lack of connection; I would add, not feeling loved. We need connection with other people. When we don't have it, we turn to food, drink, exercise, or porn. Anything to make us feel connected.

Addictions will always be the coverup for trauma. For example, the Ace Study found the more trauma you have, the more likely you are to have an addiction.

Addictions to sugar example: Sugar may be related to a good feeling of cooking pies with grandma. The unconscious mind blends the two ideas because the person wants to feel loved by grandma, but she can't stop eating pie. The truth is the pie is never going to love you. That is why we must disconnect grandma's love with pie. In Eutaptics, we teach the unconscious mind to connect to grandma's love without pie. It's annoying at times; our unconscious mind joins two concepts to form a nonsensical idea. Just like the woman who's suffered sexual abuse. The only way she feels safe is to be fat. When she was skinny, men were all over her. Logically the woman does not want to be fat, but the unconscious mind says, "We are going to be fat so no one desires us or touches us."

I have a fond memory as a coach with the Drug and Alcohol Treatment Center in Hawaii. The practitioners worked with the residents using addiction protocol training in

Eutaptics/FasterEFT. The Eutaptics founder hand-picked the individuals at Habilitat. I visited four times with other practitioners. It was such a great learning experience and privilege. The success rate was very high using the addiction protocol. Each time we worked non-stop for 10 days. We were able to see most of the residents. It was so uplifting to see them change, to see them smiling. The experience may have been the first time they felt authentic relief without drugs.

The treatment center was a 2-year program; many were there on the condition they'd be going to jail or getting help. We saw the worst of the worst addictions — meth and heroin. These drugs had completely destroyed residents' lives. Our job was to release their painful traumas as well as releasing them from their "ritual" drug of choice. There was not one person we treated who didn't endure horrific trauma. I remember one person who, at 5 years old, lost his parents and was left to live on the streets.

I have heard people say, "Well, I am eating too much sugar, but I'm not like a heroin addict." I disagree. No matter what the substance or behavior is, the reason is the same. The person is trying to escape the pain. Addicts feel comforted by different things. The sugar addict and heroin addict are more similar than we realize. One does have more severe consequences, but both are unable to handle their emotions sober.

Addictions are proof we're partly empty inside. Workaholics are great escape artists. If they just stay busy enough, they don't have to look at _____. Whatever you are running from, there will come a day when you cannot run anymore. You will have to face your fear.

If you have an addiction, you may ask yourself, "What am I trying to cover up or run away from?"

While I've shared many reasons for addictions, we must not forget their outcome. The outcome allows Lucifer to use our weakness against us, to lead us farther away from God. Satan is a master deceiver. He entices us at first. "It's ok, there's nothing wrong with just one little time." Then eventually we find ourselves down a path of self-destruction while Satan and his minions are laughing to victory. One more soul destroyed.

Some people have learned to disconnect from the addict, causing heavy shame and isolation. There is a time when disconnection must occur for safety reasons. But all too often, a family member's judgment and condemnation *is* the only response to an addict. This will never help the addict to quit. He already feels worthless. If you want an addict to stop, the root cause must be tackled. When the reason is found, the emotional pain can be released, and the addiction disintegrates.

All things are possible with God's help. Finding the right tools to address the addiction is imperative. If you don't release the underlying cause, the smoker who quits will turn to food, the drug addict who quits will turn to caffeine. The addiction will always find something to ritualize unless you find the pain's root cause. Releasing the emotional pain is KEY!

I believe some addictions cannot be overcome without God's help. Of course, people must realize addiction means demonic attachments or unclean spirits will come.

There are some addictions that require the casting out of demons and dead human spirits who had addictions while living. On the other side, the spirits refuse to accept Jesus Christ. They roam the earth for just one moment of ecstasy and your body is their target.

Sometimes we pray for relief from our addiction, but it doesn't come right away. Don't give up. The help will come and it may be in baby steps. If the addiction has lasted years, it may not be an overnight recovery. You may fall many times before healing. Just never give up.

If you're a survivor of mind control, the programming may have to be removed to halt the addiction. Alcohol and drugs are powerful tools for programmers. If you can't stop and you don't understand why you're doing it, check if your programming includes the habits you can't stop. I was drinking, and I didn't even like it, but I had to drink. I couldn't say no. That is programming. Every time the survivor consumes the drug, the mind is wiped clean all over again.

A common energy drink called Monster is used in programming. Monster becomes the signal and anchor, often connecting to an alter monster. It may trigger many other instructions. Cults commonly do this with Red Bull and many other drinks and foods. Each substance will mean different things to the alter inside. Pornography or video games are often used in MK Ultra programming. I have a friend who said military men are hooked on video games about war and murder.

When I was updated with NWO programming, the cult installed a complex addiction program to hold the programming in place. It contained multiple substances. Shortly after the programming, I developed a ferocious desire to drink a beer. I could not say no. I will never forget that.

Every survivor must be hopeful. The Lord will help you. Rest assured there will be days when Satan will whisper, "You will never be free, you can't do it, just give up." Turn to the Lord then and cast out Lucifer. You will never be alone if you call out to the only being who can save. You will receive strength and knowledge about how to triumph. YOU ARE NOT ALONE!

Programming with Substances

The following piece shows how drugs and alcohol are used in a programming system.

An alter can receive drugs for the system, activating it. If the system has not been fed in a while, alarms go off, making the cult member feel as if she'll die without a drink. The system is triggered, sparking agony, panic, a flood of memories. A survivor may go berserk if he begins to remember. The urge to inject himself becomes overwhelming. The anxiety, the fear may even lead to suicide. Drug and alcohol programming will have codes, alarms, symbols, etc. Remember this is a program.

Drugs act as a buffer between the conscious mind and memories of trauma the system carries. The drugs flow to an alter, revealing information to the unconscious mind. Flooding occurs as the cult member takes his drink or injects her drug. The rush may snowball to five times the amount a programmer intended. A dark, growing formation brings a hazy forgetfulness upon the cult member, convincing her to forget what lies behind the wall. Many alters begin drowning in the system's bath of drugs and alcohol, while other parts can't reach the substance they depend on.

Alters can manipulate people into feeling drunk or drugged when they've taken nothing. Different systems may have different directions regarding what each substance means. One system may be programmed with food and energy drinks, another with drugs, and another with alcohol. Obviously, this creates quite the problem for survivors.

If cult members do not remember or do not do what they're told, they won't have the urge to use narcotics. A drug may only be triggered if survivors are remembering.

Cults may even program individuals to not eat healthy — no vegetables, fruit, or even water.

Each substance may have a different meaning according to specific times; cults may also turn an addiction program on and off based on the person's behavior. Cults may program members to gain or lose weight according to a member's mission. Indeed, programmers unearth and exploit the individual's weaknesses. Some people are drawn to sex.

What the survivor and professional can do is ask for all codes and alarms to be removed, then deliver healing codes and conduct the usual techniques to heal all alters from all substances. I've seen intricate addiction and substance trigger programs. Cult members may have a built-in system to kill themselves with a drug without making it look suspicious.

EXAMPLE OF TRIGGERS IN SYSTEM OF PROGRAMMING

Drug---Keeps System in place---There is threat to system---Threat to system's triggers---Take Drugs---Alters are activated---Reminder to forget---warning if you remember you will die---Person forgets---Person begins to remember---Urge to take drug---Overdose feelings---System in danger, shut down, reminder of death or may even be killed.

One thing triggers the next until a person is brought back under control or killed.

MISCELLANEOUS

MIND WIPING

M ind Wiping is done to all survivors of the Illuminati Programming/Military, and it's been highly effective for decades. Cults are achieving the same objective as portrayed in movies. The technology leaves the victim with no memory. Cult groups also mind wipe with drugs. Do you remember the movie *Men in Black*, when Tommy Lee Jones pulls out his shiny Neutralizer tool to wipe bystanders' memories clean? Well, this is similar. The refined technology preys on all five senses to complete the task.

The following information is from my experience, though my guess is cults have developed more advanced technology to cover their crimes. They can wipe out hours, weeks, and years in some cases. Most programming sessions are followed by mind wiping.

Additionally, cults may use demons to manipulate the hypothalamus, transporting it to another dimension or underworld. They also train alters to withhold memories from other parts. In programming, many amnesia walls created in the survivor's mind may actually be programs. Not only are cults effective in erasing the past, they also implant false memories. As long as the unconscious can be tricked into believing illusions, the conscious makes it real.

Every three to four years, cult members are reconditioned. A person's memories are never really gone, just deeply hidden in the unconscious. Satanic cults devote great attention to mind wiping. If you can't remember, the group controls you.

What's more, cults fear members who begin recalling their special skills, training, or foreign languages. Survivors' expertise in many areas can be shocking, whereas cults want members to blend in. There were many times a prominent politician employs an odd sexual desire or is sexually perverted; a fellow cult member will be created just for him under mind control so the person never remembers what was done.

The handler, programmer, slave owner, and others involved in sexual perversion can't be known. Leaders of the Illuminati, Druids, Military, and Fertility cults rely on mind wiping to protect them from victims remembering. Over recent years, survivors are truly proving them wrong.

That is why cult leaders are so addicted to power. Think about it. A leader may brazenly do anything to another person, violating her in the most awful ways. The next day she attends a party with her rapist but does not even know his identity. Mind wiping allows the evil cult members to have great power over another person. Like a perfect dream for secret societies.

Some programmers are better than others. A careless programmer's mistake might cause the system to crumble — a great day for the survivor. Henry Kissinger was brilliant at mind wiping. He wanted to make sure I never remembered him. It worked. I did not remember him until I was in my 50's. I was the perfect sex slave to the many clients he had. I wonder how much they paid for the services Kissinger provided. What a career! Like so many of them. A successful career in politics; behind closed doors, however...

Joseph Mengele was probably one of my major programmers while I was young. Because my programming started in the womb, it seemed that every cult group had been trying to install programs. From the womb to 7 years old, I was heavily programmed. Every cult wanted to install its beliefs, false gods, entities, programming, and Satan himself to own me. A true battle for a soul. The Illuminati, Freemasons, Fertility Cult, Military, they all use witchcraft.

The easiest to remember is Satanism. I next remember the Military, the Illuminati, and Fertility Cult programming.

Demons are a huge part of programming and not remembering. Fallen angels are great at mind wiping. If you start to remember, demons will distract you or cause misfortune, so you don't try anymore. They will absolutely attempt to disrupt professional counseling sessions. They also make you hear voices. They want you to think you're crazy, that all you recall could have never happened. Demons can make you fall asleep if you start to remember. Distract, distract, distract until you forget! If nothing else works, demons will persuade you to use drugs and alcohol to forget.

Can our unconscious mind do its own mind wipe to keep us safe? Yes, it can and it does!

Recap:
1. Tool to wipe the mind.
2. Trauma and programming to forget.
3. Demons.
4. Unconscious mind's natural ability to suppress trauma.

When you consider these points, it may seem impossible to get free, but there is hope. There is one truth that stands above all: God can heal anything. The power of the human soul is much stronger than anything Satanic cults can muster. Our soul they cannot touch. Then let's start relying on the soul. No matter how much cults invest to remove it, they CANNOT EVER! Think about this for a minute. Millions all over the world and their families before them have survived this horrific torture. Here we are against all odds. Yes, we are a little beaten up, but we survived.

Cults may microchip everyone, program people to all kind of machines, make us suffer indignities, and torture us to the point of death. Still, cults will never capture our souls.

God the Father created us well before this earthly experience. We are his. We lived before, and after this mortal existence we will live again. Not any of Lucifer's tools or minions can stop that. Lucifer did not give us life despite cults persuading our many parts it's true. Lucifer cannot create or procreate; therefore, he cannot give life.

A meme said, "We just implant the idea and expect the people to create it for them." Exactly. That's exactly what programming is. If the unconscious mind believes it as truth, the mind creates whatever it is told. We were the ones who created their sick illusions. Without us doing the programmers' work, cults would have no power at all. Cooperation mandates torture. Evil organizations torture people until they submit. "Create or die." So, we create to stay alive. It ends when we stop creating for them.

The truth is the cults are weak and powerless. Get real. Do you mean cults resort to the excruciating torment of individuals to coax those people into agreement? Not only that, but the cults are so powerful they have to make you forget everything you know about them. Wow, that is real power *alright*. Not really. It actually proves exactly how weak, pathetic, and sickly Lucifer and his minions are. Weak cowards torturing people to convince them of the company's many good ideas.

An individual becomes powerful because she wins others' respect by using her free will to allow others to use theirs. The individual honors a person's wishes when he says, "No." She is mighty because she loves and values the other souls. They lift him up. God made us to be that powerful. When we love others, value their free will, and listen to them, we have learned to be a leader.

So, it's time to own your mind and memories. You are powerful! You are a child of God!

As the recovering survivor begins to heal, the unconscious mind's walls will topple. The healthy, conscious mind can begin to remember the bits and pieces that will transform into the long seasons, the childhood, a marriage made in heaven. The process does take time. Most survivors were hurt every day, maybe numerous times a day. It's important to understand that healing takes place in layers. By the same token, I don't think healing should take years either. I believe God is giving us ways to heal quickly. There's not much time left.

If you are wondering, "Do I have to remember everything?" Of course not. That would require the rest of your life. Although we don't have to remember every detail, I do believe we must know our past. I've also had clients ask, "Do I really have to remember?" My belief is yes. A woman once told her story and I'd like to paraphrase what she said. She explained the memories stolen from her are *hers*. She said she must know what's been done, otherwise the cults may control her. The programmer counts on obedience by annihilating memory. That is why it's so, so important to know the pieces of the puzzle — what's been done — inside of you. If you don't know the cult's misdeeds, how can you undo the programming in your unconscious mind? They will still be able to turn and twist you in any direction they want.

Let's take back the stolen goods so no one can manipulate us. This is *your* life, *your* memories. Don't let the cult hold your memories because you are afraid of knowing what really happened.

SEX MAGIC

What is sex magic? First of all, it's witchcraft. Satanic cults use entities to desecrate sex and what God ordained it to be. All sex magic is to honor Lucifer and is in all training of the Illuminati, Fertility Cult, and Freemasons. Sex magic is using sex in evil ways.

I would like to explain something called *Tantra Sex*. Clients have expressed that when they're sleeping, they can have an orgasm. This happens for many reasons. Witches may be sending curses to someone, which causes the orgasm. As orgasm is reached, the receiver of the curse has just opened the portal to receive it.

This kind of sex training is done at a very young age, considered a skill of training that must be mastered. Orgasms in the middle of the night will happen with a dream that some-one wishes to create in another person. This can be done at rituals when the spirit has left the body.

Everything is about the orgasm in Lucifer's kingdom. Ev-ery evil thing is created around sex. The orgasm is sealing up something and making it valid. It is like an oath that seals the deal.

If an individual wants to stop a curse from being sent to them, the person cannot have an orgasm. If an orgasm occurs, it is a sign of victory for the opposite side and accep-tance of the gift.

Tantra Sex can be used at other times by consenting adults. The practice will be expected in the training of witch-craft groups.

Sex is used as a weapon to control another person. The sex partner of a witch will find his energy is under the witch's control via demons. The witch may use her partner's body for many purposes. A person may complain that unusual things are going on. The individual may experience mood changes, feel demons' presence, and be confronted by dark events.

Partners having sex are creating an energetic tie, which is different. If you've been with partners, you need to destroy all energetic connections to the partner even if the relation-ship ended years ago. Witches search for victims to have in-tercourse with and may stir up nasty conflicts. Orgasm is sacred and believed to have magical power in the cults. They utilize sex as a gateway to control the unconscious.

In witchcraft, orgasm may become a pathway to transfer demons to a partner. The witch will summon demons to enter and behave recklessly. Permission is granted when a person agrees to have sex. Unfortunately, most people will be oblivious to a witch's meddling even as their lives deteriorate. The energy bond may last years; that is, until a partner breaks all ties and permissions.

This kind of witchcraft is used by occultic groups that worship the orgasm in the interest of evil. The orgasm is in all programming and considered to carry great power. Perverts obsessed with sex believe they're downloading power for Lucifer's purposes.

Many survivors have been taught to *not* have orgasms or be punished. Monarch training includes performing a job but not having pleasure. There are parts for every occasion. Some alters in the same person will love sex and have many orgasms at once. Many people breaking loose from cults will have a sex addiction or a celibate life. The same is true for sexual abuse victims not in cults.

XXIII

STORY FROM A
SURVIVOR

I asked this survivor to share his journey due to his incredible, rapid healing. He experienced and I witnessed many miracles in this last year with him. Because his wife helped him to devote great effort to his program removal, he recovered faster than most survivors. Further, he went to Jesus Christ, speeding up his recovery even more. The story reveals the appalling horror of survivors of Satanic Ritual Abuse. His particular history is deeply rooted in Freemasonry. Even though David has been through the worst things imaginable, he is healing in unbelievable ways.

Never give up hope! You can overcome what's been done to you. Jesus Christ will help to heal you!

"I am a 58-year-old male Satanic Ritual Abuse/DID survivor and have come to realize I'm from a multigenerational Satanic family with links to Freemasonry.

"From early adulthood I'd have flashbacks and memories of evil occurrences involving rituals and sacrifices. I never fitted in and always knew I was different, but I used to bury the flashbacks and gruesome images and just got on with my life as a long-distance lorry driver. I never really understood the images that would flash into my mind and did not realize they were actually true-life memories of events I'd been involved in.

"I often suffered anxiety attacks when in crowds, feared walking through doors first, and often wasted time when going out and about and driving along in my truck. I always scanned the environment I found myself in, planning the quickest, safest exit. I spent many years confused, not only about my sexuality but also my gender. I had no friends. My father, then my first two wives, controlled all my money and told me I couldn't be trusted with it. I just would accept it. I couldn't bring myself to buy any new clothes or shoes and would even buy all the dented tin-can food to be consumed immediately. I could never look at myself in the mirror, not even when shaving. I was obsessed with removing body hair. I adored my dad and didn't like my mum. I just did not understand myself or even like myself and never thought of myself as worthy.

"I now know that all the above was from being tortured, abused, electrically shocked, and under complete mind control — the result of being Satanically and ritually abused and programmed right from conception and upon birth right up to my early adult life and beyond. I've since become aware I was last accessed in 2012 at 48-years-old (and in my third marriage). I had no idea I was being accessed as an adult; I believed I'd *gotten away from all the weird stuff that happened to me. I'm aware now that when I've been accessed, they've activated a younger "identity" of me that had been called forward.*

"I can't express enough the struggles I've battled with trying to comprehend the extent of my abuse and mind control, and the realization is quite heartbreaking. I still find it all very difficult thing to live with and it certainly demands the right person to share it with, which, luckily for me, I've found in my third wife.

"I was no more than a sex toy, from 3 years of age, to many men including men of high standing and importance in respectable positions of authority. I wasn't just used as a sexual object at rituals and ceremonies, I was sold and trafficked out to men and women, couples, and groups for sexual purposes, where anything went, including being forcibly raped and beaten, suffocated, strangled. I obliged, no questions asked. Not only would I not complain, but I was even programmed to beg for more and say things such as, "You are the best." I also had to make pornographic movies over a period of years from about 6-8 years old till about 17 years old, and so much more.

"I also discovered I'd been trained as a soldier for the One World Order and was sleeping till they activated me so I could help them usher in the New World along with other sleeping mind-control slaves. I was a trained mercenary waiting to carry out whatever orders they'd give me. I had several hidden identities trained in military arms, by Russians concealed behind big firewalls inside me that were booby trapped with suicide and self-harm programs. It's been a process to dismantle the firewall and alarm systems. As a young child, I had many action-men

dolls that each had a military ranking along with a name, all were used in programming individual identities of mine for the One World Order. During torture, sodomy, and electric shocks I was made to hold an individual doll and I would take on the character of that doll. In my One World Order training I was taught that the New World would usher in:

"One Ruler. One Infiltrator. One Army of Enforcers. One Medical System. One Child System. State-Owned Children. Manageable Hybrid Human Race. Documents to Move. One Food Maker. Sickness Deletion. Age Deletion. One Religion.

"My parents handed me over to the Satanists. The father I adored helped torture and abuse me and actually would rape me along with the others. My mother also compiled by keeping me sleep-deprived and shutting me away in dark boxes as a tiny baby. It's all been really difficult to process and absorb the extent they all went to shape and mold me into a non-questioning, compliant, and obedient mind-controlled sex slave and toy. I spent a lot of my life actually being referred to as a Bendy Toy and I now know that was a sex program where they could get me to bend and flex to any position they wanted me in.

"I'm aware they've used many mainstream songs in program-ming me, and childhood nursery rhymes, which should be joyous and fun. Those have been used to wipe my memory clean, help me to forget, keep things in place and oblige. When I think about it all, it's mind blowing, the lengths they've gone to, the time, money and effort gone into making me a person shaped into their toy and weapon.

"I'm aware of all the Bible Scriptures they've also used in my

programming, twisting and perverting it to fit Lucifers agenda and kingdom. I was made to desecrate a Bible at 3 years old and had to hold its burning covers in my hands just before a major ceremony. It is only recently that I've been able to actually pick up a Bible as I believed it would burn my hands. With Laura's help, I can now read the words in the Bible; before, they all jumbled around and the words Christ, Jesus and God were just blank spaces and I could not even see them.

"I have memories of being told when I was a teenager that I'd signed over the rights to my body at just 3 years of age. I'd signed a deal with Lucifer; he owned my body, I no longer had rights to it, my body was to be used for the work of Lucifer as a high honor. I was chosen by him and he gave me a chance to be part of him and that made me special. I was told many children didn't get that special honor and I was to be grateful.

"An analogy of my life would use a theater and stage setting. I use this example as I used to work backstage in a theater until recently. The audience sitting in the auditorium has no idea what is going on backstage to make the show come to life. Their reality is just what is happening on the stage. That's what is real for them. So, the front of the stage is your life. Yet so much is happening backstage that's never seen or even considered or thought of, but it's those very actions making the reality of the front happen. The backstage is never appreciated.

"Virtually my whole life was spent under a spell, but one day my third wife, in a moment of anger, hurt, confusion and frustration towards my behavior, slapped me several times around the face. It broke the spell of mind control I was under. I saw

a fork in the road I had to take. One was bright and inviting, the other dark with warnings. I decided to take the dark road with warnings and blurted out, "I've been sexually abused." The journey to recovery has been dark and twisted with plenty of warning bells going off, but it was the correct path to take.

"No one should have to go through what I went through and what all the other countless Satanic Ritual Abuse survivors had to go through. My whole childhood was stolen from me. Most of my adult life was taken from me, My first marriage was a pre-planned, full-on Satanic marriage. It's only these last 10 years I believe I've been able to find myself and only just recently started becoming the person I should have been. My third wife and I have come to Christ and have been baptized by full immersion. We both do a daily Bible teaching and attend Church regularly. I believe my healing has only come through Christ being in my life. I've had to dismantle the lies and false truth. I believed that Lucifer was the only true God and that the True God/Jesus Christ were the evil ones not to be trusted. I can't change any of my past and I have physical reminders of my past, such as a broken little finger and broken toes and countless scars. After constantly being cut at ceremonies and rituals, I'm angry with the people who did this to me, and finding it difficult to forgive them. I am still in the process of repentance and asking for forgiveness and there are days that I worry God won't find it in his heart to wash me clean of all my sins, but, as I say, it's still all a process.

"My justice will be to help stop it happening to other children. I want to bring awareness to the world of the corruption

of those involved in the Satanic world from the very top, including the royal family and head of the church. I also want to bring awareness of child trafficking through the Freemasons, and awareness of the sheer extent of money being through children. If I can be part of bringing this awareness to people, then I will feel I've turned evil into some good.

"When I broke out of my first Satanic arranged-marriage, I survived three attempts on my life. One of those attempts was a suicide program triggered by my own dad.

"All I craved was to be normal, and to pull my life together. I would fight the images in my head, which I now realize were actual memories. The only way I could cope with life was to distance myself from as much human contact as possible. I would push back what was coming into my head, seal it away, and not deal with it. As I got better at doing that, I thought I'd be able to carry on my life and not deal with my past or tell anyone about it, but it was actually keeping me under Satanic control. I was obsessed with masturbation and doing things to myself, not realizing they were programs to keep me controlled by the Satanists.

"When I met my second wife, I got her pregnant and married her even though I did not have feelings towards her. I spent most of my time away from home, her, and my child through my work as a long-distance truck driver. It was my way to cope. Through therapy, I became aware they'd accessed me during my second marriage, which came as a shock as it had been a well-hidden memory.

"When I met my third wife, Carol, I felt for the first-time feelings I'd never felt before or had known. My DID parts tried their hardest to wreck our relationship even though I really wanted to be with her. Being in my relationship with Carol has allowed me to break free and tell her of my past. She's helped tremendously and found me therapists and eventually found Laura. Carol's 24-hour, round-the-clock work has really helped to break so much down and discover identities and programs, which Laura then helps me to integrate and dismantle.

"During my sessions with Laura and when my identities have come forward to speak, I never have any recollection of what was said and what happened. Carol will tell me what happened and it certainly is fascinating to learn about my identities, but it makes me very sad.

"I know that I cannot change my past, but I do have a future now with God and my wife Carol. Many of my identities have been integrated and I believe possibly all of them. They all seem to be tired and weary of life. Even the cult's loyal identities, though at first reluctant to integrate, have watched and listened to other identities integrate and eventually decided to join them.

"With Laura's help, we have dismantled a lot of programming and have started to dismantle the Kabbalah trees.

"I feel a lot calmer since writing my first piece for inclusion in Laura's book and I'm not constantly under demonic attacks. I don't have identities coming in and out and taking over my body. For the first time in my life, I've made friends and I'm able to talk to them about SRA and I have spoken at my Church on the subject and given another talk to a local group of interested

people. I have a podcast lined up and I have someone wanting to include me in their documentary on SRA and may even do a feature just on my life. Out of all the SRA survivors they've met and spoken to over many years, 98% have been female. The future's looking brighter now that I have decided to break free of my nightmare."

David Wakefield

Testimony from A Survivor's Spouse

My name is Carol and my husband, David, is a survivor of Satanic Ritual Abuse.

"When I met David, I wasn't aware of his past and we had been together for eight years before he even mentioned anything about sexual abuse he'd experienced as a child and did not mention Satanic rituals. To begin with, he just focused on a 2-year span in his life between 14-16 years old. It all came about when we were not agreeing on a subject and I got angry and felt hurt and confused. I slapped him around his face several times, screaming and shouting at him as I just could not understand why he'd been behaving in the way he had. Two years leading up to this moment had been quite a strain in our marriage, and I finally had had enough and my emotions just showed in a fit of rage and outburst. As soon as I slapped David, he burst out that he'd been sexually abused and raped as a teenager by his school teacher. I calmed down and everything that had been happening

in our life up to then all made sense. A light bulb moment went on in my mind and I became immediately sympathetic towards his pain and I forgot my pain.

"I asked David questions. He was quite candid in his answers. He did take me to the house where his perpetrator [had lived]. To the dismay and horror of David, I went and knocked on the front door and explained to the person who answered that I was looking for the man who lived in the house many years previously. They had just recently purchased the house but suggested I ask a neighbor as they had been there for years and knew everyone. I knocked on their neighbor's door and he told me the previous owner had moved, but he also suggested there was something strange about the guy. After a Google search, I found one article that said this man had been charged for sexual offenses on a 15-year-old boy many years after David had known this person.

"Between December 2014, when I found out about my husband's abuse, and June 2020, David never really elaborated on his abuse, and I trod carefully around it, but also during this time I would often have images in my head during times of intimacy with David of other men being involved, other children being involved, women being involved, and images of such things as children kept in cages and posh dinner parties with children under the tables servicing the adults seated around the table. I never discussed these images with David and thought I was just becoming really perverted sexually in my thoughts and mind. At this point I had never heard of Satanic Ritual Abuse and David never really spoke much about his actual sexual ex-

periences with his school teacher. I did become very conscious, though, at this point, in how David and I were intimate with each other. I would no longer go along with the fantasy games we had played together up to that point. I became aware that some of those acts had been inappropriate and that we had been acting out some of the things that he had really experienced in his previous life. I realized we were not doing these things out of love but out of a perversion of what he had experienced and re-enacting some of those experiences for whatever reason. Our whole relationship changed from 2014 and we became closer and more stable. David gave up touring in the music industry towards the end of 2015, and for the first time in our relationship we were spending each and every day and night in each other's company and truly enjoying each other.

"The real turning point for David was in June of 2020 when mandatory face-mask wearing was introduced. It was a time he finally had to expose more of the extent of his abuse, when he started to tell me he had had two choices: To speak to me or commit suicide, which he had planned in great detail. People wearing face masks were triggering him daily with several flashbacks each day, and he could not even bring himself to leave our home in the end, he just could not cope seeing people in masks. I had asked him over the years if there had been other men, children, or women involved because of the images I had been having but he had always said no. I had even asked if his dad had ever abused him because of something odd he used to say about his dad at the beginning part of our relationship. Always, the answer was always no. I never pushed, but something

inside was telling me he was not being completely truthful. I just remained by his side and always told him he could discuss anything with me. I think our love for each other grew stronger and, unbeknown to me, David's internal DID identities were growing more and more relaxed in my company, observing and learning to trust me. I hadn't realized David had DID, but I did see a different side to David than others did including my children. Towards others, he could often be cold, heartless, and grumpy and really unsociable, but towards me he was loving and caring and chatty. Do not get me wrong, there were occasions when he could also be cold and heartless towards me, but I was privileged to see another side of him. David often would say to me, even right at the beginning of our relationship, that he felt relaxed with me and he'd never felt that before with either of his two other wives.

"Gradually, David started admitting there were other men, sometimes women, but it never came as too much of a surprise as I had already had a variety of images in my head. Sometimes I could even finish the description, as I had already seen it, and my description would take David by surprise. We don't know if David somehow had transferred the images into my head or I had turned into him or it was just God Divine. It was a relief for me, as I started to be aware that I had not become sick and perverted in my thoughts during intimacy, but I was actually being shown experiences which allowed me to show understanding and compassion when he started to reveal the details. I think, because of this, it's allowed me to somehow detach emotionally to some extent and not get too caught up in the reality of it all, and

not feel hurt, confused, unbelieving or frightened of the things my husband experienced.

"The new exposure of David's abuse spurred me to find him a therapist. At this point, I still was not aware of his Satanic Ritual Abuse, and I still wasn't even aware of SRA myself. Laura Worley is David's fifth therapist since 2020, and we've spent thousands of pounds of our savings on therapists. David feels guilty all our money's gone to him finding help and healing. I assure him it's ok as his health, being, and welfare is far more important than just having money in the bank. Obviously, David's not being open and truthful with his previous therapists didn't help him in helping himself to heal. He spoke about abuse but never spoke of the SRA element until I found him Laura. For the first time, he was speaking to someone who could fully understand what he had experienced and was never shocked at anything he told her, and helped him understand and uncover the depth of his torture.

"In December 2021, the Lord spoke to me through my art, and I produced a piece of artwork that was of a large cross and fragmented stained-glass windows. I was told to give it a title of Christ the Redeemer and Fragmented Worlds. I had no idea what it all meant and it was something completely different to any art I had ever produced. I fought doing that piece of art all the way, wanting to abandon it, but something inside me made me finish it. I was confused by what I had drawn and colored and put it to one side. When I finished this art, I had an overwhelming thought that David and I both needed cleansing and needed to be baptized with full immersion. At

19-years-old, to marry in the church, I had to be baptized, and I wondered if you could be baptized twice. The next day a video came up on my Facebook feed on SRA and something made me click on it and watch. It was the first SRA video I had watched and something resonated in it for me when they mentioned the words "fragmented souls." Only the day before, I had titled my art piece with the words "Fragmented Worlds." Still, I did not understand what it all meant. I made a note in my diary of the words mentioned in the video and wondered what I could do with all the information I now held in my hands. How would I broach the subject with David? The other thing that entered my head was that David and I had to do much praying together, something neither of us had ever done individually let alone to-gether. I just left it to one side until a couple of weeks later when David started talking about gatherings and ceremonies he had attended where men were wearing hooded gowns and chanting and candles were burning. I then knew this was the correct time to bring out my art and the note I had made in my diary, and about the baptism and praying. I started coming across videos on SRA and DID and finally I started to understand the frag-mented worlds and souls. I fully immersed myself into helping the man I loved by researching and trying to understand it all.

I would never share my research with David so as not to influence him in anything, and would only reveal my research with him as things started to be revealed that were similar or the same as what I had read or known. I'm fully committed to helping David. It's been tough at times as some of the things he's revealed are quite horrifying. I think the Lord has helped me to cope and given me the strength and courage I've needed to not turn my back on David. It has been the Lord who's helped me in my prayer life to help David in moments of darkness and when the demons have attempted to take him over. I've had to learn to be vigilant and alert as David's therapy proceeded. Then his DID identities started to come through during daily interactions and sometimes the identity was cult-loyal and told me I was not wanted, that I needed to go, and that I was causing damage to the inside. I believe the Lord has led me on how to respond and react to the variety of identities. The more the demons attempted to scare and intimidate me, the more stubborn and determined to not let them get the better of me. I spent many nights in prayer, rather than sleep, combatting the demonic attacks. I've had to battle with David and pin him down to the bed when he seems to be taken over. I've prayed over him, preventing him from completing a task given to him by an identity determined to finish. I will always let David know what's happened, and I have always been truthful to him. I have never sugar-coated what he's said or done as I truly believe the conscious David, whom I am married to, needs to know the truth so he can pray and repent. I help him in his prayers and I encourage him to pray without my help. I've always listened carefully to his prayers as sometimes during prayer an identity might come through and twist the wording. I would bring conscious David back and get him to change the words to worship and glorify Jesus Christ rather than Lucifer. It has been quite a journey in such a short time (since the SRA's been addressed), but I do believe that because we both committed our life to Christ and because we both love each other, the journey has sped up. In reality, I would need to say that, unknowingly, David's been in therapy with me since 2006 when we met. His identities, even though they tried many times over the years to destroy our relationship, there obviously have been identities inside of him who liked me and fell in love. His identities have learned over the years that I was not going anywhere and that I wasn't going to leave him. They've learned how to be loved and how to love because I've always treated David with love. Once, an identity asked me how long we'd been together and said David met a light 16 years ago, and the light never left his side. He was referring to when we first met. I love my husband very much and I've never once felt I would be better off in life without him."

Carol Wakefield

XXIV

IN CLOSING

This manual has been written through a great deal of heartache and spiritual warfare. My husband and I have suffered many spiritual attacks from the very pits of hell. The legions working for Satan have done a great deal to stop this book from being written and published.

The pain and loss we have gone through will never really be understood by anyone other than my husband and myself. The more the cults and Satan attack, the more determined we've become. As a matter of fact, they've pushed us to a greater resolve to make sure this information goes public.

The occult crossed a line by destroying that which mattered the most to me. Now there is no more fear of bringing their dark secrets into the light. Everything the cult did to my husband and I culminated in our eyes being more- wide open to cults and military secrets.

The occult has many secrets, but the most important to a

survivor is the Tree of Death. Cults and the military attempted to ensure no one would understand the truth of their organized template and all it represents. That concealed truth
made it likely most programming survivors would never be
free.

It is only recently that the truth of The Tree of Death
been revealed. People can now understand what's at the core
of Lucifer's kingdom. Why would my husband and I be so
viciously attacked if this truth did not represent all survivors
getting free of their programming?

Assaults came from every cult group at every level of evil.
We've repelled vicious attacks to murder me. People have
urged me to keep my mouth shut. A time arrived when I
knew the cults and demons wouldn't kill me until my work
was finished. God is in charge of my life.

I know a great deal more than I was able to share in my
first book, *Puzzle Pieces to the Cabal, Mind Control, And
Slavery*. I know more than I shared in this book *Puzzle Pieces
Together*. I've been asked if a trilogy may emerge. But having
knowledge is not the same as the Lord telling me to write another book. I'm reluctant to face those words at the moment.

I would like to thank a very special person who gave me a
voice to announce my abusers' names and to share my expertise of MK Ultra, the Illuminati, and military programming.
His name is Lewis Herms. Speaking in Herms' Truth Tour
2022 emboldened me to share essential information with a
wider audience. Speaking at seven public events inspired me
so much. Many people at each event came up to me, saying

"thank you" for sharing my story. Many at the Truth Tour said they'd been learning about MK Ultra programming and cult abuse. I think some people were shocked when I discussed military abuse, including how I witnessed military personnel under mind-control programming. Survivors and professionals of various backgrounds thanked me for sharing. Without speaking at the Truth Tour, I don't think I would have realized the vital nature of spreading my information publicly, to a wider audience than only therapists and survivors.

On the Truth Tour, Lewis Herms was very gracious to me; it meant so much to hear the kind words he spoke. Lewis has no idea what he's done to help me, so I wanted to thank him in my book. I know the Lord had us meet. Lewis and his lovely wife, Araceli, have come to mean so much to me. Both of them are true warriors in this fight of taking our country back — for God, family, and friends.

Puzzle Pieces Together is necessary for cult survivors to find freedom and for professionals to be successful working with Satanic Ritual Abuse clients. This last year, I was blessed to be interviewed, which allowed me to share knowledge about the various groups that utilize programming. My husband and I recently taught a seminar on how to remove core foundational programming. I have only begun to be a witness against Lucifer's kingdom.

After 30 years of learning, I know how the mind works and the many ways holistic modalities can heal. I must fulfill my calling to educate people. I no longer can refer to myself as a survivor. I'm a witness. A witness of Jesus Christ. A witness of the darkness in Lucifer's kingdom. I stand as a witness against those members of Lucifer's kingdom who delight in harming children. I stand as a witness to every evil act done to me and others. I stand as a witness against the fiends owning the so-called right to experiment on me.

I stand as a witness for truth. Finally, the world will know of the Luciferian system behind the curtains.

I stand as a witness against the darkness. I have witnessed the deepest hell where Lucifer resides. I am a witness to the greatest Light of Jesus Christ. I know how both run their kingdoms. No one can ever tell me they don't exist because I have seen them. I know them both. While the cults were downloading demons, I was on the other side talking to Jesus. Jesus strengthened me. My soul knew Jesus Christ. At a soul level, I knew who Jesus was, that he loved me, and that he was helping me. I don't remember his face, only his presence. I cannot and will not deny him.

I will not be silent about either kingdom. We are in a war. Lucifer against God. Lucifer's kingdom is represented by the Illuminati, Freemasons, Fertility Cult, Witchcraft, and some in the military, government, and business. We must take down the builders of Lucifer's kingdom.

The time has come for the earth to shake and the truth to be released. All of us were sent here to be Light bearers, to stand not as survivors of hell but witnesses against it. Will you stand as a witness against the darkness with me?

If you are a survivor, it's important you begin to see who you are and to tear down the cult's illusions in order to control you. Take authority over what's been done, and do not ever give up.

I want all survivors of Satanic Ritual Abuse to know you are some of the strongest human beings on earth. You are not weak. Lucifer and his demons want you to believe you're weak so they can beat you down and destroy you. Stand up and fight back. There is a way out of all things. Your unconscious mind knows how to undo all the programming and break down the lies. You are the one who created the illusions for the programmers. You can now destroy them.

You are not alone. We must all stand up together and support each other and become an army of witnesses. I believe it's our mission to not only be a survivor, but to be a witness against the criminals who thought they'd go scot-free after torturing and raping you. Survivors will take down the globalist Cabal. We know all their secrets and weaknesses. We know what they do in the dark. We must now destroy the Globalist Cabal Luciferian agenda. We must be an army.

Survivors, however, need an army of professionals to help them. Worldwide, if professional therapists understand how cults have programmed Satanic Ritual Abuse survivors, they can assist millions of people.

Stand as a witness against the dark as God intended.

My greatest wish is that my two books will help you find a pathway to freedom. I am grateful the Lord has entrusted me with this information at this moment. Much content in my two books came from the Lord and Savior. I give Him the credit and will go forward as he directs.

May the Lord also walk every step with you on your healing journey.

My dear brothers and sisters, I respect you all for what you've been through. I love you all; my prayers will never cease until every survivor of Satanic Ritual Abuse has been freed.

Your fellow warrior,
Laura Worley

ACKNOWLEDGMENTS

First of all, I would like to thank my husband for supporting me every step of the way in writing this book. I would not have finished this book without him.

Many thanks for the editor, Rich Trout who worked hard to make sure my book was ready for publication. Rich did fully put his heart into helping me and I really appreciate him navigating through the various issues that arose. I felt like he was on my team and helped the book to be the best version possible. (Dr. Richard Trout is an Assistant Professor of English holding a Doctor of Business Administration (DBA) from the University of the Southwest (USW) in Hobbs, NM. Trout works as a Freelance editor. Trout was a business reporter, assistant editor, and managing editor at the Hobbs News-Sun from 2001 to 2012.) (richtrout@gmail.com)

There were three artists/graphic designers who created all artwork in the book. All three are very talented individuals. I am very grateful each had their own unique style which fit perfectly in my book.

I would like to thank Nic Youngblood for the illustrations of the many ages of a survivor. Nic is a very talented artist who all I had to do was share my ideas and he just made it happen. As you can see from the pictures; Nic captured the essence and the meaning of the hell the survivor goes through. Nic brought out facial expressions in such a real way. Nic has also designed both book covers which he was able to express the theme of each book exactly how I had envisioned. (Graphic Design/Photo Manipulation/Illustration) (niceyoungblood@gmail.com)

K.T. designed the Water World Characters and the picture of Rose. The design worked out perfectly to bring out the illusions of the programming.

D.G. used his talent as a graphic designer and created many charts and pictures that had to fit exactly with specific details and measurements.

Gabbi Choong wrote the summary of the book on the back cover. Gabbi is a very talented writer. Gabbi is an SRA survivor who also helps other survivors in the country of Australia.

I would like to give a big thank you to Heidi Caperton for putting this book together and making it look phenomenal. We had to some extra work to pull it together. Heidi is awesome at her job and I know I can count on her to pull difficult projects together because she pulled my Book 1 and 2 together beautifully.

Everyone did such a great job and I am very thankful to each person for their contribution in making this book a reality.

REFERENCES

Buys, A. (2020). *Recap, refresh, and recalibrate for the journey forward!!* Kanaan Ministries. (Page 177)

Buys, A. (2020). *Book 4 Advanced Training DID SRA, Recap, refresh, and recalibrate for the journey forward! Kanaan Ministries. (Page 28-30)*

Buys, A. (2019). *DID/SRA training video 15 of 19.* Kanaan Ministries.

Buys, A. (2020). *Restoring the shattered soul: Step-by-step DID.* Kanaan Ministries.
Buys, A. (2020) *Recap, refresh and recalibrate for the journey of the soul. (Pages 50-52)*

Buys, A. (2020) *Restoring the Shattered Soul. (Pages 66)*

Day, M. (n.d.). *Unclean Spirits research paper.*

Hale, H. Q. (1920, January 20). *Heber Q. Hale in the spirit world.* In Despain, B. D., *Works of wonder.* (2021). https://bdespain.org/frontier/progress/proghale.htm#S17

Hall, M. P. (1973). *An encyclopedia outline of Masonic, Hermetic, Qabbalistic, and Rosicrucian symbolical philosophy.* Philosophical Research Society. https://www.amazon.com/Encyclopedia-Qabbalistic-Rosicrucian-Symbolical-Philosophy/dp/B0006W6Y7K

Henderson, R. [Robert Henderson Ministries]. (2022, June 24). *Secrets to a successful bloodline cleansing w/ Robert Henderson* [Video]. YouTube. https://www.youtube.com/watch?v=cChVWHseB-U&t=88s

Henderson, R. [Victory Christian Centre]. (2019, November 13). *Robert Henderson 1. courts of heaven* [Video]. YouTube. https://www.youtube.com/watch?v=A-MANcu-JwVo&t=94s

Henderson, R. [Victory Christian Centre]. (2019, November 13). *Robert Henderson 2. courts of heaven* [Video]. YouTube. https://www.youtube.com/watch?v=Ww4L1yjc5G0

Henderson, R. [Victory Christian Centre]. (2019, November 13). *Robert Henderson 3. courts of heaven* [Video]. YouTube. https://www.youtube.com/watch?v=6bIv14RGkWg

Kerstein, B. (2018, September 27). Kabbalah. In the *World history encyclopedia*. World History Encyclopedia. https://www.worldhistory.org/Kabbalah/

King James Version Bible. (12/2006). The Church of Jesus Christ of Latter-day Saints

Mclymont, A. (2012, September 22). *10 Facts about the great beast Aleister Crowley*. Listverse. https://listverse.com/2012/09/22/10-facts-about-the-great-beast-aleister-crowley/

Nachtigal, Y. (2014, February 21). *Aleister Crowley and Adolph Hitler — The ideology of evil*. Christian Observer. https://christianobserver.net/?s=Crowley&id=40986

Nelson, B. (2020). *Take a tour of the body code healing system*. Discover Healing. https://discoverhealing.com/the-body-code/

New International Version Bible. (2013). Holman Bible Publishers.

Oglevie, S. (XXXX). *Mind control: An Introduction*. (2004) 08/20/2004-8/22/2004

Parry, D. W. (2012, July 31). *Angels, chariots and the Lord of hosts*. BYU Broadcasting. https://www.byutv.org/cdd115bc-27fa-4382-b1a2-8344cc81d700/byu-devo-tional-address-donald-w.-parry-(7-31-12)

Pontius, J. (2012). *Visions of glory: One man's astonishing account of the last days*. Cedar Fort.

Pratt, P. P. (1891). *Key to the science of theology* (5th ed.). George Q. Cannon & Sons.

ABOUT THE AUTHOR

Laura Worley is a Speaker, Trainer, Coach, and Author. She has successfully helped thousands of people around the world address issues stemming from complex trauma and ritual abuse. Laura's goal is to train an army of professionals and survivors on how to use powerful techniques that lead to freedom. Laura believes if we all work together; we can defeat those who keep people under mind control and slavery.

As the creator of the Worldwide Transformational Summit, Laura has interviewed over 85 of the top global authors and motivational speaker in the field of transforming lives.

Currently, Laura Worley is being interviewed on podcasts to share her story and the secrets of the Cabal and MK Ultra Programs.

Printed in Great Britain
by Amazon

20656072R00322